Modern China

Modern China

A History

THIRD EDITION

Edwin E. Moise

Harlow, England • London • New York • Boston • San Francisco • Toronto
Sydney • Tokyo • Singapore • Hong Kong • Seoul • Taipei • New Delhi
Cape Town • Madrid • Mexico City • Amsterdam • Munich • Paris • Milan

Pearson Education Limited
Edinburgh Gate
Harlow CM20 2JE
Tel: +44 (0)1279 623623
Fax: +44 (0)1279 431059
Website: www.pearsoned.co.uk

First edition published 1986
Second edition published 1994
Third edition published in Great Britain in 2008

ISBN: 978-0-582-77277-9

British Library Cataloguing-in-Publication Data
A catalogue record for this book is available from the British Library

Library of Congress Cataloging-in-Publication Data
Moise, Edwin E., 1946–
  Modern China, a history / Edwin E. Moise. — 3rd ed.
    p. cm.
  Includes bibliographical references and index.
  ISBN-13: 978-0-582-77277-9
  1. China—History—20th century. I. Title.
  DS774.M58 2008
  951.05—dc22
                          2008001019

10 9 8 7 6 5 4 3 2 1
12 11 10 09 08

Typeset in 10/13.5pt Sabon by 35
Printed and bound in China WC/01

The publisher's policy is to use paper manufactured from sustainable forests.

Contents

Maps

Illustrations

Acknowledgements

We are grateful to the following for permission to reproduce copyright material:

Plates 1.1 and 10.2 Sally and Richard Greenhill Photo Library/SACU; Plates 1.2, 2.1, 2.2, 3.2, 4.1, 4.2, and 10.1 Getty Images; Plate 3.1 David King Collection; Plates 5.1, 8.1, 8.2, 9.1, 9.2, and 11.3 PA Photos; Plates 5.2 and 7.1 Magnum Photos; Plate 6.1 Camera Press London.

In some instances we have been unable to trace the owners of copyright material, and we would appreciate any information that would enable us to do so.

Chinese names and Chinese geography

Writing Chinese names

This study will emphasize general policies more than the individuals who made those policies. This will be helpful to readers not already familiar with China, since variations in the way Chinese names are spelled in English, and cases in which none of the spellings seem to the English speaker to match the way the name is actually pronounced, can cause considerable confusion. A few years ago the English-speaking world used what was called the 'Wade–Giles' system to write most Chinese names. In the Wade–Giles system the pronunciation of consonants often shifted drastically depending on the presence or absence of an apostrophe. Thus the word pronounced like 'bye' was written *pai*, while the word pronounced like 'pie' was written *p'ai*. The names of provinces and major cities, however, were written in a different system. Sometimes the same sound was written in two different ways depending on whether it appeared in the name of a person or a place, and neither spelling corresponded to the way it was actually pronounced.

Recently we have shifted to a new system called *pinyin*, for the names of both people and places. The *pinyin* system is a bit more rational, but there are still some cases in which the sound indicated by the letters is not what the average English speaker would guess. The table below shows the relation between the new spelling, the old spelling, and the actual pronunciation for the letters most likely to cause confusion. The *pinyin* spellings will be used in this book, but the first time a particular name appears the former spelling will usually be added in parentheses. Names will also appear in the index under both spellings.

Pinyin spelling	Wade–Giles spelling	Pronunciation
a	a	a as in papa
b	p	b as in boy
c	ts', tz'	ts as in shots
d	t	d as in dog
g	k	g as in good
i	i, ih, u	ee as in feet after b, d, j, l, m, n, p, q, t, and x
		i as in shirt after c, ch, r, s, sh, z, zh
ia	ie	ye as in yes
iu	iu	yo as in yoke
j	ch	j as in jeep
p	p'	p
q	ch'	ch as in cheap
r	j	approximately, though not exactly, like the English letter r
t	t'	t
x	hs	sh as in she
ya	ye	ye as in yes
z	ts, tz	ds as in odds
zh	ch	j as in joke

The names that will appear most often in this book in *pinyin* are:

- Beijing, pronounced 'bay-jeeng', the capital of China. In Wade–Giles it would have been Pei-ching, but it was traditionally written Peking.

- Deng Xiaoping, pronounced 'Dung Shyao-peeng'. A leading member of the 'moderate' wing of the Chinese Communist Party (CCP), he was twice purged by the radicals, but returned to become the most powerful figure in the Party after Mao Zedong died in 1976. Formerly written Teng Hsiao-p'ing.

- Guangdong, pronounced 'Guahng-dong', the south-coast province that was headquarters for the Guomindang and the CCP in the mid 1920s. Formerly spelled Kwangtung.

- Guangzhou, pronounced 'Guahng-joe', an important seaport, capital of the south-coast province of Guangdong. It is often called Canton.

- Guomindang, pronounced 'Guo-meen-dahng', the name of the Nationalist Party that ruled China from 1927 to 1949. Formerly written Kuomintang.

- Hu Jintao, pronounced 'Who Jean-tao', became head of the CCP in 2003.

- Jiangxi, pronounced 'Jyahng-shee', a province in South-central China where the Communist Party established a base area in the early 1930s. Formerly written Kiangsi.

- Mao Zedong, pronounced 'Mao [a single short syllable] Dzuh-dong', head of the CCP from 1935 to 1976. Formerly written Mao Tse-tung.

- Qing, pronounced 'Cheeng', the Manchu Dynasty that ruled the Chinese Empire from 1644 to 1911. Formerly written Ch'ing.

- Shanghai, pronounced 'Shahng-hai', the largest city in China, on the coast near the mouth of the Yangzi River. Former spelling the same.

- Yanan, a city in Shaanxi province (Northwest China) that served as headquarters for the CCP from 1937 to 1947. Formerly written Yenan, which matches the actual pronunciation.

- Yangzi, pronounced 'Yahng-dzih', the great river that flows from west to east through the middle of China. Formerly written Yangtze or Yangtse. Also called the Changjiang, formerly written Ch'ang Chiang.

- Zhao Ziyang, pronounced 'Jao Dzih-yang', became premier of the People's Republic of China in 1980. Purged in 1989, as punishment for being too sympathetic to the democracy movement and the demonstrators in Tiananmen Square. Formerly written Chao Tzu-yang.

- Zhou Enlai, pronounced 'Joe En-lie', Chinese premier until his death in 1976. A moderate leader who managed to stay on good terms with Mao Zedong all through the Cultural Revolution. Formerly written Chou Enlai.

- Zhu De, pronounced 'Jew Duh', commander-in-chief of the Chinese Red Army, later the People's Liberation Army, until 1954. Formerly written Chu Teh.

There are a few people and places that have long been known in the West not simply by a different spelling, but by a significantly different name from that given them in modern standard Chinese. To avoid excessive confusion, this book will use the familiar English names for Hong Kong, Tibet, and Manchuria, for the Guomindang Party leaders Sun Yat-sen and Chiang Kai-shek, and for the philosophers Confucius and Mencius, rather than giving the names currently used in China (Xianggang, Xizang, Dongbei, Sun Zhong-shan, Jiang Jieshi, Kongzi, and Mengzi).

Chinese names almost always consist of a one-syllable surname, which comes first, and is followed by a two-syllable personal name. Thus Mao Anying was the son of Mao Zedong, and both of them would be found, in an alphabetical index, listed under 'Mao'.

Regional geography

China proper, the area that has for centuries had a dense population of ethnic Chinese, can be divided into three major regions:

1   North China. The most conspicuous feature of this region is the Yellow River. It follows a wide, looping path through the arid hills of the northwest, and finally crosses the North China Plain (largely created by the silt it has laid down) to reach the sea. It is not navigable, and it is very difficult to control; it lays down so much silt that the bed of the river tends to rise with the passage of time, and the water must be kept in its course by high dikes on either side. Eventually, the bed of the river may rise until it is considerably higher than the surrounding countryside. When the dikes break and the river flows down onto the lands around it, the task of putting it back in its elevated channel is difficult, sometimes impossible. Thousands die in the resulting floods. Three times in the past 150 years the river has changed its course very drastically, with the point at which it flows into the sea being altered by hundreds of miles. (The dotted line on Map 1 shows the course before 1853, and from 1938 to 1947.)

   The area along the Yellow River is the original home of Chinese civilization. The soil is relatively rich, but harsh winters and sparse rainfall limit agricultural production.

2   Central China. The dominant feature is the Yangzi River (Changjiang), which is navigable far into the interior. The provinces along the Yangzi and its tributaries form the most populous region of China.

3   South China has no single unifying feature; it is cut up by a number of small mountain ranges. However, despite the uneven terrain, its generous rainfall and mild climate have made possible a productive agriculture that supports a large population.

In addition, there are peripheral areas that have not been inhabited by many ethnic Chinese for most of history, but that have been controlled by the Chinese government when that government was strong. The main ones are:

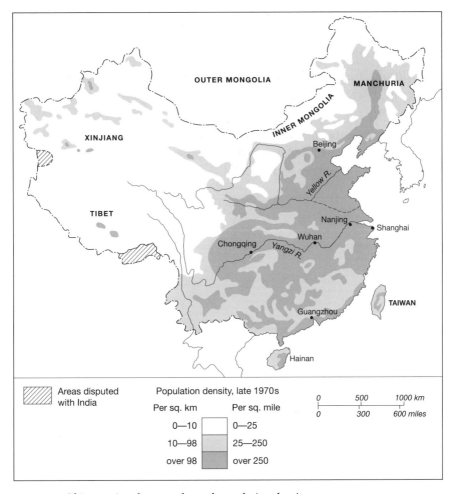

MAP 1 *China: regional geography and population density.*

4   Manchuria. This was a fringe area for the Chinese Empire for most
     of its history, but a flood of Chinese settlers during the past 100 years
     has made it essentially Chinese today. The principal unifying feature
     in modern times has been not natural but manmade: the South
     Manchurian Railway, running north from the port of Dalian (Dairen)
     through the major cities of Manchuria. This region used to be one of
     the main centres of Chinese industry, but it has fallen behind since the
     1980s.

5   Mongolia has always been too arid to support a dense population. It
     was under the control of the Chinese government for a considerable

time, but early in the twentieth century Outer Mongolia became a separate country, the Mongolian People's Republic, under strong Russian influence. Inner Mongolia has remained part of China.

6 Xinjiang (Sinkiang) is mostly mountain or desert, with a few areas of fertile oases. The indigenous population, quite sparse, is largely Muslim.

7 Tibet is mountainous and inaccessible; the population is very sparse. Of all the regions listed, this is the one where Chinese influence has traditionally been the weakest.

CHAPTER 1

The Chinese past

Most of the world has changed very drastically in the past 100 years, but few areas have been altered more than China. First the imperial government was brought down by internal decay and foreign pressure, and replaced by a republic. Then central authority collapsed completely, and the country was divided among provincial warlords. Incapable of organized defence, China became the prey of foreign powers whose 'spheres of influence' sometimes approached the status of outright colonies. Corrupt officials, marauding armies, and natural disasters periodically ravaged the peasantry.

China's recovery began under the Guomindang, or Nationalist Party, which ruled from 1927 to 1949. It eliminated most of the foreign spheres of influence and unified significant portions of the country. The Communist Revolution of 1949 carried on with these tasks, creating the first really effective central government since the middle of the eighteenth century, and pushing economic development far enough to eliminate mass starvation if not poverty. The Communists, however, then began struggling savagely among themselves.

A large proportion of this book will be devoted to events after 1966, simply because so much happened in China after that year. China underwent greater changes just from the 1960s to the 1990s than Britain or the United States did from the 1920s to the present.

At first glance, everything in China seems new. The groups that have struggled for power in the past fifty years have been modern in their essence. Those who have ruled since the late 1970s regard modernizing China – creating a strong, wealthy, technologically sophisticated nation-state – as their main goal. We can find roots for such an attitude reaching back to about 1860, but its main development came after 1900. The group in power before 1976 had been preoccupied with Marxian class struggle; such attitudes had only become a factor in Chinese politics after about 1920.

Much of this book will be devoted to the interaction between these two trends, with the advocates of Marxian class struggle found within the Chinese Communist Party (CCP), while the advocates of modernization and nationalism have been found both inside and outside the Party. For a while, in the 1940s and 1950s, the CCP seemed to have learned to reconcile the two approaches to revolution, and apply both of them simultaneously. In the 1960s, however, a savage conflict broke out between advocates of the two approaches. The advocates of radical class struggle, led by CCP Chairman Mao Zedong, seemed victorious at first. After Mao's death in 1976, however, Deng Xiaoping led a resurgence of the group called pragmatists, moderates, or rightists – the people who thought of Communism essentially as a technique for making China a richer and stronger nation.

The groups that had opposed the Maoists during the 1970s then fought one another during the 1980s over an issue almost as characteristically modern as the previous one: whether the political domination of the Communist Party should be preserved, or whether substantial elements of Western-style democracy should be introduced. The group now called the conservatives, the defenders of Party power, triumphed in the Tiananmen Massacre of 1989, but it remains to be seen how long this triumph will endure.

Given that China has changed so much in recent decades – far more than Britain, France, or the United States – one could almost consider writing a history of modern China without reference to the past. Everyone writing a history book must decide how far back in time he or she will go in searching for the causes of later events. Some date must be the earliest date mentioned. Why not write a history of modern China in which the earliest date mentioned is 1900, or even 1921 (the year in which the CCP was founded)?

The simplest and most obvious reason why we should not do this is that not even the most drastic upheaval changes everything. Continuities with the past do exist, especially in thought and attitudes. The concern for stability and order that China's leaders showed in 1989, when suppressing the democracy movement, was very traditional even if the nature of the order they were trying to stabilize was modern.

An equally important reason for remembering the past history of China is that the Chinese themselves remember it, and react to it. They are a historically minded people. If we wish to know why Chairman Mao and his radical followers attacked the intellectuals so savagely between 1966 and 1976, it is not enough to understand what the role and status of the intellectuals had been in 1966, or even in 1936. We must also know the role of the intellectuals in the imperial governments of past centuries, because Mao himself knew, and this knowledge helped to shape his actions.

It is sometimes said that the Chinese 'abolished history' during the years of the Cultural Revolution, from 1966 to 1976. This is true in the sense that there was not much historical writing done in this period, and that what little was published was mostly propagandistic hackwork. However, this did not mean that the Communist Party leaders no longer cared about the past. On the contrary, they were sure that events of the distant past could have a direct and immediate relevance to the present; the reason they clamped down on historical research was that they feared *the wrong things* might be said about the past.

One fairly important official of the CCP was disgraced and imprisoned partly for having written a play about a Ming Dynasty official who had died in 1587. His enemies charged that it was in fact an allegory about a 1959 power struggle in the CCP.

In 1974, the CCP declared that contemporary political issues had roots going back to ancient times. The political struggles surrounding the collapse of the Qin Dynasty, in the third century BC, were solemnly rehashed in the press. When the workers in a railway station in the city of Tianjin (Tientsin) formed a historical study group, the *People's Daily* declared:

The struggle between the Confucian and Legalist schools over the past 2,000 years or so still has its influence at present and has continued to this day . . . The workers, peasants and soldiers can use Marxism to study and learn history. Liberate history from the confines of the historians' lecture rooms and textbooks, and turn it into a sharp weapon in the hands of the masses.

A Chinese-American woman who visited China during this period found that her hosts, trying to decide whether she was still basically a Chinese, or had been so westernized as to be just an American with the ancestry and physical appearance of a Chinese, used knowledge of Chinese history as their touchstone. When the train on which she was riding passed a location where something important had happened more than 1,000 years before, would she know what had happened there and be excited about actually seeing the place? If so, they would consider her to be a real

Chinese. This is not the behaviour of people who have abolished history, or would even consider abolishing it.

If we wish to understand modern China, therefore, we should start by learning at least a little about the origins and development of this very ancient culture.

The birth of China

The civilization we know as China originated in the area of the Yellow River, in the northern part of the country. Traditional texts list rulers going back to almost 2700 BC, but the earliest walled towns do not seem actually to have been built until the second millennium BC, and the earliest individual kings whose existence has been verified by archaeology lived probably between 1300 and 1200 BC. Their dynasty, the Shang, ruled a substantial portion of northern China. The people of the Shang used a writing system recognizably related to the characters of twentieth-century Chinese, but in other respects (such as frequent human sacrifices) they were strikingly different from later Chinese cultures.

The Shang rulers were overthrown by a group called the Zhou (Chou), who had lived on the western fringe of the Shang domain and had a similar culture. This probably occurred around 1040 BC, though estimates of the date range from 1122 BC to 1018 BC. The Zhou kings maintained fairly effective control of the area around the Yellow River for a few generations, but then gradually lost their grip. After 770 BC, real power was divided among a number of states. The typical state was a city, with some greater or lesser amount of the surrounding territory under its control. The rulers of these various states paid nominal allegiance to the Zhou kings, but the kings retained only a small territory under their actual control. The culture of Zhou China, however, was spreading even while its political structure was disintegrating. As time went on, areas along the coast and the Yangzi River, which had not been part of the Shang or the early Zhou, began adopting some cultural traits of the Yellow River states and joining their political struggles.

The period from the sixth to the third centuries BC, although characterized by interstate warfare that had many Chinese in despair, was intellectually one of the most productive eras in Chinese history. A tremendous variety of philosophers and thinkers propounded various ideas. Chinese tradition refers to 'the Hundred Schools', but three major groups eventually emerged, which remained central to Chinese thought down to the twentieth century: Confucians, Daoists (Taoists), and Legalists.

Confucianism

Confucius was an itinerant teacher of the fifth century BC. He travelled from one state to another, talking with his disciples and with any rulers who might be willing to listen.

Our knowledge of Confucius' actual teachings is somewhat vague. Like Socrates, he taught face to face rather than writing books, so we are dependent on accounts by his students. Even for these we cannot be sure we have reliable texts. A considerable portion of the book known as the *Analects* really does come from accounts of his teachings written by his students, but other sections were inserted into the works long afterwards. While scholars today can sort much of the *Analects* into genuine and spurious sections, there are some passages about which doubt still exists.

Confucius was sure that his teachings provided the key to good and effective government, but no ruler was sufficiently convinced to give him a position of real power and let him show what he could do.

Confucian doctrine evolved gradually as later writers, of whom the most important was Mencius, extended and modified the original teachings. The general thrust of Confucianism was the importance of proper human relationships. Subordinates should be reverent and obedient towards their superiors, while superiors should be benevolent and just. In one sense, it was an optimistic doctrine – it claimed that human beings have a natural sense of what is good. However, Confucianism did not support the idea of progress; it suggested that people wanting to improve society should look to the past for their models, rather than trying to devise something new. Confucius advocated adherence to old customs and old rituals. Among the Confucian ideas that have particular importance for the later history of China are:

1 Confucianism treated the family as the key unit in human society, and filial piety – loyalty and reverence towards one's parents – as the most important part of family relationships. A man's loyalty to his parents was supposed to take precedence over everything else, including loyalty to his children, his wife, or his ruler.

2 Confucianism took a basically hierarchical view of society. One should note that of the five key human relationships in Confucian doctrine, four are relationships linking a superior to a subordinate: father to son, ruler to subject, husband to wife, and elder brother to younger brother. Only the relationship of friend to friend is between equals.

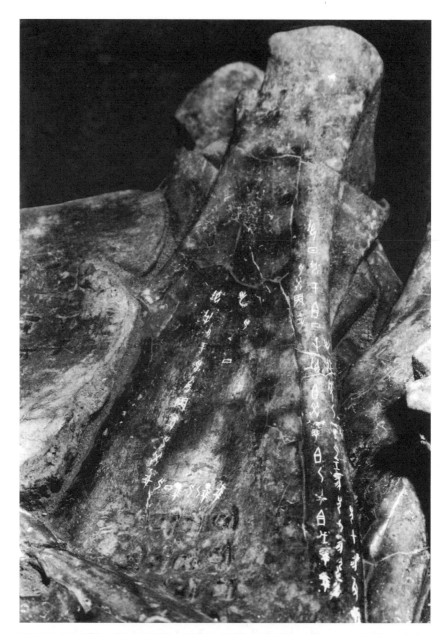

PLATE 1.1 *Shang Dynasty 'Oracle Bone'. When the Shang kings wanted knowledge about the future, they had a question inscribed on the flat-bottomed shell of a tortoise or on the shoulder bone of a cow. Heat was then applied until the shell or the bone cracked; the shape of the cracks was supposed to indicate the answer to the question. (© Sally and Richard Greenhill/SACU.)*

3   Confucianism argued not only that a ruler has an obligation to behave in a good and humane fashion, and provide decent living conditions for his subjects, but also that this is profitable for the ruler: the subjects will respond with loyalty and obedience. It is imperative that a ruler keep the confidence of his people. If they are poor and miserable the ruler will lose the mandate of heaven; he deserves to be overthrown, and he probably will be.

4   Power should be exercised by people who have been educated in the proper way of exercising it. Confucius himself never attained the position of power for which he yearned, but he felt that he was training his students to be officials, and eventually (many centuries later) a Confucian education became, in fact, the main pathway to power in the Chinese government.

Few rulers actually behaved in the high moral fashion that Confucian doctrine prescribed. Many Confucians, therefore, developed a low opinion of the governments with which they had to deal, although the Confucian prescription of loyalty to rulers usually kept them from engaging in active opposition.

There is an anecdote about Confucius, which, though it probably is not true, illustrates this strain in Confucianism. According to the story, the sage was once passing through a mountainous area with some of his disciples. They came upon a woman mourning by the grave of her son, who had been killed by a tiger. She told them that her husband and her husband's father had previously suffered the same fate. When asked why she lived in a place that had so many tigers, she explained that in this place there was no oppressive government. The moral Confucius is supposed to have drawn for his disciples is that oppressive government was worse than a tiger. The unspoken implication was that governments were so universally oppressive that the only way this woman's family had been able to escape oppression was to live in the wilderness where there was no effective government at all.

Legalism

Another school preached not moral obligations but naked self-interest. The legalists argued that human beings are fundamentally amoral, and that they cannot be moved by moral example. The only way to make them behave correctly is by a strong legal system, which enforces correct behaviour through rewards and punishments. If even minor infractions are ruthlessly punished, then nobody will dare to commit serious crimes. The philosopher Han Fei Zi (Han Fei Tzu) argued that while there might occasionally be an individual who was naturally good, and did not need to be coerced into good behaviour, 'the intelligent ruler will not prize him. The reason is that the law of the state must not be sidetracked and government is not for one man.' The ruler must apply coercive laws to everyone; what difference does it make that this one individual would have behaved properly without being forced to do so?

Han Fei Zi was contemptuous of the idea that the ruler should consider the opinions of his subjects. He claimed that legalist government would benefit the people, but he was sure that the people were too stupid to recognize good government even when living under it. His contemporary Li Si (Li Ssu) went further, and argued that the ruler could ignore not only the opinions but also the welfare of his subjects. The purpose of government was to serve the interests of the ruler, not the common people. 'If a ruler will not . . . utilize the empire for his own pleasure, but on the contrary purposelessly tortures his body and wastes his mind in devotion to the people – then he becomes the slave of the common people instead of the domesticator of the empire. And what honour is there in that?'

The legalists were future-oriented; they had no respect for tradition, and felt they could devise techniques of government superior to anything that had been known in the past.

Daoism

The Daoists preached harmony with the forces of nature. They doubted the value either of will-power or of too much thinking; life is to be enjoyed, and should be kept as simple as possible. They agreed with Confucius about the deplorable quality of existing governments, but where Confucius had been eager to achieve high office so he could carry out reforms, the Daoists rejected position and power. They argued that the wise man minds his own business, ignores the government, and hopes that it will ignore him. There is a story that the King of Chu, a very powerful state on the Yangzi River, once sent two officials to offer a senior position in his government to the sage Zhuangzi (Chuang Tzu). He was sitting by a river, fishing, when they found him and made their offer.

Zhuangzi held on to the fishing pole and, without turning his head, said, 'I have heard that there is a sacred tortoise in Chu that has been dead for three thousand years. The king keeps it wrapped in cloth and boxed, and

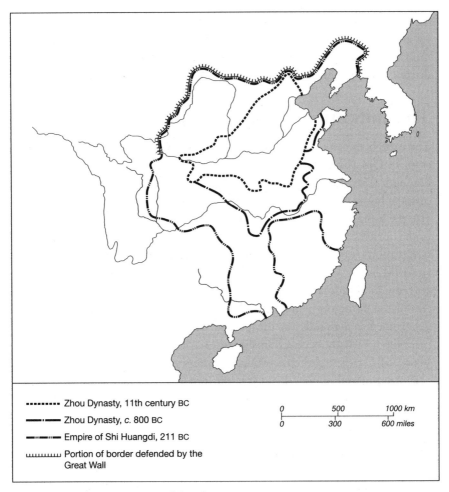

Zhou Dynasty, 11th century BC

Zhou Dynasty, c. 800 BC

Empire of Shi Huangdi, 211 BC

Portion of border defended by the Great Wall

MAP 2 *The early expansion of the Chinese state.*

stores it in the ancestral temple. Now would this tortoise rather be dead and have its bones left behind and honoured? Or would it rather be alive and dragging its tail in the mud?'

'It would rather be alive and dragging its tail in the mud,' said the two officials.

Zhuangzi said, 'Go away! I'll drag my tail in the mud!'

On another occasion, offended by a rumour that he was scheming to attain the position of prime minister in the state of Liang, he wondered why a person of taste and discernment should be suspected of lusting after a piece of carrion.

Daoist philosophy later mingled with medical knowledge, popular religious beliefs, and other elements of folk culture. The products of such mingling included a Daoist religion, with organized worship of numerous deities, and also the martial arts discipline known to the West as Kung Fu.

The unification of China

The wars between the various states grew increasingly violent. Finally, the state of Qin (Ch'in) conquered the others and its ruler became Qin Shi Huangdi (First Emperor of the Qin Dynasty). He controlled not only the original home of Chinese culture – the area around the Yellow River – but also the Yangzi Valley and even a portion of the south coast, reaching down to the borders of Vietnam. This new empire benefited from improved communications, standardized coinage, a standardized writing system, and so forth, but it was soon groaning under a legalist regime of unparalleled severity. Li Si (quoted above on the foolishness of trying to serve the interests of the common people) was the First Emperor's prime minister. The government's demands on the people were massive, and any failure to meet them brought severe punishment. Earlier rulers of several states had built walls to guard their northern borders against attack. Shi Huangdi organized incredible numbers of labourers to strengthen these walls, and link them together, to form what we know as the Great Wall of China. Many of those conscripted for this work failed to survive; their sufferings became part of Chinese legend.

The First Emperor launched a ruthless persecution of Confucianism. He was probably motivated partly by worries over the political threat posed by any comparison between his own savagery and the Confucian doctrine that a tyrant would lose legitimacy in the eyes of heaven, and partly by the intolerance of an arrogant man for any ideas different from his own. He may also have been egged on by legalist bureaucrats who resented the Confucians as would-be competitors for office. Confucian books were burned, and Confucian scholars were executed.

The Qin Dynasty lasted less than twenty years. Its fall was caused partly by power struggles between top officials after the death of Shi Huangdi in 210 BC, and partly by revolts of subjects who found the savagery of legalist government unendurable. According to tradition, the first major uprising was begun by some men who had been ordered to report for duty at a military post on a certain date. When floods rendered the roads impassable, they realized that they would not arrive in time. In accord with the legalist principle of ruthless punishment for even minor infractions, the penalty for tardiness was death, and no excuses were accepted. The men decided to rebel, despite the likelihood that they would fail and be killed, because they had nothing to lose.

The fall of the Qin Dynasty did not destroy the idea of a unified China under a single emperor. A new dynasty succeeded the old one and, despite occasional periods of division, unified imperial government existed for most of the next 2,000 years.

Major dynasties showed a fairly regular life-cycle. Every dynasty started out with competent and vigorous leadership; without such strengths a dynasty could not obtain control of China. However, the vigour of imperial leadership generally declined sooner or later, and the bureaucracy decayed. Great landowners were increasingly able to evade taxation, and such taxes as were collected tended to remain in the hands of corrupt officials instead of being passed on to the Emperor.

The wealth of the great landholders usually increased during the course of the dynastic cycle. In the beginning, if many such landholders of the preceding dynasty had lost their wealth during the collapse of the preceding dynasty, most of the land might be in the hands of small farmers. This eased the problem of tax collection; the land had to support only the government and the farmers themselves. Small farmers generally lacked the power and influence to evade taxation effectively. As time went on, however, families influential in the new dynasty accumulated land, and the surplus produced by the peasants who worked that land had to support them as well as the government. The richer these families became, the better they were able to bribe or otherwise influence tax-collectors, and shift their tax burden on to people having less influence than themselves. Government revenues therefore declined, even as the burden placed on the remaining peasant smallholders grew heavier. Some peasants were driven into banditry, which a decaying government with declining revenues could not easily suppress.

The pattern of decline might be reversed only briefly by strong leadership in the capital. Hunger and anarchy would soon be spreading again, and the dynasty would lose the 'Mandate of Heaven'. After its fall the country would go through a period of conflict, seldom very long, at the end of which a new dynasty would arise. The fact that the overall history of any particular dynasty was a history of decline encouraged the tendency of the Confucian scholars to praise the past rather than thinking in terms of progress.

One should not be misled by the recurring patterns of the dynastic cycle; China was not fundamentally an unchanging society. Every major dynasty came eventually to suffer from most of the same weaknesses, but in other ways they were very different from one another. The structure of government, the economy, and the relationship of government to society underwent substantial long-term changes.

The first major dynasty to go through the dynastic cycle was the Han. A man named Liu Bang (Liu Pang), one of the rebels who overthrew the Qin, founded the Han Dynasty in 206 BC. Shi Huangdi's ban on heterodox philosophical writings was lifted, and various scholars either removed old texts from places of concealment or tried to write them out from memory. Confucian ideas eventually became quite influential at the Han court, even though much of the Han government structure was legalist.

The Han Dynasty lost power for a few years in the first century AD, but was soon restored under the same name, and did not finally disappear until AD 220. Central government collapsed with the Han, and was not restored for almost 400 years. However, the Chinese Empire, unlike the Roman, did not fall back into barbarism when it lost its political cohesion. When the brief Sui Dynasty (581–618) restored central authority, it controlled a civilization on roughly the level of the Han. The Tang Dynasty (618–907) carried Chinese culture to the highest peak it had yet attained in art and poetry as well as in wealth.

The coming of Buddhism

In the late years of the Han, and during the period of division that followed, the Buddhist religion was filtering into China from India. This was the only occasion before the modern era that Chinese culture was heavily influenced by the culture of a foreign country.

Buddhism had originally been essentially a set of prescriptions about how humans should approach the world. Buddhism taught that life in this world is essentially miserable, and that there is nothing that can be done to make it other than miserable. Nothing endures; everything changes, decays, and is eventually destroyed. People are born, grow old, sicken, die, and are born again in other bodies in an endless cycle of misery. The goal of all sensible people should be to break the cycle of reincarnation, to free themselves from the ties that bind them to the world. Upon attaining true enlightenment, a person will lose all desire for the things of this world. The lack of such desires means that after death, such a person will not be pulled back into this world to be born in another body for another life of misery. Instead, he or she will remain forever in the state of bliss known as nirvana. The man known historically as 'the Buddha', who is believed to have lived in northern India around 500 BC, was supposed to have been such a one.

This original doctrine, known as Theravada or Hinayana, was individualistic; it showed how each person could save himself or herself from the misery of earthly existence.

The schools of Buddhism that spread most widely in China and Japan, known as Mahayana, gave more emphasis to the ways human beings could obtain help from outside themselves. Mahayana thinkers criticized Theravada doctrine for its selfishness. Surely a person who had attained enlightenment would not simply escape from the world to enjoy the peace of nirvana as an individual, but would remain active in the world to help those less fortunate. He or she would become a Bodhisattva. Most Mahayana sects worshipped Bodhisattvas as if they were gods, and ascribed to them the sort of supernatural powers that other religions ascribe to gods. Ordinary humans could pray to them for assistance in matters both earthly and spiritual.

The Bodhisattva Amituofo (A-mi-t'o-fo, Amitabha, Amida) presided over what was in effect a heaven – a 'Pure Land' into which people could be reborn after death, in which they could be permanently safe from the suffering of earthly life. To be reborn in the Pure Land, by aid of the Bodhisattva, seemed a far more attainable goal than to achieve enlightenment by one's own efforts and thus avoid any rebirth. Chinese Buddhism eventually became more preoccupied with praying for the aid of Bodhisattvas than with efforts to achieve nirvana.

The doctrine attained its greatest strength during the Tang Dynasty. It declined thereafter, but it did not disappear; instead it was absorbed into the mixture of traditions that came to characterize China.

Some Chinese were exclusively Buddhist or exclusively Confucian, but most saw no reason to choose a single set of beliefs. The Chinese worshipped a tremendous variety of gods. Many were Bodhisattvas. Some were Daoist in origin. Some represented a combination of Daoist and Buddhist ideas. Each city had its own city god. The 'God of War' Guandi, who in fact owed much of his popularity to his roles as a god of wealth and a healer of the sick, was an actual general of the late Han Dynasty, deified long after his death.

Few Chinese felt compelled to restrict themselves to a single deity, and there was seldom friction between worshippers of different gods. Guandi had temples of his own, but his statue was also placed as a guardian figure at the entrances to both Buddhist and Daoist temples. A Buddhist tradition held that the ghost of the general had fallen into conversation with a monk, and been converted to Buddhism, more than three centuries after his death.

The Confucian scholar could work all day as an official in a government that was essentially legalist in structure, then go home, have some wine, and write poetry that was Daoist or Buddhist in inspiration. The various schools learned to get along so well, in fact, that people sometimes forgot that there ever had been serious conflict. The legalist attack on Confucianism under Shi Huangdi was too dramatic to be forgotten, but men accustomed to the idea that the Confucian bureaucrat became a Daoist when the working day was over have sometimes had difficulty understanding certain old documents containing Confucian criticisms of Daoist ideas.

Popular religion remained strong, if not well organized, down to the twentieth century. Élite culture and élite philosophy became essentially secular, however, as they had been in the Zhou period. Confucius, when asked about the gods, had simply refused to answer. By about AD 1000, the strength of Buddhism had faded enough so that serious philosophy was coming once more to be concerned primarily with things of this world.

The later dynasties

Chinese urban culture reached a peak in the late Tang and then in the Song (Sung) Dynasty, AD 960–1279. A wealthy and vigorous merchant class developed commerce both within China and with Southeast Asia. The apparatus of government came for the first time really to be dominated by educated civil servants, men who had passed state examinations based on the Confucian classics. However, while civil culture throve, China's military strength declined. During the late Song period the nomads to the north began moving south into China. Finally, in 1279, the Mongols under Kublai Khan conquered all of China. Under the Mongol rulers (referred to in Chinese as the Yuan Dynasty), China was incorporated into a Mongol Empire, which for a while covered most of Asia.

Mongol rule lasted less than a century. In 1368, Chinese rebels were able to expel the Mongols and establish the Ming Dynasty.

Chinese society was dominated by Confucian scholars under the Ming Dynasty even more than it had been under the Song. Almost all positions in government were filled by men who had passed written examinations, administered by the government, which tested literary ability and knowledge of the classics. The scholar-bureaucrats who had passed such examinations formed the main ruling class of China from the early Ming up to the nineteenth century. However, the structure of government retained a strong legalist element. The Ming emperors, who used Confucian scholars in government more than most previous dynasties, were at the same time more brutally and arbitrarily despotic in their own behaviour than the rulers of the Han, Tang, or Song.

Confucian doctrine stressed harmony, loyalty, and trust. Actual government practice under the Ming involved elaborate techniques of 'divide and rule' by which despotic emperors broke up all concentrations of power and maintained their own control over their subordinates. The emperors worried that if bureaucrats were appointed to important positions in their home provinces, or if they served in any one place for too long, they might use the networks of contacts and friendships they built up to serve their own interests rather than the interests of the throne.

Rulers had learned the tremendous value of Confucian officials as tools of government, but a man true to Confucian ideals of moral government could find himself facing the same dilemma that had frustrated Confucius – immoral rulers may not be enthusiastic about officials who want to practise moral government. One famous clash occurred in 1565, when an official of legendary rectitude, named Hai Rui (Hai Jui), submitted a written protest to the Emperor about his disgraceful behaviour. Realizing what kind of reaction he could expect, Hai Rui had first purchased a coffin for himself and made arrangements for his funeral. He was indeed arrested and tortured; his life was saved only by the timely death of the Emperor he had offended. Most officials, however, were more flexible.

In the view of the scholars, society was made up of four major classes. In the order of their worth, these were: (1) The scholars themselves, who by virtue of their education and culture were fit to rule over the others. (2) The peasants, who grew the food without which nobody could survive. (3) The artisans, who made things somewhat less vital than food but still of considerable value. (4) The merchants, who made nothing, and lived simply by shuffling goods around from one place to another.

The real status of the merchants was higher than this theoretical scale would suggest; their wealth guaranteed them a certain amount of respect. However, the merchant class never regained the position it had held in Chinese society under the Song. Many successful merchants, instead of wanting their sons to follow in their footsteps, had them educated as scholars in the hope that they could join the bureaucracy, the real ruling class of China.

The Chinese reaction against Mongol rule gave Chinese culture an isolationist bent. The Ming rulers were less friendly towards foreigners than the Song rulers had been. Furthermore, the high proportion of foreigners among the merchant community at the time when China was under Mongol rule may have contributed to a decline in the prestige of the merchants.

Under the Song, Chinese diplomats had been quite active in Southeast Asia, promoting Chinese commerce in the area. The Ming Dynasty was not interested in encouraging such commerce. Early Ming emperors built a large navy, and sent fleets through Southeast Asia and on across the Indian Ocean as far as Ceylon and East Africa. However, they quickly lost interest in such projects. In the end they not only stopped maintaining a powerful navy but also forbade Chinese merchants to build large ocean-going vessels.

China's relations with lands overseas were conducted through the tribute system. Other countries were expected to acknowledge the superiority of Chinese civilization and the Chinese Emperor, and present tribute. The Ming Dynasty's expectation that other cultures would actually recognize the superiority of Chinese civilization, and emulate it, was encouraged by the extent to which Korea and Vietnam really were patterning themselves after China. Bureaucrats came to be chosen there, as in China, through written examinations based on the Confucian classics.

China continued to enjoy a good deal of commerce, some of it conducted by foreign missions whose official excuse for coming to China was the presentation of tribute. However, the Chinese government did not place a high enough value on commerce to treat it as a purpose of the tribute system.

It was unfortunate that European ships began to arrive at this particular time, when Chinese attitudes towards both foreigners and commerce had become so negative. The first Portuguese sailors reached the south coast of China in 1514, and soon they were trading on a regular basis. The Chinese regarded them as barbarians; they looked odd, had a strange language and customs, and showed little respect for Chinese law. They also smelled disgusting, since sanitary conditions aboard most Portuguese ships were terrible. They were eventually allowed to establish a trading base at Macao, a peninsula on the south coast near the city of Guangzhou. The peninsula was walled off from the mainland of China.

Contact was restricted essentially to commerce until the 1580s, when a Jesuit missionary named Matteo Ricci began a determined effort to penetrate China. He studied the Chinese language, adopted the clothing and to some extent the customs of the Chinese upper class, and carefully dissociated himself from the disreputable Portuguese merchants at Macao. By 1598 he won permission to visit the capital at Beijing for a short period, and lived in Beijing from 1601 to 1610. He made a number of converts to Catholicism at the imperial court. Jesuit priests became a fixture at the court from Ricci's time onward, though they had little impact on Chinese culture.

The overall rate of advance of Chinese civilization slowed dangerously during the Ming Dynasty. Under the Song, China had been among the leading cultures of the world, far superior to Western Europe in wealth, technology, and science. By the Ming period, stagnation was setting in. The causes are numerous and some are still subject to dispute. The decline in the position of the merchant class and the reduction in foreign contacts were probably important factors. The scholars' concentration on study of the classics diverted their interest away from science and technology. Changes in the structure of the Chinese economy have also been blamed. But, whatever the causes, Chinese technology and science lost their previous dynamism.

The Ming Dynasty, like previous ones, eventually fell into decline. The Manchus, a semi-civilized and quite un-Chinese group living to the northeast, took advantage of this situation. Raiding parties were getting past the Great Wall into China proper by 1629. Manchu leaders progressively strengthened their political and administrative system, and in 1636 they began calling themselves the Qing Dynasty. In 1644, taking advantage of the collapse of the Ming (Chinese rebels had actually seized Beijing), they launched a massive invasion of China. Their control was fully consolidated by 1681.

Government and society under the Qing

The Manchus got along with their Chinese subjects far better than the Mongols had. They adopted many Chinese cultural patterns and were to a considerable extent assimilated by the people they had conquered, so by the year 1800 the empire was run in much the same way that indigenous dynasties had run it in the past. The Qing Dynasty emperors were Manchu, but Chinese was the language of administration, and many of the officials, even in very high positions, were Chinese.

Chinese emperors had traditionally worried about the danger that officials who became too strong might someday turn against the throne. This problem was especially serious when the Chinese officials in question were serving an alien Manchu emperor. When the Manchus first established their control in China they allowed some of the Chinese who had collaborated with them in the conquest to control substantial regional power bases, and substantial armies. These men turned against the Manchus in 1673, in the Rebellion of the Three Feudatories. Eight years of warfare

PLATE 1.2 The Great Wall. The Ming Dynasty rebuilt and strengthened the Great Wall for defence against the Manchu nomads to the north. However, the Wall could block invaders only if it were effectively manned. In 1644, with the Ming Dynasty collapsing, the Chinese general assigned to defend a crucial section of the Wall decided to let the Manchus in, and to join their conquest of China instead of fighting to keep

were required to put them down. From this point onward, the Qing rulers were more careful to keep their officials from becoming too strong. The form of government organization was determined as much by the need to prevent certain things from happening as by the need to make sure that the things that were supposed to happen did happen.

The empire spread far into central Asia; it was larger than it ever had been under an emperor who was actually Chinese. Aside from the areas where the Chinese people themselves had traditionally lived, it included Manchuria (the home of the Manchus) in the northeast, Mongolia in the north, Xinjiang (Sinkiang) in the northwest, and to some extent even Tibet in the southwest. The great majority of the empire's population was Chinese, but the sparsely populated non-Chinese border areas made up more than half of its land area. The Manchus also conquered the island of Taiwan in 1683; the island had not previously been part of China.

Governmental power was as centralized as the emperors could make it. Provincial officials were not local leaders; they were men who had passed the civil service examinations based on the Confucian classics, and had then been appointed to office by the central government, usually in some location far from their original homes. However, this bureaucratic system did not stretch down below the county level. The county magistrate appointed by the Emperor had to work through local people in actually running the villages. The most important of these were the 'gentry', the people who had enough education to have passed at least the lower stages of the civil service examinations. (Note that the Chinese 'gentry' did not bear much resemblance to the gentry of traditional England.) At any given time the number of people who had passed the lower examinations and thus acquired gentry status was much larger than the number actually holding bureaucratic appointments; the ones not in office formed the leadership of local society.

The emperors tried to emphasize impersonal norms, but purely personal relationships played a tremendous role. The Chinese élite was bound together by a web of personal relationships (*guanxi*) based on kinship, shared educational background, and past favours given and received. Doing favours for one's friends often took precedence over adherence to imperial policy. The emperors made a point of not appointing civil servants to positions in their home provinces, because this was where they had the most and the closest personal relationships.

By the nineteenth century, as the Qing Dynasty weakened and its officials grew lax or corrupt, the gentry became a little more independent of the central government, but they still, to a considerable extent, formed a national rather than a local élite. A member of the gentry had far more in common with people of his own class in other provinces than with peasants who lived in his immediate neighbourhood. The main factor setting the gentry off from the masses was knowledge of classical Chinese,[1] the language of literature and scholarship. There were many dialects, sufficiently different really to constitute separate languages, spoken in different areas of the country. Scholars communicated in an ancient tongue, no longer spoken by the common people anywhere, but known to educated men everywhere. All respectable literature, and writing on politics, philosophy, and other important subjects, was in classical Chinese. It was used much the way Latin was in medieval Europe, but classical Chinese was a more difficult language than Latin.

The way the élite used a quite different language from the common people, which could be acquired only through long and usually expensive study, was symbolic of the great social inequalities that existed throughout Chinese society. Class structure was not frozen by heredity. If the son of a poor peasant were sufficiently intelligent, and somehow managed to get a good education, he could be accepted as a full member of the ruling class. Many children of the gentry, conversely, sank down among the commoners. However, the fact that individuals could cross the gap between élite and masses should not lead us to suppose that the gap was small. People who laboured with their minds felt they were born to dominate those who laboured with their hands. In most human relationships it was clearly understood that one person had a higher rank than the other, and the differences in rank were very important.

Simple inequalities in wealth were substantial (though not nearly as great as in some other societies of the same period, notably Russia). The landlords and officials could live in luxury while many of the peasants were on the edge of starvation. Living standards for the common people were not very good even in the eighteenth century, the high point of the Qing Dynasty. In later years, as overpopulation and a low level of technology were exacerbated by corruption and decay, things became very unpleasant indeed for them.

---

[1] Classical Chinese is also called classical Mandarin, literary Chinese, and *wenyan*. Do not confuse it with modern Mandarin, which is the everyday language of most of northern China, and is the main language of education and government in China today.

Psychological inequalities – differences in status – were even more extreme. One hears a lot about 'face' in Chinese society. The Chinese were very sensitive about their personal dignity, and would go to great lengths to avoid situations in which they were likely to 'lose face'. In most contexts, people were careful not to arouse enmities by causing others to lose face. However, the other side of the coin was that people with a high rank were sometimes quite ruthless in feeding their own pride by humiliating their inferiors. It is no accident that China, a place where people were extraordinarily concerned about their personal dignity, was also the place where top government officials were expected not merely to bow but to prostrate themselves on the floor when presenting themselves before the Emperor.

The central institution of Chinese society, the primary locus of loyalties, was the patrilineal family. For a man not to have a son was a disaster; there would be nobody to carry on his family line, nobody to care for him in old age, nobody to perform the ancestral ceremonies for him after his death. In order to have a son a man needed a wife. While some Chinese men were simply unable to marry, hardly any remained single by choice. However, marriage did not mean that bride and groom were creating a new family; it meant that the bride was becoming a member (not necessarily even an important member) of the family into which her husband had been born. Family structure was supposed to be based not on the bond between husband and wife, but on the line of descent from father to sons. If possible, husband and wife were supposed to live with the parents of the husband, or with his brothers if his parents were dead. In such an extended family, a young married man's primary loyalty was supposed to be to his parents and brothers rather than to his wife. In practice, however, the extended family was found mostly among the well-to-do; young men of limited wealth were often forced by circumstance to set up households separate from those of their parents.

Most marriages were arranged by the parents of the people involved. It was considered perfectly normal for the bride and groom to be strangers, and to meet one another for the first time during the marriage ceremony.

The status differentiation in Chinese society extended to family relationships, where old people ranked higher than young ones and men higher than women. The worst treatment was reserved for young females. As infants they were sometimes killed, or just allowed to die of neglect, if the family did not feel it could afford to feed the extra mouth. As children, most of them had to bind their feet – to wear tight wrappings that prevented the feet from growing to normal size, and distorted the skeletal structure. The result was 'lily feet', which made them sexually more attractive to their future husbands, but made walking difficult. As young wives they could be abused unmercifully, especially by their mothers-in-law. They were sometimes regarded less as members of the family into which they had married than as property owned by that family. A family containing a young man in need of a wife might buy one for him, and if things went wrong she might even find her husband, or her husband's family, selling her again to some other family.

The only way a woman could attain a position of power and security was through a relationship with a male. Sometimes she could attain a sufficiently good relationship with her husband, but the system of arranged marriages and the subservience most husbands showed towards their parents, especially their mothers, kept this from being the norm. The typical woman had to endure years of abuse by her mother-in-law, and achieved a strong position only when her son became important enough in the family to give her some leverage. When her son became the nominal head of the family she might in fact rule it through her control over him; she could then shower on younger women, if she chose, the sort of abuse she had once endured.

By the nineteenth century, the Qing Dynasty was beginning to decay as others had before it; Chinese who knew their own country's history could recognize the signs. However, Chinese society and culture seemed very stable. Hardly anyone in China suspected that the fall of the dynasty, when it came, would be accompanied by massive alterations in the whole structure of their civilization.

Study questions

How was China different in the Ming Dynasty from what it had been in the Song Dynasty?

How did the role of Confucian scholars in China change over the centuries?

How much difference did it make that the emperors of China in the Qing Dynasty were Manchu, rather than Chinese?

CHAPTER 2

The collapse of the old order

By the middle of the nineteenth century, the Manchu government of China was under severe pressures both internal and external. Its longstanding policy of isolationism was beginning to break down in the face of European military superiority; the Opium War of 1839–42 was only the first of a series of Chinese military defeats. In the 1850s and 1860s, the Taiping Rebellion almost destroyed the dynasty from within.

The Manchus were very reluctant to carry out any extensive reforms in the face of these threats. They had barely begun to attempt serious modernization when they were overthrown by the Revolution of 1911. The revolution aroused high hopes, but within about five years central government collapsed completely, and China was divided among various warlords. The challenge of establishing an effective government, capable of restoring order and defending the country against foreign encroachment, remained unmet.

The first Western impact

The general attitude of both Manchus and Chinese was that China had the highest, and in a sense the only, true civilization. They were willing to have contact with foreign cultures only on the assumption that the foreigners were barbarians who acknowledged the superiority of Chinese culture and the Emperor of China, and presented tribute to the Emperor as a sign of submission. Ambassadors received by the Emperor were expected to perform the 'kowtow', touching their heads to the floor, just as high officials of the Chinese government were required to do.

China's immediate neighbors, such as the Koreans, Vietnamese, and Burmese, were tributary states, willing to give at least lip-service to the idea of Chinese supremacy. The Jesuits won acceptance partly through their scientific knowledge, especially in astronomy, but the main key to their success was that they complied with Chinese expectations by adopting many aspects of Chinese culture. Eventually, in fact, the Pope became disturbed by the question of who was converting whom. In the early eighteenth century, when the Pope ordered the Jesuits to behave more like Christian missionaries and less like Confucian scholars, their influence at the imperial court declined.

However, in the early nineteenth century the Europeans, and in particular the British, became unwilling to accept the system and the rather insulting restrictions that went with it. Western trade was permitted only at the south-coast port of Guangzhou, and the European merchants were not permitted year-round residence even there. The British East India Company's representatives were not permitted direct contact with provincial officials in Guangzhou; they had to pass messages through Chinese merchants. When the Company tried to go around this system by sending a delegation headed by Lord Amherst directly to Beijing in 1816, the Emperor refused to receive him. The East India Company accepted this. But in 1834, the Company was stripped of its monopoly of trade in Asia, and soon direct representatives of the British government, less willing to tolerate Qing Dynasty officials' assumption of China's superiority, were arriving in Asia. Britain, the greatest trading power in the world, wanted the right to trade more freely, to maintain an ambassador in Beijing, and to send missionaries into China.

Friction over these issues was exacerbated by the problem of opium. For many years European merchants seeking tea, silk, porcelain, and other luxuries had bought more from China than they sold, and paid for the difference in gold and silver. This was where much of the wealth that the Spanish had taken from Latin America had eventually gone. But early in the nineteenth century the British had begun selling tremendous quantities of opium, acquired from their new possessions in India, to China. Soon the balance of payments had shifted, and gold and silver were flowing out of China. This caused an economic crisis as well as a tremendous drug-abuse problem.

In the late 1830s the Chinese government made a serious effort to eradicate the opium traffic. An energetic and competent administrator named Lin Zexu (Lin Tse-hsu) was sent to Guangzhou to manage the campaign. Officials there had already launched an effective drive against the Chinese smugglers who had been distributing opium within China; Lin decided also to go after the foreign merchants (most of them British, but some from the United States and other nations) who had been supplying the Chinese smugglers. In March 1839, Lin placed about 350 foreign merchants under a polite sort of siege in their compound in Guangzhou. They were not physically harmed, or cut off from food supplies, but their Chinese servants all had to leave the compound, and the hostage merchants were not allowed either to trade or to leave until the merchant community had handed over its opium stocks to be destroyed. The British government's representative on the scene, Captain Charles Elliot, collected more than 1,000 tons of opium from the merchants and handed it over to Lin.

Lin had a more sophisticated understanding of the foreigners than most Chinese officials, but he had no conception of how important the opium trade was to the economy of the British Empire, or of how powerfully the British could and would react to any threat against their merchants. He had started what became known as the Opium War. For China it was a disaster from beginning to end. The British navy roamed the coasts at will. Even on land the Chinese army was inferior in weapons, training, and discipline, besides being riddled with opium addiction. Most of the officers were hopelessly incompetent; the most talented young men in China had been encouraged to study the Confucian classics rather than training themselves for war. By 1842 China was forced to submit. Britain acquired the island of Hong Kong and an indemnity. Missionaries and merchants were henceforth allowed to live, trade, and preach in five 'treaty ports' along the coast. Other Western powers soon signed similar treaties with China.

For more than a decade, the results were minimal. The government of China was still determined to minimize contact with the Westerners. It did not interpret the opening of the port of Guangzhou to British trade as implying that Englishmen could enter the walled city of Guangzhou, and those who tried to do so were threatened with mob violence. Of the five treaty ports, only Shanghai saw much growth in foreign commerce. Britain and other powers attempted to negotiate a revision of the treaties, opening China to much more Western contact, but had no success. They concluded that another war would be needed to persuade China to submit.

The incidents that triggered what became known as the Second Opium War came in 1856. Britain's excuse for war was very thin. Chinese officials had boarded a vessel in the harbor at Guangzhou, the *Arrow*, and arrested most of the crew (who were Chinese) for piracy. The British consul treated a report that the Chinese officials had hauled down a British flag flown by the *Arrow* as having represented an insult to Britain, despite the facts that (1) the report may well have been false, and (2) the right of the vessel to fly a British flag had been dubious (the *Arrow*'s owner, a Chinese rather than a British subject, had registered it in British Hong Kong but had allowed that registration to lapse). The French had a better excuse: the execution of a Catholic missionary, Fr Auguste Chapdelaine, whom Chinese authorities had caught far outside the small area that the treaties had opened to missionary activity.

British forces raided Guangzhou in October 1856, but it was not until the end of 1857 that substantial British and French forces began operations against China. They seized Guangzhou, and then went north. They seized the coastal forts at Dagu and moved inland towards the major city of Tianjin, about 125 kilometres from Beijing. Chinese negotiators signed the Treaty of Tianjin in July 1858. The following year, however, the Emperor retracted his initial acceptance of this treaty, which would have opened a number of new treaty ports, allowed Westerners to travel in the interior of China, allowed the British to station an ambassador in Beijing, and granted the Westerners an indemnity. The British and French once more took the forts at Dagu, and then moved inland through Tianjin to Beijing, where the Emperor's summer palace was looted and then burned. They then imposed a new treaty. In addition to everything the Emperor had found unacceptable in the 1858 treaty, China had to grant the addition of further territory to the British colony of Hong Kong, a further expansion of the list of treaty ports, the right of missionaries to buy land and build churches in the interior of China, and an increase in the size of the indemnity. The Emperor's despair over these events probably contributed to his death the following year.

Later negotiations involving various Western powers, and later wars in which China was defeated by France (1883–85), Japan (1894–95), and Britain, France, Japan, Russia, the United States, Austria-Hungary, and Italy all together (1900), led to further elaboration of what the Westerners called the 'Treaty System'. Chinese authors referred to the 'unequal treaties'. The list of treaty ports expanded steadily; by 1917 there were ninety-two of them. (Most of these 'ports' were in fact ports, either along the coast or on the Yangzi River, but some were landlocked cities.) Foreign influence was substantial in all treaty ports; portions of Shanghai and fifteen other treaty ports were placed under outright foreign administration, mainly British.

Christian missionaries could move freely throughout China, and merchants could circulate to a considerable extent. The 'most favoured nation' principle ensured that any privilege given to one European power also went automatically to the others. Under the principle of extraterritoriality, no Westerner accused of a crime in China could be tried under Chinese law; Western courts were established in the treaty ports to try such cases. The tariff that China could collect on its imports was limited by treaty to 5 per cent, and in practice it often was below even this limit. The Maritime Customs Service, which collected the small permitted tariff, was run by foreigners (mainly British). Eventually, significant numbers of Western troops began to be stationed in China as protection for Western residents and as guards on foreign-owned railroads. Foreign warships operated not only off China's coast, but even on her inland waterways.

Internal problems

The dynastic weakness that made China vulnerable to these foreign incursions also increased her susceptibility to internal rebellion. The population had increased dramatically under the Qing; it probably reached 400 million some time between 1800 and 1850. Traditional forms of technology were not capable of providing a decent living for so many people. At the same time the government was growing lax. Local officials, who had collected taxes primarily as agents of the central government early in the dynasty, were now keeping most of what they got and passing on only a fraction of their take to the Emperor. Wealthy individuals acquired greater influence over local administrators and thus became increasingly able to evade taxation, throwing the burden onto the poor. The peasants, short of land, paid increasingly heavy taxes while the amount of revenue actually reaching the Emperor declined. Poverty drove thousands to banditry. The Manchu army, its original spirit sapped by generations of garrison duty within China, had deteriorated badly; many units were almost useless. As the government's ability to maintain order declined, local leaders began raising their own militias to protect their villages.

Dynastic decay had gone far enough to permit a serious rebellion by the 'White Lotus' Buddhist sect in Central China at the end of the eighteenth century. The outbreak of the Taiping Rebellion in the mid nineteenth century led to an even greater crisis. It began in the hills of South China, where a religious visionary claiming to be the younger brother of Jesus Christ founded a Christian sect. His movement spread, came into conflict with the government, and developed its own army. Soon it was calling itself the Taiping Tianguo, or 'Heavenly Kingdom of Great Peace'. Sweeping north and east into the basin of the Yangzi River, the richest and most populous region of China, the 'Heavenly King' established his capital at Nanjing (Nanking) in 1853. He could not take the Manchu capital at

Beijing, but the government armies proved equally incapable of destroying the rebels.

The Manchus then turned to regional militias formed by the local gentry, and allowed some of these militias to develop into real armies. The man who initiated this development, Zeng Guofan (Tseng Kuo-fan), had originally been a civilian rather than a military official; he had won entry to the bureaucracy by the usual means – success in the civil service examinations. He had served in a number of important posts in the central government in Beijing, but at the beginning of 1853 he was at his home in Hunan province, having been released from his duties for the customary period of mourning following the death of his mother. He received an imperial order to supervise the organization of local militia forces in his home area, to resist the Taipings. He quickly began to build a much larger and more powerful force than the men who had sent him this order had intended.

This was not something the Manchus could afford to take lightly; they had not forgotten the lesson their ancestors had learned from the Rebellion of the Three Feudatories in 1673. However assimilated they might be to Chinese culture, the Manchus knew that they were a small number of aliens dominating a huge number of Chinese; any concentration of power in Chinese hands was potentially dangerous. The typical Confucian scholar's lack of respect for soldiers and military affairs (there was a saying, 'one does not waste good iron by making it into nails, or good men by making them into soldiers') had been a comfort to the Manchus, since it had left bureaucrats trained in the Confucian tradition poorly qualified to lead rebellions. The Qing Dynasty's armies had always included Chinese soldiers under Chinese officers, but these officers had not usually been conspicuous for their intelligence, and they had been rotated from unit to unit to keep them from building excessively strong personal bonds.

So here was Zeng Guofan, long known for his intellect and now showing himself to be aggressively innovative as well, operating in his home province (where he could never have been given any normal bureaucratic appointment), recruiting out of the local élite officers who had personal ties with him and with one another, officers who in turn led troops from the same area, with whom they had personal ties.

When the Emperor and his Court learned what was happening they hesitated. Eventually they not only tolerated what Zeng was doing, but allowed him the financial resources to pay his men better than regular imperial troops were paid. The fact that top officials in Beijing knew Zeng, from the years he had worked there, may have helped them make the decision to trust him. Soon others were organizing similar armies in other provinces. For the Dynasty the gamble paid off; the regional armies that grew up outside the regular chain of command put down the Taiping Rebellion, and other smaller rebellions in other regions of China, and remained loyal. The Westerners also provided the Qing government with some useful support against the Taipings, feeling that it was worth working with the existing government despite the fact that they did not really like it. One should particularly note the 'Ever-victorious Army', a small Chinese force commanded originally by an American named Frederick Ward, and later by a British officer, Major Charles Gordon. It was very successful in fighting against the Taipings near the mouth of the Yangzi River. Such Western intervention, however, was much less important than the support provided for the Qing by the regional armies.

The leaders of these regional armies acquired tremendous power. The greatest of them was Li Hongzhang (Li Hung-chang), a native of Anhui province who had worked for a while under Zeng Guofan in the Hunan Army, but then had gone to Anhui to establish a similar force. After the defeat of the Taipings, he took for many years a large part of the responsibility for conducting China's foreign relations. He had his own army, under officers he had chosen and promoted, equipped to a considerable extent from his own arsenals. He also controlled much of China's naval forces. He was governor-general of a province, and had privileged access to tax revenues from other provinces to pay for his military forces. He sponsored several efforts to introduce modern technology into China.

Some Chinese were beginning to feel that they needed to learn from the foreigners, but this awareness developed very slowly. The idea of learning from foreigners seemed very abnormal in the light of Chinese tradition. In the English-speaking world today, most children grow up knowing that they use an alphabet developed in Italy, a political system whose origins go back to Greece, and a religion that comes from the Middle East. Their very ancestry can be traced more often than not to immigrant stock – Angles, Saxons, Danes, Normans, and so forth – who invaded Britain after the fall of the Roman Empire, and various groups that have migrated to the United States, Canada, and other English-speaking countries within the past 400 years. The ancestors of the modern Chinese, by contrast, had lived in China for all of recorded history. They had only once in their history engaged in large-scale borrowing from abroad, when they had adopted Buddhism. As far as most Chinese knew, the biggest foreign-inspired modification that had occurred in their culture in the past thousand years had beep the imposition by the Manchus of a new hair style on their subjects (male Chinese were required, under the Manchus, to wear their hair in a single braid, called a queue, hanging down the back). Most Chinese still believed that it was the foreigners who needed to copy the superior civilization of China.

The Chinese had been shocked by the defeats they had suffered at the hands of the West, but they did not respect the military profession enough to feel that someone who was militarily strong was necessarily worthy of respect or imitation. What they most valued was the literary and philosophical knowledge, especially of the Confucian classics, that both defined the gentleman and formed the qualifications for high office in the government. When the Manchu warriors had conquered China, it had been they who had imitated and been absorbed by the Chinese, rather than the other way round.

Initially some men, especially leaders of the regional armies, tried to introduce particular Western devices without imitating the West in any more basic way. Rifles and Western-style cannon came first; steamships, railroads, and telegraph lines followed. The policy was to use Western techniques as tools while retaining Chinese culture as the fundamental basis for all activity. This policy showed a distressing lack of success. For one thing, the foreigners had to be handled and dealt with, and this required far more than knowledge of a few techniques. Chinese officials had to know Western languages, commercial practices, behaviour patterns, and concepts of international law before they would be able to understand what the foreigners wanted, and how it could be either granted or refused with minimal cost to China. Moreover, even simple matters of technology did not work very well when taken out of their cultural context. The Chinese could manufacture artillery to Western designs, but it was not actually much use in battle as long as it remained, to the troops, an essentially alien device. The same applied in other areas. Superficial adoption of a few Western techniques could not even begin to save the country from the degree of peril facing it.

By the end of the century a few influential people were beginning to realize that China would have to copy the West in fundamental matters, but they did not find their position popular; most Chinese who had an opinion of the foreigners detested them. This was partly a response to genuine injuries and slights suffered at the hand of the West, ranging from the Opium War down to incidents of petty racism. The Europeans showed a conspicuous lack of respect for Chinese law and the Chinese people. In Shanghai, the richest city in China, there was a public park for the exclusive use of Europeans. (There is dispute among historians as to whether there was actually a sign at the entrance stating that 'No Dogs or Chinese' were permitted in the park.) But beyond such issues, which created much well-founded Chinese resentment, there were rumours attributing quite imaginary crimes to the foreigners. Many Chinese were convinced the Christian religion was based on black magic, and that Western missionaries were using Chinese children as victims in rituals involving human sacrifice. The notion that the Chinese should become students of Western culture seemed odd even to many of the more sophisticated Chinese; to those who believed the wilder of the anti-foreign rumours, it appeared positively obscene.

The Empress Dowager Cixi (Ts'u-hsi) dominated the imperial court. She had not been particularly powerful as the wife of an emperor, but when her husband died in 1861 and her five-year-old son inherited the throne, she was able to seize effective control of the government. When her son died some years later she arranged, in violation of the normal rules of succession, that the throne should go to a three-year-old boy who was her adopted son (originally her nephew), and she continued to rule in this young Emperor's name. Certainly she was intelligent and strong-willed. Otherwise she could hardly have dominated a society as male-centred as China for forty-seven years. However, she was also short-sighted, self-centred, and thoroughly ignorant of the Western world, which posed such a threat to the country she ruled. She would not willingly support any drastic programme of reform or modernization.

Islands of modernization began to appear in some places, under the aegis of various Chinese officials. Regional leaders like Li Hongzhang not only tried to modernize the armed forces under their control, but sometimes went beyond to sponsor commercial enterprises – shipping lines, factories, and so on. However, the merchants who managed such enterprises were subjected to much interference from their political masters, and many of the enterprises suffered from corruption and nepotism.

A more vigorous and far-reaching form of westernization occurred in the treaty ports and in Hong Kong, where Western influence was strongest. Christian missionaries set up schools and colleges. Chinese businessmen not only learned foreign business techniques and technology but also were able to apply their knowledge in a environment far more friendly to commercial enterprise than that found in the bulk of China. The competition of Western business firms with superior financial resources was sometimes a problem, but on the other hand many Chinese businessmen were able to borrow operating capital, through intermediaries, from Western banks. In any case, foreign competition posed fewer problems than the extortionate bureaucrats of cities not under foreign control. Later nationalist scholars have looked down on the 'compradors', Chinese businessmen who acted as agents or partners of foreign merchants, but these people played an important role in introducing Western knowledge to their country.

China had two great gateways to the outside world. One was Shanghai, at the mouth of the Yangzi, the headquarters for Western penetration of the huge Yangzi basin and economically the most important city in China.

The other was Guangdong province in the south, the first area that had been significantly influenced by Westerners. This was the province that sent by far the largest number of settlers overseas, to Southeast Asia and even to more distant lands like the United States. Many of these 'overseas Chinese' stayed in contact with relatives at home. Aside from having this huge network of informal contacts abroad, Guangdong was also host to the British colony of Hong Kong. The island of Hong Kong, near the mouth through which the province's major rivers reach the sea, had been ceded to Britain in 1842. British Hong Kong had been expanded by the cession of a small area of the mainland opposite the island in 1860, and then by the British acquisition of a much larger area of the mainland, called the New Territories, on a ninety-nine-year lease in 1898.

It was a native of Guangdong named Kang Youwei (K'ang Yu-wei) who in 1898 gained the car of the young Emperor and initiated the first major effort to modernize the central government of China. Kang was a Confucian scholar, but of a very innovative sort; he had reinterpreted the classics to make Confucius an advocate of reform and change rather than a preserver of tradition. Kang and the Emperor launched a remarkably broad campaign of reform and modernization. Military forces were to be modernized. The bureaucracy was to be streamlined. Western technology was to be promoted in many areas. Ancient texts were no longer to be stressed in the civil service examination system; practical knowledge would become more important. Traditional academies, and some temples, were to be converted into modern schools. Within a few weeks, however, conservative elements at the court, led by the Empress Dowager, had regained control. The brief period of Kang's ascendancy was later known as the 'Hundred Days'. Kang fled abroad; other leading reformers were executed, and the Emperor spent the rest of his days as a prisoner of his aunt the Empress Dowager.

Foreign pressure increases

The Qing Dynasty, even after its defeat in 1860, retained hopes of functioning as a regional power in Asia, defending its traditional tributary states against foreign encroachment. Its efforts to protect Vietnam from

French conquest led to the Sino-French War of 1883–1885, in which China was defeated but did not suffer huge losses.

The effort to defend Korea against the Japanese went much worse. Japan had become sufficiently modernized to begin serious penetration of Korea, emulating the patterns of European imperialism, in the 1870s. In 1884, Li Hongzhang negotiated an agreement under which Japan and China shared influence in Korea, but this did not end competition between them. The Sino-Japanese War broke out over this issue in 1894. On the Chinese side, it was fought primarily by Li Hongzhang's forces. Li's army was defeated on land. His navy, very badly commanded and with outdated ships, was defeated at sea and the surviving ships captured when the Japanese took, by land assault, the ports where the ships had taken shelter. Li then had to negotiate a humiliating peace in 1895, under which China was to lose its influence in Korea, pay a large indemnity, and hand over substantial territory to Japan, including the island of Taiwan and the Liaodong Peninsula, the southernmost part of Manchuria. A few months later, France, Russia, and Germany intervened, forcing Japan to give up the Liaodong Peninsula.

The Sino-Japanese War was followed by a sudden surge of foreign penetration in many areas of China, leading to the creation of what were called the 'spheres of influence'. One motive for the French conquest of northern Vietnam had been a desire for access to the southwestern Chinese provinces of Yunnan and Guangxi. Between 1895 and 1898, the French obtained the rights to open mines in this area, and to build railroads from Vietnam into both provinces. They also extended their sphere into the western part of Guangdong. The Germans went into Shandong province. Once in firm possession of Taiwan, the Japanese began to penetrate the nearest part of the mainland of China, Fujian province. The British extended their influence in the Yangzi basin, though they could not establish as tight a grip on this huge area as other powers did in smaller spheres of influence.

There were, of course, conflicting claims. The British, coming through Burma, competed in Yunnan against the French coming through Vietnam. But a more dangerous situation developed when the Russians, who had helped to block the Japanese out of Manchuria in 1895, went in themselves. First came an agreement for construction of the Chinese Eastern Railway, running from Russia's Pacific port of Vladivostok across northern Manchuria to link with the Trans-Siberian Railway, leading to European Russia. This was nominally a joint Russian–Chinese project, actually under firm Russian control. The Russians are believed to have paid Li

PLATE 2.1 *Public execution during the Boxer Rising. A Boxer is beheaded in front of European troops. (© Hulton Archive/Getty Images.)*

Hongzhang a hefty bribe for arranging the deal. In 1898, the Russians leased from China the southern tip of the Liaodong Peninsula, including the naval base of Port Arthur and the commercial port of Dalian (Ta-lian, Dairen, Dalny). They also won the right to build the South Manchurian Railway, running northeast from Dalian through the heart of Manchuria to link with the Chinese Eastern Railway. The Japanese were infuriated.

The final outburst of traditional Chinese xenophobia came in 1899. A group generally called the Boxers, basically a secret society, began attacking missionaries and foreigners in general. They claimed that the mysterious powers of Chinese martial arts could defeat the firearms of the foreigners and drive them out. The Boxers originally had anti-Manchu tendencies, but the Empress Dowager and the court, hating the foreigners and in any case fearing to antagonize the Boxers, decided to co-opt them and gave them a certain degree of support. The Boxers killed missionaries and Chinese Christians, and besieged the foreign legations in the capital of Beijing. The result was what might have been expected, given China's repeated defeats earlier in the nineteenth century. A joint force of the major Western powers plus Japan marched in, defeated the Boxers and the government army that had been half-heartedly supporting the Boxers in their attack on the foreign legations, captured Beijing with much destruction and looting, and extracted a massive indemnity from the government.

Fortunately, the fighting was limited to the northern part of the country. Key provincial governors in central and southern China understood the power of the European far better than did the Empress Dowager; they ignored her decision to support the Boxers, and maintained the fiction that the Boxers were rebels against the Qing Dynasty. They were thus able to avoid becoming embroiled in the hostilities. Eventually the victorious Westerners also decided to accept this fiction, which is why books published in the West often refer to the whole affair as the 'Boxer Rebellion'. The Westerners did not want to destroy the dynasty, but simply to manipulate and exploit it, so they allowed it to save face by disavowing its erstwhile Boxer allies.

The foreign threat to Chinese independence had become acute. It seemed for a time that China might be carved up into colonies. Within their spheres of influence, the foreign powers' investments and commercial activities were usually backed up by control of communications, especially railways, and by the presence of military forces. Foreign naval vessels operated not only along the coast but also a considerable distance up the Yangzi River. China's helplessness was revealed when the Japanese seized the Russian sphere of influence in southern Manchuria in the Russo-Japanese War of 1904–05. Some Japanese troops entered Manchuria by land from Korea; others landed on the Liaodong Peninsula to take Dalian and Port Arthur. From there they pushed more than 200 miles northeast along the South Manchurian Railway to defeat the Russians in a bloody battle at Shenyang (Mukden). In this war fought mostly on Chinese soil, the Qing Dynasty government remained an essentially passive spectator, and even issued a formal declaration of neutrality.

In the end China was not carved up; the spheres of influence did not become colonies. Partly this was because China was too large for any one power to take, and for a foreign power to convert influence into total control was difficult, in any particular area, as long as there existed a Chinese national government lying outside the foreign power's sphere of influence. Partly it was because the various powers interfered with one another's ambitions. Complete control of an area by any of them would have implied locking out the others. The 'Open Door Policy', announced by the United States in 1899 and 1900, was the most formal statement of this principle. This policy ordained that the control exercised by foreign powers over their spheres of influence should not be carried to such a point that the commerce of other nations was excluded, or that the sphere of influence ceased to be a part of China. One should not overestimate the impact of this American policy. The USA was not prepared to enforce it, but only to declare a wish that other nations should obey its principles. Furthermore, even had it been enforced, it would not by any means have constituted a guarantee of Chinese independence. Chinese enthusiasm for the Open Door was limited; most Chinese, given a choice, would have preferred a closed door with the foreigners on the outside.

In the first years of the twentieth century, shaken by the disaster of the Boxer incident and by the scramble of the imperialist powers for concessions in China, the Qing Court finally took drastic steps to preserve China's independence. The court tried not only to negotiate an increase in tariff levels, but also to regain control of the Maritime Customs Service that collected those tariffs. It tried very hard to negotiate an end to foreign importation of opium into China. It began modifying the principle of extraterritorality, under which Westerners in China were immune to Chinese law. It pushed effective administration into remote border areas to which it had previously never paid much attention, to make sure that they would not be nibbled away by the foreigners.

Even more important, the Qing Court embarked on a drastic programme of modernization and westernization within China. The traditional system of civil service examinations was abolished, and the education system was modified to take in Western knowledge. Students (some sent by provincial governments, others acting on their own) went to various foreign countries, especially Japan, to study. As Western ideas began to spread more broadly in China, some families abandoned the custom of foot-binding. Significant numbers of educated people began attacking traditional religious beliefs as superstition.

Efforts were made to modernize many military units. These 'New Armies' differed from the traditional units not only in their training and equipment, but also in that their soldiers were better educated and came in many cases from fairly respectable backgrounds. Administrative structures were reorganized on Western lines, and the court even announced a plan to introduce constitutional government. Provincial assemblies were elected in 1909; the following year a National Assembly was convened, with half the members selected by the provincial assemblies and the other half chosen by the court.

These steps towards modernization, however, weakened the dynasty's political position rather than strengthened it. The Manchu ruling class had neither real enthusiasm for the changes that had been forced on it, nor great skill at carrying them out. It was not capable of carrying the westernization programme through to rapid and massive success; it is hard to see how any national leadership could have done so. The government's initial steps towards modernization drastically increased the number of people who expected rapid progress, and many of them turned against the dynasty when their expectations could not be met. Soldiers of the New Armies, because of their higher educational level, were much more receptive to revolutionary propaganda than the soldiers of traditional units had been.

Talk of constitutionalism inspired the provincial gentry to hope for a considerable expansion in their political power. Voting for the provincial assemblies had been limited to people of considerable wealth or education, and not surprisingly the gentry had emerged with control of these assemblies. Representatives of the gentry were then able to take control of the National Assembly also, despite the fact that half its members had been appointed by the court. However, the provincial assemblies had been given only limited powers, and the National Assembly had not yet been given any real power. Members of the assemblies, and their supporters among the gentry, petitioned for the National Assembly to be converted into a genuine parliament, and were deeply offended when the court not only rejected the petitions but also forbade further petitioning. Promises of constitutional government lost much of their credibility as conservative Manchu leaders at the court restricted the newly elected assemblies mainly to advisory functions. Indeed, these leaders, increasingly worried about threats to their control of China, seemed to be tightening their grip on the government rather than loosening it.

Forty years earlier, during the suppression of the Taiping Rebellion, the court had allowed the rise of regional leaders like Li Hongzhang. These men, usually holding the title of provincial governor or governor-general, had their own armed forces backed up by substantial economic resources. They were entitled to most of the credit for whatever dynamism, and whatever capacity to learn from the West, the Qing government had possessed in the late nineteenth century. By the time of the Russo-Japanese War, the ones who had defeated the Taipings were gone, but there were two men occupying the same sort of position. Zhang Zhidong (Chang Chih-tung), in Wuhan, was governor-general of Hunan and Hubei provinces – a huge area in the heart of the Yangzi Valley. A younger man, Yuan Shikai (Yuan Shih-k'ai), had taken over what had been Li Hongzhang's power base in the north, after Li's death in 1901. He was governor-general of Zhili, the province today called Hebei, immediately around Beijing. He commanded the Beiyang Army, the most powerful of the New Armies.

Both Zhang and Yuan were brought to Beijing in 1907, to occupy high positions in the central government. This stripped them of their provincial power bases; their armies were placed under Manchu commanders. In 1909, Zhang died and Yuan was forced into retirement.

The court was trying to strengthen its position when it removed them from their governor-generalships. It no longer wished to allow any regional official to be so powerful. However, the actual effect of this move was to weaken the government. Such great regional lords had been bulwarks of the dynasty for the previous forty years. Zhang and Yuan had both played key roles in saving the Manchus from the consequences of their decision to support the Boxers against the Europeans a few years before. They possessed the greatest concentrations of power outside Beijing, and the court, following the longstanding Chinese tradition that the way to attain safety in politics is to break up potentially hostile concentrations of power, wished to be rid of them. However, if they had been allowed to remain they might have been very useful to the court in its efforts to control the other elements of the Chinese élite – lower-ranking government officials, merchants, gentry, modern-style intellectuals, and officers of the New Armies. Most of these people had fewer ties to the national government, and far less sympathy for the problems it faced, than Zhang and Yuan. They had been growing stronger for decades; the creation of elected assemblies was about to give them a public forum, and help both to unify and to legitimize them.

The Revolution of 1911

The final collapse of the Qing Dynasty was to a considerable extent inspired by a revolutionary from Guangdong named Sun Yat-sen. He was a Methodist Christian who had travelled widely outside of China, had received much of his education in Hawaii and Hong Kong, and had been almost totally converted to Western ideas. He wanted to make China a republic on the European model. His belief in the easy conversion of one civilization to the practices of another was rather naïve, but he was able to build up a secret society called the Tongmenghui (T'ung Meng Hui, in English usually called the Revolutionary Alliance). Its optimistically vague programme called for overthrow of the Manchus, restoration of Chinese independence, establishment of a republican form of government, and development of a modern economy. Its membership remained small, and it was riven by factionalism. Much of Sun's financial support came from the Chinese communities in various foreign countries; dislike of the Manchus was a longstanding tradition among the overseas Chinese, and as a native of Guangdong, Sun was well qualified to establish contacts among them. Between 1906 and 1911, his followers failed in numerous armed uprisings against the Qing. None of these efforts drew in many participants, but the revolutionaries kept trying. There were beginning to be Chinese cadets studying in military academies in Japan. The Tongmenghui was able to recruit a significant number of them, including the man who was eventually to become Sun Yat-sen's successor, Chiang Kai-shek.

The final crisis began with a dispute over the control of China's railways. Many Chinese regarded foreign control of the railway network as one of the major threats to Chinese independence, and they had succeeded in having the right to build some key lines returned to Chinese ownership. These lines were intended to link the city of Wuhan, on the Yangzi River in Hubei province, with Guangdong in the south and with Sichuan in the west. Members of the local gentry had then put up substantial amounts of capital for railroad construction. The amount raised, however, would not have been adequate even if properly managed, and much of it was dissipated through inefficiency and corruption. In 1911 the central government, which could see that financing and management organized on a provincial basis were not getting the lines built, and which did not care to see such vital facilities under provincial control in any case, obtained a foreign loan to pay for nationalization of the lines.

There was immediate rage in the provinces affected, both because the foreigners whose money was now paying for the railways seemed likely to emerge with ultimate control, and because those among the gentry who had already put in capital to begin construction were not being given what they regarded as fair compensation. In Sichuan province particularly, disorders and riots had escalated to outright rebellion by the autumn of 1911. The government moved in troops from neighbouring Hubei province, and rebellion then broke out there also.

Units of the New Armies in Wuhan (actually a collective name for three adjoining cities, one of which is the capital of Hubei province) had been heavily infiltrated by revolutionary organizations. The revolutionaries there called themselves a branch of the Tongmenghui, but they had in fact no contact with Sun Yat-sen and only a loose sort of liaison with some other Tongmenghui leaders. They had originally planned to spend a long time preparing for an uprising, but the crisis in Sichuan forced them to speed their schedule. Then the police arrested several of the ringleaders and captured a list of those involved in the plot. The remaining conspirators decided to move immediately, in however disorganized a fashion, rather than wait to be arrested in their turn.

No top leader of the revolutionary movement was in Wuhan, and many of the second-level leaders were in jail, so the rebels went to the highest-ranking army officer they could catch, a colonel named Li Yuanhong (Li Yuan-hung), and forced him to accept the role of leader in the uprising. He had no previous record of sympathy for the revolutionary cause, and had to be threatened with execution before he agreed to take command of the movement, but he became more enthusiastic as it gained strength. (From this unlikely beginning, he rose over the next five years to become the nominal president of the Republic of China.) China was ripe for even such a weak and disorganized revolutionary movement as this. There was no effectively organized opposition in Wuhan, because both the commander of the armed forces of the province and the head of the civil administration had fled in panic when the rebellion began. The successful uprising in Hubei quickly inspired imitation, and within a few weeks revolutionaries of various sorts had taken much of central and southern China. A revolutionary government, established in the city of Nanjing about 300 miles down the Yangzi from Wuhan, elected Sun Yat-sen as its president.

The imperial court, in desperation, turned to Yuan Shikai. He had built the strongest army China then possessed, and he was now the best man the Manchus could think of to command this army, despite the way they had removed him from command four years before. Yuan extracted very broad powers from the court before accepting command. He then made a deal with the revolutionaries, under which he supported the conversion of China into a republic in return for being made its first president. The true weakness of the revolutionaries now revealed itself. The Manchus had fallen because they were weak, not because Sun Yat-sen or any other revolutionary leader was strong. The armies of the Qing Dynasty, now commanded by Yuan Shikai, controlled much of northern China. In many areas where the Qing had been overthrown, revolutionary regimes were led by officers of the New Armies, or by members of the gentry who had organized themselves through the provincial assemblies. Most of these men were not affiliated with the Tongmenghui and did not take orders from it. In Wuhan itself the Tongmenghui had little influence over the revolutionary government, and the main power struggle was that between the forces of Li Yuanhong and Yuan Shikai. Sun did not control China and saw no way he might obtain control; the best course available to him was to make a deal with General Yuan.

Yuan Shikai and the warlord era

The Republic of China operated on an *ad hoc* basis for about a year; an elected Parliament finally convened in February 1913. The most powerful party in it was the Guomindang or Nationalist Party, which was in large part derived from Sun's old Tongmenghui, reoriented and drastically expanded. Sun himself was no longer the central figure; he did not have the skills of a party politician, nor any great desire to acquire them. Sun took a nominal post in the Guomindang but devoted most of his attention to planning the development of China's railway network, while a man named Song Jiaoren (Sung Chiao-jen) became the effective head of the new party.

Unfortunately for the Guomindang, having control of Parliament did not confer control of China. The holders of real power, notably the military commanders, had little desire to submit to any elected body, and support for Parliament within Chinese society was not sufficiently massive to force the military to recognize its authority. The electorate had been much more broadly based than in the elections of 1909, but those who qualified, by wealth or by having completed elementary school, still came to somewhat less than half of the adult male population. They were not distributed evenly across China. There would have been areas, and not just those inhabited by minority nationalities, that the elections did not reach at all.

Yuan Shikai took advantage of divisions in the Guomindang, and quickly established full control over the central government. In March 1913 Song Jiaoren was assassinated, probably at Yuan's instigation. Guomindang sympathizers in several central and southern provinces rebelled against Yuan in July, but were easily suppressed. At the end of the year Yuan outlawed the Guomindang, and in January of 1914 he dissolved Parliament. The political machine Sung Yat-sen and Song Jiaoren had built was capable of winning elections, but it was not capable of forcing a man like Yuan Shikai to hold elections if he did not wish to. Even when Yuan overreached himself by assuming the title of Emperor, and then died in 1916, Sun Yat-sen could do little to influence events.

Yuan had never really been dictator of China; his control over most provincial governments had been too weak. When he died, central authority in China collapsed completely, and the country was divided up among various generals. China entered a decade of warlord rule. There continued to exist in theory a Republic of China, with a president and a prime minister in Beijing. It had one duty of real importance – handling China's relations with the foreigners. This gave it access to the customs receipts from the foreign-operated Maritime Customs Service, or at least to foreign loans for which the receipts were pledged as security. (In some years the customs receipts went entirely for debt payments.) It contained a certain number of capable officials who genuinely wanted to use their positions to promote the national welfare. However, over most of China it had no genuine control whatsoever. On the contrary, it often seemed little more than a pawn of whatever warlord or coalition of warlords controlled the city of Beijing.

Sun Yat-sen tried in 1917 to establish an alternative national government at Guangzhou, in his native province of Guangdong, and assemble under its banner an army capable of marching north and reunifying China. He was heavily dependent, however, on the forces of South China warlords of dubious loyalty. When they turned against him in 1918 he could not fight them; he ended up taking passage on a ship to Japan. He returned to Guangzhou in 1920, tried again, and once again saw key generals turn against him; by late 1922 he was on a ship headed for Shanghai.

For China as a culture the warlord era was one of great progress. Businessmen were taking over foreign production techniques, especially in the treaty ports where foreign influence was strongest. The First World War temporarily distracted the Europeans and allowed Chinese capitalists to make considerable strides, with much less competition from foreign imports. The new knowledge imported from the West was being assimilated, and significant numbers of Chinese were acquiring a steadily deeper understanding of it. Beijing and Shanghai were especially important as centres for the new learning. This trend was not an unmixed blessing – by the late 1920s and early 1930s, the colleges of China were turning out many graduates whose education had been so totally Western that they had little knowledge of or interest in the problems of their own society – but a substantial degree of modernization and westernization was necessary for China's survival. The number of women with unbound feet continued to increase.

For China as a nation the warlord period was a time of disaster. The upper classes, in general, lost much of their legitimacy. In the old order the core of the élite had been made up of educated men, who had acquired official status by a long and difficult course of study in history, philosophy, and classical literature. Their indoctrination had included many injunctions to care for the welfare of the common people. They had not always behaved in accord with the ideals in the works they had studied, but at least they had known that the Emperor would be annoyed with them if they abused the peasants so badly as to cause a revolt. In the warlord era

PLATE 2.2 *General Yuan Shikai, who became president of the Republic of China in 1912. (© Topical Press Agency/Hulton Archive/Getty Images.)*

almost all power was derived simply from the possession of money or military force.

A man could start out as a bandit, expand his force until he had effective control of a small area, and regularize the procedure by which he extracted wealth from the population until he could call it taxation instead of looting. He would then start to negotiate deals and alliances with the military forces in neighbouring areas. He could, in short, convert himself from a bandit to a minor warlord, and if he were sufficiently competent and lucky he might someday rule a province.

The central government no longer had either the will or the ability to protect the people against the rapaciousness of provincial élites. The poor suffered terribly, whether they were workers in the growing textile mills of Shanghai, or tenant farmers beset by landlords, tax-collectors, soldiers, and bandits.

Peace and order had been breaking down in the Chinese countryside for a long time; the Revolution of 1911 released a flood of violence. The struggles that began in 1911, most of which involved armies that were far from first-rate by world standards of the time, and in which bribery and intrigue often played a more important role than actual combat, can be described in comic-opera terms. There were extremely humorous incidents, including the cases of bandits who rose to warlord status, and Li Yuanhong being forced against his will to lead the rebellion of 1911 in Wuhan. There was nothing even faintly comic about the killing, however. People died by the hundreds of thousands, perhaps by the millions. Chinese rebels slaughtered Manchus. Soldiers of the Qing Dynasty, and later of the Republic of China and the various warlords, slaughtered rebels and people suspected of being rebels. Soldiers killed bandits or suspected bandits; the bandits killed those who got in their way. Warlord armies fought one another, seldom competently, but still with a substantial level of bloodshed, which increased over time as the armies expanded and their weaponry improved.

The collapse of central power naturally meant a collapse of Chinese control over Tibet, Xinjiang, and Outer Mongolia. Tibet and Xinjiang would eventually be recovered; Outer Mongolia would be lost permanently. Shortly after the Revolution of 1911, the Tsarist government of Russia had forced Yuan Shikai to grant formal autonomy to Outer Mongolia, which became in effect a Russian protectorate. The Bolshevik (Communist) Revolution of 1917 in Russia was followed by civil warfare between Communist and anti-Communist forces in that country. In 1920, one of the anti-Communist Russian armies launched a bloody invasion of

Mongolia. Some Mongols wishing to resist this invasion allied themselves with the Russian Communists. The outcome was the formal creation of the Mongolian People's Republic in 1924, which became the first satellite state of the Soviet Union.

What little progress China had made in combating foreign encroachment, in the last days of the Qing Dynasty, was reversed. Much of the country fell within the sphere of influence of one foreign power or another, and Western military forces were stationed rather widely within China to defend foreign interests. The Japanese were particularly aggressive. They declared war on Germany soon after the First World War began, moved into the German sphere of influence in Shandong province, and then demanded a substantial degree of control over China as a whole while the Europeans were distracted and unable to interfere. The 'Twenty-one Demands' that Japan presented to Yuan Shikai in January 1915 called not only for Japanese influence over very broad areas of China, but also for the presence of Japanese advisers in several crucial branches of the Chinese government including the police. The Japanese cannot have seen much that was extraordinary in their demands; this was the way the Great Powers had been treating less developed countries for many years. However, Japan's policy was understandably offensive to Chinese public opinion. Yuan Shikai, despite a tremendous public outcry, did not have the power to resist very effectively. He rejected the demand for Japanese advisers to the Chinese police, but gave in on most other issues. The last straw for China came at the peace conference after the war. The Chinese, who had declared war on Germany and had made some minor contributions to the war effort, had expected that in accord with Wilson's Fourteen Points they would obtain more independence and respect after the war, or at least that the German sphere of influence in Shandong would be returned to Chinese control. But the Versailles Treaty left the question of Shandong unsettled (in other words left the Japanese in control), and many of the other Chinese requests never even got on to the agenda of the conference.

The May Fourth Movement and the New Culture Movement

In the nineteenth century, resistance against foreign incursions had usually taken the form of simple xenophobia; the Chinese had expressed a general distaste for things European and had wanted the foreigners to go away. By the end of the First World War a more modern style of nationalism was spreading, phrased in Western terms and concentrated among the most westernized elements of the population. When protests broke out in May 1919 against the lack of consideration for Chinese interests in the Versailles Treaty, and especially against Chinese officials who accepted foreign encroachment on China, the students and faculty at Beijing University played a major role. The period of ferment known as the May Fourth Movement, which took its name from these demonstrations, included not only political protest but also literary and scientific developments involving considerable importation of Western ideas.

The concept of democracy gained in popularity among the intellectuals, both because of its inherent attractiveness and because they were aware that the most successful Western powers had been moving towards elected government during recent decades. In some aspects of life Western notions of equality went beyond the stage of being mere ideas for discussion, and began actually to be put into practice. The status of women rose; a small but increasing proportion of them obtained formal education. Major intellectual figures began writing in a language much closer to that spoken by the common people, thus bringing closer the day when their writings could be read by a mass audience. Within a few years modern Mandarin, a North Chinese dialect spoken as a mother tongue by a large portion of the Chinese population, and not too difficult for speakers of other dialects to learn, replaced the far more difficult classical language as the medium of communication for educated people. This shift in language made mass education far easier than it could have been before, thus reducing the difficulty both of modern economic development and of creating a more equal society. Less than fifteen years before, the imperial government (thinking in terms of education in classical Chinese) had regarded raising the national literacy rate to 5 per cent as a goal that would take several years to accomplish. Much of the new literature combined artistic quality with a strong concern for social issues. Lu Xun (Lu Hsun), one of the most highly regarded authors, had been trained as a doctor, but he abandoned medicine, explaining that he wanted to treat the ills of society as a whole through literature rather than treating physical ills one patient at a time.

The movement towards greater equality was more important than many of the intellectuals may have realized. The Chinese élite through all its history had been a thin stratum, arrogantly convinced of its own superiority, ruling over a great mass of relatively uneducated peasants. The bulk of the population, even in 1919, had hardly been touched by the currents of modernization and endured a level of poverty that the citizens of modern industrial societies can barely imagine. The economic modernization and industrialization China needed could not be carried out on such a basis. A technologically oriented society cannot be built or operated simply by a few leaders and experts; it requires informed participation, at the very least, from a large proportion of the citizenry. An élite wishing to lead China into the twentieth century, to lead what is usually called a 'nationalist' revolution, could not succeed if it cut itself off from the masses in the way its predecessors had done. The question of just how far egalitarianism should be pushed has been a matter of intense dispute up to the present day, but there can be little doubt that Chinese society needed to become much more egalitarian than it was.

Study questions

In what ways was the impact of the West destructive to China, and in what ways was it beneficial?

Why did China have so little ability to defend itself against Western pressure? Were the reasons the same throughout the period covered by this chapter, or did they shift?

China is often referred to as having become a 'semi-colony'. How much control over China did the foreigners in fact attain?

Why were the Manchus overthrown?

CHAPTER 3

The Communist Party and the First United Front

For all the developments of the May Fourth era, the advocates of modernization and progress in China had found no way to apply their new ideas to their nation's political ills. In past centuries, men educated in the Confucian system had been able to count almost automatically on a considerable degree of understanding and respect from a government most of whose officials were products of the same system. The new westernized intellectuals did not enjoy the same close relationship with the warlord governments during and after the First World War, or indeed with any later Chinese government down to the present day.

If westernized intellectuals were to apply progressive ideas to political problems they needed an institutional structure through which to work, but the political techniques of the societies that had most influenced Chinese intellectuals in the past decades – Western Europe, the United States, and Japan – had no obvious application in a warlord-ruled China. The first set of techniques for building a power structure that could function and compete in this environment came not from these countries but from the Soviet Union, and came together with a radically new ideology.

The Chinese Communist Party was officially founded, with some encouragement from the Soviet Union, in 1921. It remained fairly small at first, but soon a three-way alliance was formed between the CCP, the Russians, and Sun Yat-sen's Guomindang. With Russian advice and assistance, both the CCP and the Guomindang grew very rapidly, and by 1927 they controlled a considerable portion of China. At this point, however, the Guomindang turned against its erstwhile Communist allies, and the CCP was almost destroyed.

The coming of Communism

The Bolshevik Party, soon to be renamed the Communist Party, seized control of the Russian government in 1917. It advocated policies of class struggle, leading the poor to take control of the economy from the rich, and attempting to establish a socialist economic system. The Bolsheviks looked at revolution as a world-wide phenomenon, both out of a passionate belief that the benefits of socialism should be brought to all, and because they doubted that socialism could survive, much less reach its full potential, if it were restricted to a single country surrounded by enemies. Capitalist powers as far away as England and the United States had reacted with quick and violent hostility to the Bolshevik Revolution; the weakening or overthrow of such governments could only help the Soviet Union. The Bolsheviks therefore established the Comintern (Communist International or Third International), a world-wide organization of revolutionary parties, with headquarters in the Soviet Union. The Comintern took in some existing socialist parties, and helped to establish them in countries that had not had any.

Communist ideas found adherents in many countries. Lenin's techniques for organizing a tight, disciplined revolutionary party had proven a certain degree of effectiveness in the Russian Revolution, and infinitely greater successes were promised. The new ideology claimed the ability to solve virtually all of humanity's problems. In addition, the Comintern's hostility to the capitalist powers appealed strongly to people in countries like China, which had long been victims of European imperialism. In 1919 and 1920 the revolutionary regime in Russia offered, in striking contrast to the Western powers, to give up all the special privileges that the former Tsarist government had extracted from China. The Chinese were much impressed, though the Russians did not in the end carry out their pledge. Interest in Marxist and Bolshevik ideas spread among some Chinese intellectuals, especially in Beijing and Shanghai; the CCP was formally established in 1921. Advice and assistance from the Comintern were useful in getting the party started, but they gave the Russians a considerable degree of control over CCP policy from 1921 up to about 1935. The results of this control, as we shall see, were not beneficial to the CCP.

In theory, Communism seemed a complete antithesis to traditional Chinese patterns of thought and behaviour. It was totally dedicated to the concept of progress, not only in the sense that the socialist society of the foreseeable future would be greatly superior to anything that existed in the present, but also that the civilizations of the present were far superior to those of past centuries. According to Chinese tradition, most of history had been characterized by a downward trend.

Communism was radically egalitarian. It argued that the proletariat – the class of people who owned little or nothing, and who lived by doing manual labour for wages – was destined to rule. Even Chinese who were dissatisfied with the steeply hierarchical nature of Chinese society often found this a bit hard to swallow.

The Communists advocated socialism – placing most of the wealth of society under collective ownership. One could find traces of such an idea in Chinese tradition, but in practice the Chinese people were so committed to the family as an economic unit that most observers felt it would be impossible for socialism really to be accepted.

The Communists believed that there existed one set of true ideas and that all others were wrong. They advocated class struggle; they said that Chinese society contained major internal conflicts, and that these conflicts needed to be fought through to a conclusion, by violent means, rather than being settled by compromise. Confucianism preached harmony, generally inclined away from violence, and rejected fanaticism of any sort.

Communism was, in short, a foreign ideology totally alien to the Chinese tradition. The fact that it could gain any foothold at all in China shows the extent of the crisis China was facing, and the degree to which the old ideas had been discredited. However, it would have been naïve to expect that everyone who joined the Communist movement would actually abandon all of his or her old patterns of thought. Many individuals decided that the Communist Party as an organization offered a solution to China's problems, and therefore joined it, without actually discarding all their traditional patterns of thought and adopting the attitudes supposedly dictated by Communist doctrine.

The CCP remained very small – less than a thousand members – for several years after it was founded. Most of its members were educated people, which meant that they came from middle- and upper-class backgrounds. Many received their first exposure to Communist doctrine either in a modern school or from people they had come to know in school. The children of ordinary workers or peasants were seldom able to go to such schools. However, in accord with the Marxist ideas they were studying, these young intellectuals were soon trying to organize the proletariat – the industrial workers – as the main basis of the revolution. Chinese workers, like those in many countries just embarking on industrialization, suffered from long hours, low wages, and atrocious working conditions. Their dis-

PLATE 3.1 *Mikhail Borodin, the Comintern's representative in China.*
(© David King Collection.)

satisfaction made a considerable proportion of them willing to listen to
Communist labour organizers. When Hong Kong seamen went on strike in
1922, the CCP helped mobilize dock-workers to strike in sympathy, and
block the recruitment of strike-breakers, in ports as far away as Shanghai.

In the end, the Hong Kong seamen won a wage increase. However, there were few such victories. The proletariat was still very small, and did not have the economic power to win many battles against the employers, much less to take over the Chinese government. The CCP supported a major strike by railroad workers in 1922, but it was bloodily suppressed by warlord troops. The proletariat could not provide Communist intellectuals with enough support to make them more than a fringe group in Chinese politics.

The First United Front

Negotiations lasting from 1922 to 1924 changed this situation by creating a three-way alliance of the Comintern, the CCP, and Sun Yat-sen's Guomindang. The Communists were invited to join the Guomindang, and in some cases to take top positions in it, while retaining their Communist Party membership. They worked within the Guomindang to build up a joint revolutionary force.

Not all participants in this united front were comfortable with it. On the Guomindang side, some leaders were afraid that the unity and discipline of their party, precarious at best, would be totally destroyed if a separate group with its own goals and organization were allowed to join it.

Some Communists also had doubts. The Guomindang's ideology was vague. Although Sun allowed his Three People's Principles – nationalism, democracy, and people's livelihood – to be interpreted to fit in with Communist goals ('people's livelihood' became socialism), the Guomindang as an organization had not in the past been inclined to radical class struggle, and did not seem likely to develop such an inclination. Most of its members and leaders, like those of the CCP, came from the upper levels of Chinese society, but unlike CCP members they had not been indoctrinated with radically egalitarian ideas, and they did not seem likely to carry out a revolutionary attack on their own class. However, Comintern advisers pointed out to their Chinese comrades the obvious fact that China was still too backward for a proletarian uprising to be practical. The creation of a unified, independent national government, and capitalist economic development, would be steps in the right direction and would bring closer the day when a genuine Communist revolution would be possible.

This reflected one of the fundamental theoretical dilemmas of Communism. Marxist doctrine had originally predicted that capitalist economic development would lead to a steady growth in the power of the proletariat, and that at about the time the capitalist class had gone as far as it could in developing industry, the proletariat would take over and establish a socialist system. Lenin had created the possibility of a very different path by developing the organizational techniques that enabled the Bolshevik Party to take control of Russia long before the capitalist class had completed the development of modern industry, indeed at a time when the proletariat was still quite small. Lenin's techniques later proved applicable to countries where modern industry hardly existed at all. A Communist Party active in a country at a low level of development, such as China, had to decide to what extent it would oppose the capitalist class in the name of class struggle, and to what extent it might support the capitalists against common enemies – foreign powers attempting to dominate the country, and remnants of pre-capitalist ('feudal') ruling classes. A Communist Party actually in power in such a country had to carry out tasks such as the establishment of national unity, mass literacy, and the initial stages of industrialization, which according to earlier Marxist theories should have been largely completed by the capitalist class before the revolution. In this context, it appeared not unreasonable for the Communist Party to join with the Guomindang to overthrow the warlords and establish an effective government for China, knowing that eventually it would probably come into conflict with some of the bourgeois and petit-bourgeois elements in the Guomindang.

In more practical terms, the alliance seemed to offer considerable benefits to all the parties involved. The Russians hoped that large portions of China would come under the control of the CCP, over which they had a great deal of power through the Comintern, or at least of the Guomindang with which they were now allied. In general, any strengthening of Chinese nationalism would weaken the European imperialist powers, which were enemies of the Soviet Union. The tiny CCP, which probably had less than a thousand members, gained the prestige of affiliation with the famous Sun Yat-sen, and the cooperation of Sun's organization (which while small in the scale of national politics was still much larger than the CCP). Sun gained new recruits from among the Communists, arms and funding from the Comintern, and the invaluable services of Comintern advisers to teach the Guomindang, barely more than a secret society at this time, how to run a political party and an army. By the time Comintern involvement reached its peak, in 1925 and 1926, there were about sixty Comintern military advisers attached to the Guomindang.

From 1924 to 1926 the activities of the coalition centred on the south-coast city of Guangzhou (Canton). Both its political apparatus and its army developed very rapidly. The Huangpu (Whampoa) Military Academy in particular, whose instructors included Comintern advisers as well as Communist and non-Communist members of the Guomindang, trained military officers of a considerably higher quality than most of those found in the warlord armies to the north.

The Comintern advisers got along quite well with the Guomindang. They were tremendously useful, and they did not seem excessively pre-occupied with making China a Communist country. They were, after all, in China largely as representatives of the Soviet Union, and Soviet interests might be served very well by a friendly but non-Communist government. The CCP, on the other hand, was deeply committed to making China a Communist country, and thus was more likely to come into conflict with non-Communist members of the Guomindang. Mikhail Borodin, the chief Comintern representative in China, was therefore allowed to exercise far more influence in the Guomindang than did any of the Chinese Communists who had joined the Guomindang. Sun Yat-sen, explaining in October 1924 why Guomindang leaders unfriendly to the Soviet Union would have to be excluded from a certain important Committee, said: 'Henceforth our party must take Russia as its teacher in revolution, otherwise there will be no achievement by us.'

Sun Yat-sen died in March 1925. Tension between the various men hoping to succeed him was exacerbated when one of the most important Leftwing leaders in the Guomindang was assassinated by persons un-known in August 1925. None of the serious competitors for Sun's position was a Communist, but the apparent winner of the struggle, a long-time Guomindang member named Wang Jingwei (Wang Ching-wei), was friendly to the CCP, and appointed Communists to many important posi-tions in the Guomindang. By this time CCP membership was expanding fantastically, due both to the advantages it had gained from its united front with the Guomindang, and to the role it played in the anti-foreign demon-strations and strikes that had begun in May 1925 (see below).

Both the rise of Wang Jingwei and the growth of the CCP, however, were essentially phenomena of civilian politics. Command of the Guomin-dang's armed forces lay with Chiang Kai-shek, a friend of Sun Yat-sen who as commandant of the Huangpu Military Academy had acquired great influence among the newly trained army officers. In March 1926, Chiang decided that it was time to start cutting down the power of the CCP and the Russian advisers. Claiming that a coup was being plotted against him, he arrested the advisers and some of the leading CCP cadres. He later released them, with apologies to the Russians. However, from this point onward the activities of the Russian advisers were restricted, and most

CCP cadres were removed from the armed forces. Having consolidated his control of the army, Chiang moved to take command of the party and government. Wang Jingwei, instead of fighting to retain his position, embarked on an extended trip abroad. By the middle of 1926, Chiang had emerged as the most powerful leader of the Guomindang.

The Communist Party concerned itself mainly with the proletariat – factory workers, miners, railroad employees, and so on. Labour-organizing activities often went together with nationalist agitation, since so many of the large enterprises in China were owned by foreigners. During 1925 the police in the foreign-controlled concessions, defending the interests of foreign factory owners, repeatedly fired upon crowds of Chinese workers. These incidents inspired waves of nationalist outrage, arousing students and businessmen to support worker protests. Strikes in the summer of 1925 involved hundreds of thousands; the CCP was heavily involved in these strikes.

Only a few Communists, of whom Mao Zedong would later become the most famous, were beginning to notice that by far the largest element of the population in China was the peasantry, and that the peasants could also be very responsive to Communist appeals for class struggle.

Many of the peasants were in truly desperate straits. Hunger was a normal part of life; a major crop failure could bring actual starvation. In Northwest China, with its uncertain rainfall, famines killed millions during the 1920s. Poor peasants struggled as best they could to earn more, to acquire land, and to acquire a position of some economic security for themselves and their children, but most failed. Indeed, the average man in China was significantly poorer than his father. The poorest men in China were seldom able to reproduce themselves; to raise children, or even just to marry, took more resources than they had. This meant that most of the poorest men of any particular generation could not be the children of people as poor as themselves, because people as poor as themselves did not have children. The poorest men of each generation were mostly the children of parents higher on the economic scale, victims of a systematic pattern of downward social mobility. The fact that most families tended to become poorer from one generation to the next was most conspicuous among families that were already fairly poor, but this tendency existed at all levels of the social scale. Any revolutionary movement that could convince the peasants that it could better their lives would be able to tap a tremendous reservoir of support.

The area in which the Communists happened to be operating, around Guangzhou, was not one of the poorest, and famine was not a normal part

PLATE 3.2 *Chiang Kai-shek, Commandant of the Huangpu Military Academy and later head of the Guomindang. (© Topical Press Agency/Hulton Archive/Getty Images.)*

of existence as it was in the northwest. However, this was one of the most landlord-ridden areas of China. A tremendous proportion of the peasants were tenants, so their poverty and misery, even if not as acute as in other regions, could more easily be blamed on exploitation by the rich. Mao

Zedong is only the most famous of a number of CCP agitators who went out to the countryside to organize peasant unions and whip up class struggle, especially in Guangdong and Hunan provinces. By February 1927 Mao, who ranked fairly high in the Communist Party but was not among its top leaders, had decided that the peasants rather than the industrial workers might become the primary basis for the revolution.

In a very short time, several hundred million peasants in China's central, southern, and northern provinces will rise like a tornado or tempest – a force so extraordinarily swift and violent that no power, however great, will be able to suppress it . . . They will send all imperialists, warlords, corrupt officials, local bullies, and evil gentry to their graves. All revolutionary parties and all revolutionary comrades will stand before them to be tested, to be accepted or rejected by them. To march at their head and lead them? To follow in the rear, gesticulating at them and criticizing them? To face them as opponents? Every Chinese is free to choose among the three, but circumstances demand that a quick choice be made . . .

To give credit where due, if we allot ten points to the accomplishments of the democratic revolution, then the achievements of the urban dwellers and the military rate only three points, while the remaining seven points should go to the peasants in their rural revolution . . .

These passages contain a certain degree of youthful exaggeration. Mao had not been in the business of peasant organization very long, and within a few years he would learn that it was not as easy as he had at first thought. In the short run, however, his most frustrating problem was probably his inability to convince his superiors in the Party of the importance of the peasants. Marxist doctrine was firmly committed to the primacy of the urban working class. The CCP did not formulate a coherent land policy, or assign a large proportion of its members to the tasks of peasant organization. Indeed Mao, who under the United Front was a member of both the CCP and the Guomindang, sometimes seemed to be doing his work with the peasants primarily in his capacity as a Guomindang member.

Despite its internal conflicts, the Guomindang grew rapidly. By late 1925 it controlled the southern provinces of Guangdong and Guangxi, and it was contemplating an attack on the warlords of the north. At this point a debate broke out; many people doubted that the Guomindang should risk attacking the large, if poorly trained, northern armies. The Russians in particular, who had begun to establish friendly relations with one of the northern warlords, were afraid that this connection would be jeopardized if a Russian-backed revolutionary force should begin aggressive expansion. Chiang Kai-shek, however, pushed very hard for a campaign to the north. Chiang won, and the Northern Expedition began in July 1926. The army itself was made up mostly of the non-Communist elements of the Guomindang. The Communists concentrated on political activity among the civilian population. They worked not only in areas already under the rule of the Communist–Guomindang United Front, but in areas not yet reached by the northward advance, advertising the virtues of the Guomindang. When Chiang Kai-shek moved north into the Yangzi basin, his men behaved far better than the usual warlord armies, just as the Communists had promised the peasants they would. In particular, the Guomindang forces habitually paid for food supplies, instead of simply taking them at gunpoint. The peasants, as a result, were far more willing to supply food to the Guomindang than to its enemies; this was one of Chiang Kai-shek's major military advantages.

The Guomindang pushed rapidly north through Hunan in July 1926, and reached the Yangzi River in August. From this point onward it faced stiffer resistance; the conquest of Jiangxi took about two months of hard fighting. However, Chiang Kai-shek's forces grew stronger as the campaign went on, thanks to their capture of weapons and equipment from their opponents, and to the fact that an increasing number of warlord units were changing sides and allying themselves with the Guomindang.

Chiang fought an aggressive and mobile style of warfare. His warlord opponents had more heavy weaponry, but they were dependent on the railroads for transportation. Chiang's men, less burdened with heavy equipment and able to count on more cooperation from the peasants, could more easily move across country to bypass enemy units and threaten their rail communications from behind.

The Communist–Guomindang split

The non-Communist members of the Guomindang – both those who had been with the organization before the United Front with the Communists was established, and the much larger number who had joined later – seldom had much sympathy for Communist ideas of class struggle. Most of them came from well-to-do families, including landlords and capitalists. The idea of organizing the poor to struggle against the rich struck such people as at best unnatural, and at worst a direct attack on their own families. The potential conflict had been manageable during the earliest days of the United Front, when the Communists had not yet developed much interest

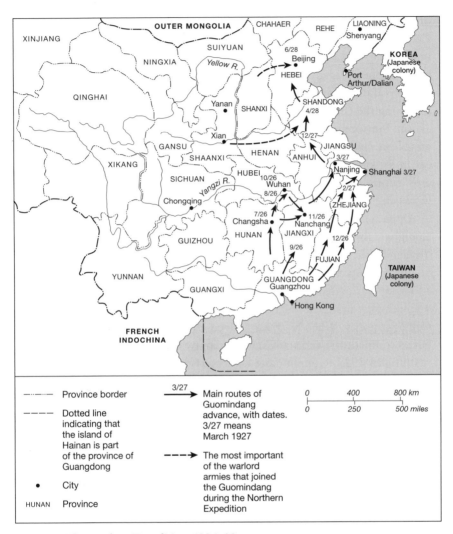

MAP 3 *The Northern Expedition, 1926–28.*

in organizing the peasants, and in any case the alliance controlled so little territory that the question of how it should be ruled did not seem worth a quarrel. What was important was united action against the warlords. But as the Guomindang acquired more power and more territory, its member factions struggled increasingly for control. When the Northern Expedition conquered vast new areas, including the homes of many Guomindang officers from landlord families, the problem became acute. Chinese Communist Party organizers set up some peasant associations and labour unions ahead of Chiang's forces as they moved north. Even more important was the rapid growth of the peasant associations in many areas after the arrival of Guomindang armies. The CCP leadership, anxious to avoid rupturing the United Front, tried to restrain the extremes of peasant radicalism, but soon the landlords and gentry of many areas were under severe attack. In the cities, Communist-led labour unions were leading the workers in strikes for higher wages. Many Communists, furthermore, while they continued to support the Guomindang as an organization, were increasingly hostile to Chiang Kai-shek as an individual.

Open violence broke out when the Northern Expedition reached Shanghai, the richest commercial city in China, near the mouth of the Yangzi River. As Chiang's troops neared the city, Communist labour unions rose up to seize it from within. Chiang treated this not as part of a joint operation to take Shanghai in the quickest possible fashion, but as a power play designed to give the Communists the predominant voice in running the city. When his army arrived it treated the workers not as allies but as competitors, and slaughtered them by the thousands.

In April 1927, Guomindang leaders associated with Chiang Kai-shek, meeting in Nanjing, decreed the establishment of a national government and proscribed the CCP. The summer of 1927 saw tangled struggles among: the centre and right-wing elements of the Guomindang mostly associated with, but by no means all controlled by, Chiang Kai-shek; the non-Communist leftist elements of the Guomindang, led by Wang Jingwei; the Communists; and assorted warlord armies. The CCP, in this crisis, was crippled by its subservience to the Comintern. Joseph Stalin, who had by this time consolidated his control of the Soviet Union sufficiently to have a dominant voice in the formulation of Russian advice to the CCP, did not want to admit that the alliance with the Guomindang was not working out well. To have done so would have provided embarrassing ammunition for his competitors for power in Moscow, including Leon Trotsky. Even after the slaughter of the Communists in Shanghai, therefore, Stalin denied the seriousness of the conflict with Chiang, arguing that the Guomindang as an institution could continue to be an ally of the Communists despite Chiang's defection. He foisted upon the CCP a policy of complacency when the party should have been trying to make military preparations for the impending struggle against an extremely powerful foe. At the same time, Stalin's visible assumption that the non-Communist leftists in the Guomindang were fools, people to be manipulated and exploited by the

Communists, offended them and helped to drive them over to the anti-Communist side.

The disarray of the Guomindang was exacerbated in August 1927 when Chiang Kai-shek resigned as commander-in-chief. Partly he may have wanted to demonstrate his own indispensibility, and if so he succeeded; no effective leader emerged to replace him during the few months he was out of command. But also he wanted to go to Japan to negotiate his marriage to Song Meiling (Soong Mei-ling), a beauty with important family ties. One of her sisters had been the wife of Sun Yat-sen, and her brother would for many years be Chiang Kai-shek's minister of finance.

Despite Guomindang disunity, the CCP met only disaster when it finally turned to open armed struggle in August and September. The uprising of 1 August 1927, at Nanchang (the capital of Jiangxi province), was carried out mainly by military units whose officers were Communists or Communist sympathizers. Their strength was inadequate and they were able to hold the city for less than a week, but the units involved in this affair later provided many of the leaders of the Chinese Red Army.

Uprisings during the following months in Hunan, Hubei, and Guangdong provinces had even less chance of success. Party doctrine held that politics was primary and that one should have faith in the revolutionary strength of the masses. This meant in practice that the Party had not devoted much effort to acquiring military forces; it expected ordinary workers and peasants to carry out an armed uprising when the time came, defeating or winning over Guomindang armies. Mao Zedong, who was assigned responsibility for organizing the 'Autumn Harvest Uprising' in his native province of Hunan, argued desperately that in order to fight against soldiers one needed soldiers. The Communists had no real army of their own, but if they were going to start a revolt they should at least base it as much as possible on winning over Guomindang units. Mao was overruled, and when the rebellion came it was primarily a civilian affair. Most of the participants were peasant union members from the countryside around Changsha, in Hunan province. Guomindang troops, though initially caught by surprise, quickly defeated the rebels. The 'Canton Commune', a Communist-led uprising in the city of Guangzhou in December, was equally unsuccessful. Mao drew from these defeats a confirmation of the view he had already held, that real military forces would be necessary for any serious uprising to succeed, and also he became more dubious about efforts to take large cities like Changsha and Guangzhou. Survivors from these affairs, and some equally disastrous ones in other areas, withdrew to the hills.

The Communist Party had been virtually destroyed; its membership dropped to less than a fifth of the level attained just before the split with Chiang Kai-shek. What might logically have been expected, given the history of Marxist and Communist movements in other countries, was that the CCP would be reduced to the same sort of weak and essentially urban movement it had been up to 1923, with some of its leaders in exile and others working underground in the coastal cities of China. Few people supposed that the Communist leaders who had chosen to retreat to the countryside, and who indeed had found themselves forced to retreat to unusually backward sections of the countryside, would be able to accomplish much there. The success of Communist guerrillas in the countryside was so unexpected that it did not attract much attention for several years.

Study questions

What benefits did the Chinese Communist party get from the United Front?

What benefits did the Guomindang get from the United Front?

What was the relationship between the Chinese Communist Party and the Guomindang, during the United Front?

What was the relationship between the Chinese Communist Party and the Comintern?

CHAPTER 4

The Nanjing decade, 1927–37

The Guomindang government of China, of which Chiang Kai-shek formally became the head in 1928, grew steadily stronger during the ten years from 1927 to 1937. However, it had serious internal problems, which limited its success in spreading its control to outlying areas. In particular, while it repeatedly decimated the Communist organizations, it never actually managed to destroy Chinese Communism. Fighting between the CCP and the Guomindang continued until 1937, when Chiang finally had to join once again in a united front with the Communists for joint resistance against Japanese encroachments on China.

The Guomindang government at Nanjing

Once the Communists had been defeated, Chiang Kai-shek continued his task of unifying China. He already held the provinces along the lower Yangzi River, the richest and most developed area in China. Shanghai was his biggest source of revenue. Nanjing, about 300 kilometres up the river from Shanghai, was his capital. By 1928 his control reached north to Beijing, which he renamed Beiping to indicate it was no longer the capital. His influence stretched even into Manchuria, where a local warlord nervous about Japanese domination looked to a restored national government for support. During the next ten years Chiang won confrontations with various warlords in more distant areas of China. He could defeat any warlord or likely combination of warlords in an open contest, but he did not have the power to move simultaneously on all fronts, to eliminate warlordism throughout China. He had absorbed warlord armies rather than destroyed them; by 1928 his army was made up mostly of warlord units, which allied themselves with the Guomindang without altering their internal structure

PLATE 4.1 *Chiang Kai-shek with two North Chinese warlords, Feng Yuxiang (left) and Yan Xishan (right), in 1928. They had allied themselves with Chiang during the Northern Expedition, but in 1930 rebelled against him. (© Hulton Archive/Getty Images.)*

to any great extent. Yan Xishan (Yen Hsi-shan), master of Shanxi province, typifies some of the problems Chiang faced. Yan had joined Chiang during the Northern Expedition, and in fact it had been his troops that completed the Northern Expedition by taking Beijing in 1928. Shortly thereafter, Yan and another major warlord rebelled against Chiang, and were suppressed only after a bloody war. Chiang, however, proved unable to impose effective Guomindang rule in Shanxi, and within a very short time Yan Xishan returned to power there, once more running the province as an autonomous satrapy.

Chiang could not count on the loyalty of his subordinates; generals tended to drift into warlordism if they got very far from the centre of his power. Guomindang generals in Guangdong province, which had been Chiang's headquarters at the beginning of 1926, slipped out of his control as soon as he moved north. One of them actually launched a war against Chiang in 1936, though this effort collapsed ignominiously when central government agents persuaded most of the warlord's air force to defect. While Chiang created the closest thing to a national government that China had had since Yuan Shikai died in 1916, and nibbled away at warlord power whenever he could, there was much that remained outside his control.

In one sense, his power was concentrated in the lower Yangzi Valley. This was the richest and most populous portion of China, and the power base it provided him enabled him to overawe local leaders in some other areas, but he never even came close to controlling the whole nation. In 1936, the area that was under at least a loose form of Guomindang rule encompassed about two-thirds of the population, but only a quarter of the land area of China. The area where Chiang's control was strong enough so that he could actually compel provincial authorities to hand over to him the land taxes they collected was much smaller.

In another sense, his control was largely limited to the cities and main communication lines. Even in provinces where he had no major rivals, his government did not penetrate the villages very deeply. He had an accommodation with local leaders, somewhat like the Qing Dynasty during its declining years, rather than a genuinely strong rural administration.

The heart of Chiang's power lay in the area around Shanghai and Nanjing, where there were many Western-educated 'Sino-liberals'. In this area he functioned to a large extent as a modern-style nationalist leader. He maintained a respectable rate of industrial growth, and built some roads, telegraph lines, railways, and so on. His armed forces acquired military aircraft. He negotiated quite successfully with the Westerners, recovering control over China's Customs Services almost immediately after he came to power, recovering some of the foreign concessions (sections of Chinese cities under foreign administration), and beginning the negotiations that finally led (in the 1940s) to the elimination of extraterritoriality. Chiang's conversion to Christianity and marriage to an attractive American-educated wife (who also happened to have been the sister-in-law of Sun Yat-sen) improved his image to some extent among 'Sino-liberals' in China, and to a very large extent in the United States. His popularity with Americans would eventually, in the 1940s, help him obtain large quantities of concrete aid.

In his political manoeuvring in peripheral areas, however, it sometimes seemed that he was functioning much like a warlord. He distrusted his subordinates, and tried to keep them from becoming too powerful even if this sometimes meant keeping them too weak to do their jobs. He had to tolerate, and negotiate alliances with, warlords in outlying provinces.

However, if he had not made China a nation-state he had at least created a nucleus, centring on Nanjing, from which a nation-state seemed to be growing.

While the Guomindang proclaimed democracy as a long-range goal, it said that the Chinese people were not yet ready for such a system, and would first have to undergo a period of 'tutelage' under a *de facto* dictatorship. Chiang, in fact, showed little sympathy for democratic ideas. He thought of a good citizen as one who gave loyal and unquestioning obedience to the government, rather than as one who thought independently about public affairs. His political style was partly Confucian, and he encouraged study of the Confucian classics. He was also influenced by Fascism; he used some German advisers in his army and accepted certain Fascist ideas, especially in regard to every nation's need for a single supreme leader. He said, 'without one leader that everyone worships absolutely, it will not be possible to reform the country to complete the revolution . . . All power and responsibility rests with the one person of the leader.' But his Blue Shirt Society was a secret organization; it did not really resemble Mussolini's Blackshirts or Hitler's Brownshirts, despite the similarity of names.

His crucial problem was that he had no strong tie of any sort – democratic, Confucian, or Fascist – to most of the Chinese people. He could not depend on the voluntary allegiance of the mass population, or even of the officials who made up his own government. Many members of the urban middle class thought of themselves as citizens, and thought of the nation as an entity naturally entitled to the loyalty of its people, but this group was too small to form an effective basis for government. The peasants, the bulk of the population, felt no identification with the government and might barely be aware of its existence. Chiang had no network of reliable cadres[1] spread out through the countryside to popularize his ideas and enforce his policies. In the early 1930s, the Guomindang had an organized party branch in less than one-fifth of the counties in China. The ruling class was preoccupied with struggles over power and personal wealth. The loyalty of many officials went more to cliques based on personal relationships than to the government as a whole.

Chiang Kai-shek was aware of the way the spirit of his organization had decayed after 1927. He commented in 1930 that 'not only is it impos-

---

[1] In standard English usage, a 'cadre' is a group of people who perform a leadership role in an organization or movement. In writings on Asia, especially on China and Vietnam, the term is used in a variant sense; a 'cadre' is a single individual who provides ideological and organizational leadership. The cadre does not necessarily hold a high rank in the organization in which he or she functions as a cadre.

PLATE 4.2 *The Bund, Shanghai. One of the more modern and westernized parts of Shanghai in the 1930s. (© General Photographic Agency/Hulton Archive/Getty Images.)*

sible to find a single party headquarters which administers to and works for the welfare of the people, but all are stigmatized by the most reprehensible practices, such as corruption, bribery, and scrambling for power'. Both idealistic dedication and simple efficiency had declined very severely. The split between the Guomindang and the Communists had contributed to this. Of those members of the Guomindang who had been seriously concerned to organize the common people and improve their lot, a large fraction had been Communists; these people had been driven out of the Guomindang in 1927 and 1928. Most of the remainder came under suspicion of Communist sympathies, since a desire to organize the masses was identified as a Communist trait; they were discouraged from continuing such activities, and often purged from the organization. The Guomindang thus cut itself off from real contact with the mass of the population.

At the same time, the Guomindang was recruiting very indiscriminately in the newly conquered areas. A great variety of people, mostly from the upper classes, swarmed to join once it became apparent that the Guomindang was now to rule China. Administrators from the North Chinese warlord regimes, and some of the actual warlords, signed up and were given senior positions. Certainly Chiang Kai-shek could not have administered his new domains without recruiting many such people, but the lack of discrimination in recruitment, the lack of indoctrination of the new people, and the lack of any serious effort to supervise them and force them to adhere to some higher standard of political morality than that to which they had been accustomed during the warlord era, allowed them to bring their political style into the new regime almost without alteration. The result was a large administration, many of whose branches never seemed to accomplish much except for the enrichment of their own personnel.

There were cliques within the power structures of the Guomindang and the government that were loyal to Chiang Kai-shek in a way that the power structures as a whole were not. The most important were the Whampoa Clique, centering on graduates of the Whampoa Military Academy (especially the first three graduating classes), and the CC Clique, named for its leaders, the brothers Chen Lifu and Chen Dafu. The CC Clique was sometimes called the Organization Clique, because it dominated the Organization Department of the Guomindang, and could thus place its members in key positions in the party bureaucracy. The Political Study Clique was considerably weaker.

The loyalty of these cliques was as important to Chiang's power as the formal offices he held in the government. This is why on the occasions when he resigned his formal positions – in August 1927, and in December 1931 – he was always able to regain them. But Chiang did not entirely trust them, sometimes deliberately playing them off against one another. Thus he had two rival secret police organizations, one affiliated with the CC Clique and the other with the Whampoa Clique.

In the past, the rise of a new dynasty had sometimes been accompanied by a break-up of large landholdings. This made tax collection easier and also eased the lot of the ordinary peasant. No such thing happened when Chiang rose to power. The amount of land in the hands of very large landlords may even have increased, though not as much as many Chinese thought it was increasing. Many landlords had enough influence to evade taxation to a very considerable extent; both the government and the ordinary peasants suffered as a result.

The Jiangxi Soviet

The tattered little groups that followed various Communist leaders into the hills after the Communist defeats of 1927 did not at first pose much threat to the government; only after several years had passed did they begin to become conspicuous. They were not in a position to obtain significant aid, or even much guidance, from the Comintern or the top leaders of the Communist Party. They were not operating in areas containing many intellectuals or industrial workers, the two groups from which Communist Parties normally recruited their supporters. Local peasants distrusted the Communists at first; they could not see how a scruffy band of inadequately armed men could represent anything but trouble.

The writings of Mao Zedong describe some of the problems he faced at this time, operating in the countryside of southern China after the failure of his effort to take the city of Changsha in September 1927. Lacking a base of political support in the villages, and hunted (if not with great vigour) by the Guomindang, he was forced to build up his forces in any way he could. He absorbed local bandits into his 'Red Army', and the former bandit leaders became officers. (Some of these men, when times later became difficult, revealed the shallowness of their conversion by reverting to apolitical banditry.) Mao took in not only Guomindang soldiers who had decided to change sides and join the Communists, but some who had simply been captured in battle. For a while the former bandits and former Guomindang troops, between them, made up a majority of his army.

Somehow he kept control of this motley group; he made the bandits become Communists, instead of allowing the Communists to become bandits. He was operating in areas where the structure of government was weak; a small and not very well-armed band could establish a local administration and have its way, at least until provincial or national authorities could bestir themselves to send a superior force against it.

In 1928, Mao joined forces with Zhu De (Chu Teh), one of the few CCP members who had held a military command in the Guomindang in 1927. Zhu had participated in the Communist seizure of Nanchang in August 1927, and then in an effort to take an important town in eastern Guangdong. After this effort failed he had retreated into the hills. Soon Mao and Zhu acquired a substantial territory, lying mostly in the southern portion of Jiangxi province. Officially named the 'Chinese Soviet Republic' in 1931, it is generally known as the Jiangxi Soviet (The term 'soviet' was used in China to describe any section of the countryside where the CCP had been able to establish a functioning government.) Zhu became commander-in-chief of the armed forces of the Jiangxi Soviet, but Mao was in fact the senior partner in their relationship. Once they had acquired their initial territory, their task was to penetrate the villages – to win the loyalty of the peasants, and place the movement on a solid mass base.

This was a far more complex problem than some Communists had supposed. Marxist doctrines of class struggle teach that the rich and the poor are natural enemies. The Communist Party is supposed to lead the poor in a struggle, inevitably destined for eventual success, to overthrow their wealthy enemies. In a society like China's, the factors making for misery among the peasants appeared overwhelming. The fundamental poverty of the Chinese economy was exacerbated, in many areas, by the rapacity, brutality, or sheer callousness of the élite. In famines, food was sometimes shipped *out* of the areas of worst starvation to places where the situation was not so bad, because in the worst areas there was no longer anyone with the money to pay for it. The poor were quite naturally dissatisfied with the state of their lives; they would have had to be insane to be satisfied. China had in past centuries witnessed repeated rebellions fuelled by their discontent, the largest recent one having been the Taiping Rebellion. Inexperienced Communists often made the mistake of assuming that the poor would see their situation in Marxist terms, would blame the wealthy, as a group, for their plight, and would join enthusiastically in a revolution based on class struggle as soon as they were presented the opportunity. This turned out not to be the case; not all the poor believed either that the existence of a class of wealthy landlords was inherently unjust, or that an attempt to abolish the landlord class would have the slightest chance of success.

The most important programme for winning the peasants was land reform. This consisted primarily of redistributing land from the rich to the poor, as private property. (A few early gestures towards the Marxist goal of collectivization were quickly abandoned; the peasants were not ready.) The CCP considered that any economic relationship in which one person enjoyed an income that came from labour done by some other person constituted exploitation; if the person who worked a plot of land had to pay rent to some other person who owned it, this was automatically considered to be exploitation, even if the rent were quite modest. The Party sorted the rural population into classes primarily on the basis of who was exploiting whom. The main categories were as follows:

- Landlords were people who did not do significant amounts of agricultural labour themselves, but lived by exploiting others. The most important form of exploitation they used was renting out land, but they also sometimes hired labourers to work their land, and made usurious loans.

- Rich peasants obtained a significant part of their incomes from exploitation, usually hiring labourers and lending money, but they also worked on the land themselves.

- Middle peasants were small farmers who lived primarily off their own labour. They might exploit others to a small extent (most frequently by hiring some supplementary labour at the harvesting season), but most of the work on their farms they did themselves.

- Poor peasants did not live so well. They were usually exploited by others; they had to rent land, borrow money at high interest, or work as hired hands on other people's farms for part of the year.

- Agricultural labourers were the poorest class; they were people who had been unable to get land even as tenants.

The 'Land Law of the Chinese Revolutionary Military Council', passed in 1930, said that the cultivated land was to be divided equally among all the agricultural population, except that landlords, reactionaries, etc., and their families, might be left with less land than the peasants or no land at all.

Carrying out land redistribution on this basis, the CCP was able to win a substantial peasant following, and by 1931 and 1932 Mao was getting peasants to enlist in his army, instead of the bandits and prisoners of war who had earlier been his main sources of recruits. However, he also found substantial numbers of landlords and rich peasants joining his organizations. When members of the village élite saw that the Communist Party had become the government of a given area, they naturally tried to fit themselves into the new power structure, just as their counterparts in other areas were swarming to join the Guomindang. When Communist Party organizers came into a village and looked for recruits, the people likely to step forward first were those with self-confidence, literacy, prestige, and enough wealth to be able to take time off from earning a living and work on political tasks – in other words people who came at least from the richest half of village society, and often actually from the landlord class. The poor peasants would *not* immediately tell Communist organizers from outside the village: 'Do not accept that man; he is a landlord.' For one thing, to do so and thus offend a powerful man would be very dangerous. For another, it took the peasants a considerable time to realize that an alternative to landlord rule existed – that village affairs might actually be placed in the hands of the poor. Even if the recruiters sent into the villages by the CCP realized that some of the people joining their organization were not poor peasants, they might not object. After all, many of the recruiters were (like Mao Zedong himself) intellectuals from well-do-do families.

This naturally affected the results of any effort at land reform. Late in 1930, Mao commented that in any given area, the first time land redistribution was attempted, the rich peasants and middle peasants played the leading role; the poor peasants had little power over the process. Naturally, this situation enabled the rich peasants to conceal some of their best land.

In June 1933, at a conference on problems of land redistribution, Mao described areas where the old village élite had been remarkably successful in adapting itself to life under a Communist regime:

Here the landlords' and rich peasants' open counter-revolutionary struggle had already been crushed by the revolutionary masses during the first stage. After this, many of them quickly altered their appearance, taking off their counter-revolutionary masks and putting on revolutionary masks. They express approval of the revolution and of land redistribution. They claim that they are poor peasants, and are entitled to share in the distribution of land. They have been very active, relying on their historic advantages: 'They are the ones who can speak, and they are the ones who can write.' Therefore, during the first stage they were able to snatch the fruits of the land revolution. The facts from countless localities prove that they are controlling the provisional administrations, infiltrating local armed forces, manipulating revolutionary organizations, and [in land redistribution] receiving more land and better land than the poor peasants.

This was a problem that Communist Parties in Russia and Western Europe had never really faced. It is a truism that one does not find many poor peasants or industrial workers running a Communist Party. The leaders are generally intellectuals from middle-class backgrounds. But in the rather depersonalized atmosphere of a city, the main centre of action for previous Communist movements, this seldom caused direct personal conflicts of interest. Such people were rarely in the position of deciding the fate of their own families or even close friends. In the smaller and tighter environment of the village such things happen all the time. When the CCP obtained recruits who came from the upper classes it had to worry more than previous Communist Parties both about the possibility that those who had joined the revolution sincerely would become involved in conflicts of interest, and that some would have joined for reasons of self-interest rather than conviction.

The Communist base area that Zhu De and Mao were building up did not follow the previous patterns of Communist revolution. The most obvious innovation was the idea of basing the revolution on the peasants. Marxists had always thought of themselves as representing the most advanced, developed sectors of society. Their base of support was supposed to be the industrial workers, especially those in the largest factories. The peasants were uneducated and technologically primitive; with each family a separate economic unit, the peasant economy provided no natural basis for united political action. Few Marxists expected that the peasants could do more than become junior partners in the revolution, following the lead of the industrial workers. The Bolshevik Revolution in Russia had moved beyond this pattern to acquire a considerable degree of peasant support, but its real base remained in the cities. Mao wrote as if the proletariat were the leading force in the Chinese Revolution, and the Communist Party a party of the proletariat, but this was a verbal gesture towards doctrinal orthodoxy. His actual policies placed the main theatre of the revolution in the countryside.

Even more fundamental was the shift in the way the Communist Party appealed for support. The previous assumption had been that a Communist movement would spread propaganda among the people, and when enough had been converted there would be an uprising and the Communists would come to power. Communist movements had sought support by making promises. Furthermore, the propagandists making the promises lacked genuine experience with the realities of economics or administration, so even if they were attempting to be honest they had no way of knowing which of the things they were promising could actually be delivered. Promotion within such a movement was not – could not be – based on actual ability to run a government, since the Party had no way of testing the abilities of its members. A talent for making idealistic speeches was likely to be at a premium.

This had been the pattern of revolution European Marxist parties had always expected to follow, and the Russian Revolution had indeed followed it for the most part. Lenin and the Bolshevik Party had had virtually no experience in running either a government or an economy when they suddenly became the rulers of Russia in the autumn of 1917. Some things they learned fairly fast once they were in power, but others took years. In March 1922, more than four years after the revolution, Lenin reported in despair that the Communist Party still was not capable of running the economy, and that if it did not learn to do so, very quickly, it could not expect to survive.

*And the greatest danger is that not everybody realises this . . . The time
has passed when the job was to draft a programme and call upon the
people to carry out this great programme. That time has passed. Today
you must prove that you can give practical economic assistance to the
workers and to the peasants under the present difficult conditions, and
thus demonstrate to them that you have stood the test of competition . . .*

*[Even] responsible and good Communists . . . do not know how to run
the economy and, in that respect, are inferior to the ordinary capitalist
salesmen, who have received their training in big factories and big
firms . . . The responsible Communists, even the best of them, who are
unquestionably honest and loyal, who in the old days suffered penal
servitude and did not fear death, do not know how to trade, because they
are not businessmen, they have not learnt to trade, do not want to learn
and do not understand that they must start learning from the beginning.*

Mao was following a very different path to power. He had taken control of a small area, and was recruiting followers from villages that either
were already under Communist rule, or were close enough to Communist
areas to have heard something about the situation there. The revolutionary
struggle was being carried out mostly by people who had already experienced life under a revolutionary regime. The result was a far healthier
process than that which had occurred in Russia. The Chinese Communist
Party was appealing for peasant support not just on the basis of promises,
but on the basis of an actual, demonstrated ability to run local administrations in such a way as to benefit the peasants. Furthermore, promotion
within the Party could be based not only on 'revolutionary attitudes' but
also on proven administrative ability. No Communist Party could ever
hope to come to power with its personnel fully competent to handle all the
problems of economics and administration. Still, Communists like Mao
and Zhu De had begun facing some of the problems of rule, and promoting
cadres at least partly on the basis of their ability to handle administrative
and economic problems, as soon as they began establishing base areas in
the back country in the late 1920s. This was fully twenty years before they
became responsible for running China as a whole.

Mao's departure from Marxist tradition caused repeated conflicts with
his superiors in the Party. During the Autumn Harvest Uprising in 1927,
they had reproved him for lacking confidence in the masses when he tried
to centre the uprising on army units, instead of relying on civilian mobs.
After he and other similar leaders had built up significant armies over the
next few years, the Party command urged that these armies come down out

of the hills and try to take over towns and cities. Such efforts were utterly hopeless given the small size of the Communist forces, and caused them heavy losses; after 1930 the rural guerrilla leaders refused to try for the cities again.

Friction grew worse when top Party leaders began to arrive in the Jiangxi Soviet. For several years after the disaster of 1927, much of the Party leadership had operated outside China, especially in Moscow. This had seemed necessary simply to keep the organizational machinery safe from destruction by the Guomindang, but it both kept Party leaders out of touch with conditions in China, and increased the degree of Russian control. Joseph Stalin, who in the late 1920s had firmly established his control of the Soviet Union, also had considerable control over both policy formation and the selection of leaders in the Chinese Communist Party. By 1931 a group of young Chinese known as the '28 Bolsheviks', who had been of no great importance in the CCP before they went to the Soviet Union for training, had risen, with Stalin's backing, to control of the Party. When they found that Mao and similar organizers in some other areas had brought significant sections of the Chinese countryside under Communist rule, they began filtering back to China. Since they were officially the top leaders of the Party, they were able to take over the Jiangxi Soviet.

Their policies were doctrinaire and inflexible, as one might expect given their background. They had won control of the CCP not in the turmoil of actual revolutionary struggle, in which the relative merits of different leaders could be judged by the actual results of their policies, but in Moscow where displaying a correct revolutionary attitude was the important thing.

Mao had been willing to compromise a little on class struggle in the countryside, in order to maintain agricultural production. He favoured redistributing wealth from the rich to the poor, but he did not want to reduce large numbers of people to absolute destitution; he felt most of the rich should be left enough land to make a living. In contrast to Mao's views the Land Law of the Chinese Soviet Republic, heavily influenced by the 28 Bolsheviks and passed in October 1931, said that the landlords should be stripped of all the land they had, and the rich peasants reduced to extreme poverty (reduced to below the average level of wealth in the countryside).

Mao also said that redistribution should not be carried out in too disruptive a fashion. The easiest way to equalize landholdings in a village would have been simply to pool all the land of each village, divide it into equal parcels, and assign one parcel to each peasant. Mao felt that this would cause too much confusion, shift peasants from plots whose exact characteristics they understood to plots they did not know, and undermine the morale of peasants who had an emotional attachment to a particular plot of land and would not be happy if shifted arbitrarily to another. He said that one should take the existing situation as a basis, and shift the ownership of as little land as possible, trimming down the landholdings of those who had more than their proper share of land by Communist standards, in order to give to those who had less. A rich peasant could more easily evade the land reform and retain excess land under Mao's policy than under a policy of simply resdistributing all land in a village, but Mao thought this was a price worth paying in order to avoid disrupting production too much. He had noted that agricultural production in many of the areas under his rule was well below prerevolutionary levels, and he did not want further decreases if he could avoid them. The 28 Bolsheviks, less concerned with the maintenance of agricultural production, attacked Mao for following a 'rich peasant line'. This was a very serious accusation at this time, when Stalin was waging all-out war against the rich peasants (kulaks) in the Soviet Union.

Even more important were conflicts over military strategy. The Guomindang had too many other problems to be able to keep up continual pressure on the Communists, but every so often provincial or national authorities would send a force, always far larger than the Red Army defending the Jiangxi Soviet, in an attempt to destroy the Communist base area. There were five major 'extermination campaigns' between 1930 and 1934. Mao's strategy for dealing with these attacks had been to fight only when he could win a quick, decisive victory. He did not defend the borders of the base area, trying to keep enemy troops out. Instead he would withdraw, avoiding contact while enemy armies advanced into Communist territory. Given the poor coordination that usually existed between Guomindang units in the field, Mao could expect that sooner or later the enemy units manoeuvring to surround him and force him to battle would become separated and he would be able to concentrate his full force on one section of the enemy force and destroy it. He was willing to retreat and wait for as long as necessary for such an opportunity to arise, despite the amount of harm the invading forces might be doing to Communist organizations, and to peasants who had sympathized with the Communists, in the countryside through which Mao was allowing them to pass. For one thing, he was always so outnumbered that if he tried to fight the whole enemy force, instead of just an isolated section of it, he would probably be obliterated. For another, he could not afford major battles that ended with the enemy retreating in defeat. He depended on capturing guns and ammunition to keep his army supplied, so he had to surround enemy units and destroy them in order to capture their equipment; this required that he wait until he could fight a battle in which he outnumbered the enemy locally. The 28 Bolsheviks considered this policy politically unsound and perhaps even cowardly. The Red Army should not retreat and allow Guomindang troops to enter the base area and abuse pro-Communist peasants; it should defend the borders.

This was not, as some people have supposed, a matter of Mao favouring guerrilla warfare and the 28 Bolsheviks favouring conventional warfare. Guerrilla warfare is a strategy in which much of the fighting is done either by peasant guerrillas, who spend most of their time farming but occasionally participate in raids or ambushes, or else by trained soldiers who operate in small groups, mixing with the population in such a way that it is very difficult for a regular army to find them. It is a matter of many very small battles, raids, and ambushes. But if we look at Mao's analysis of the policies he followed in the Jiangxi period, we will find little indication of fighting done by part-time peasant soldiers, or even by regular Red Army troops operating in units of less than 1,000 men. The fighting he describes is a matter of standup battles fought by very large units of the Red Army. He just wanted these units to operate as mobile forces rather than trying to defend fixed lines. As a matter of fact the 28 Bolsheviks, preoccupied with revolutionary purity and respect for the masses, may have attributed a greater importance to peasant militiamen than Mao did.

One interesting aspect of the difference was that Mao's ideas were more firmly rooted in Chinese tradition. The 28 Bolsheviks were trying to fit themselves to an image of revolutionary heroism forbidding retreat or compromise, which was largely European in origin. Mao's much more flexible tactics, and even some of the language he used to describe them, have parallels in Chinese documents going back more than 2,000 years to the Zhou period.

Mao had fought off three major attacks before the 28 Bolsheviks arrived in Jiangxi. A fourth was also beaten off in 1933. But the fifth, launched in 1934, was different. Chiang Kai-shek had observed the failures of poorly coordinated efforts in the past, and had decided that this one should be not only far stronger but also more methodical. He slowly strangled the Jiangxi Soviet, by surrounding it with a cordon of blockhouses and fortified positions and then constricting the ring. Formerly, when Guomindang units had tried to move relatively fast, it had proven difficult or impossible to coordinate the movements of different units.

Under the new strategy, Guomindang units moved so slowly that co-ordination was not a serious problem.

Mao later said, in line with the strategy he had been following for the past few years, that what the Red Army should have done was to concentrate its forces, break through the ring, and then take the attacking troops in the rear. They would then have been forced to choose between sitting in their fortified positions with the Communists astride their supply lines, or moving out of their positions and fighting in the open. This might not have worked, against a stronger and better equipped Guomindang force than Mao had ever fought before, but at least it would have had a chance. The strategy the 28 Bolsheviks followed had none. Arguing that it was the obligation of the Red Army to defend the population of the Soviet areas, they spread their troops out and tried to hold their borders. Heavily outnumbered, even more heavily outgunned, and following a strategy that gave it little chance to surprise or confuse the enemy, the Red Army soon found its position hopeless. It was forced to abandon the Jiangxi base area and flee.

The conflict pitting the 28 Bolsheviks' stress on correct revolutionary behaviour, against Mao's desire to choose policies that worked, was a conflict that would be repeated many times in the CCP; it is often described as a struggle of Red against Expert. Crises occurred in the years 1947–48, and again in 1966–76, when some Party leaders decided that the preservation of a correct revolutionary spirit was being neglected, and de-emphasized expertise in their efforts to restore a proper level of 'Redness'. Even during these periods, however, the Party had available plenty of people who had training and experience in running a government and an economy. Revolutionary spirit was not the only tool the Party had for maintaining its rule, as it very nearly had been for Lenin after the Russian Revolution.

The Long March

In October 1934, something on the order of 100,000 people broke through the Guomindang forces encircling the Jiangxi Soviet. At first they tried to take all the paraphernalia of a government – printing presses, files, and so on – but they soon tossed aside the excess baggage and ran for their lives. They moved westward, away from the centres of Guomindang power, and then turned north. This took them through mountainous and thinly settled areas, in some of which the population was not even ethnically Chinese. Casualties inflicted by the pursuing Guomindang forces, by

MAP 4 *The rural soviets and the Long March.*

local tribes that hated all Chinese, by disease, starvation, and the injuries inherent in forced marches through rough terrain, were heavy. The force that finally arrived in the northwestern province of Shaanxi (Shensi) in 1935, momentarily free of pursuers, was less than a tenth the size of the one that had set out from Jiangxi. However, this small group was the nucleus from which the Communist movement was reborn. The Party would be dominated by veterans of the Long March for the next thirty years.

It was during this march that Mao Zedong rose to command the Chinese Communist Party. At its outset he had not even been among the leaders of the Party; the 28 Bolsheviks had stripped him of his position and may have had him under arrest. But the defeats the Party had suffered under their guidance, defeats that would finally leave the CCP with its membership reduced from around 300,000 to around 40,000, made the demand for new leadership overwhelming. In January 1935, during the third month of the Long March, those CCP leaders making the march stopped to confer and made Mao the effective head of the party.

Mao did not, however, try to establish one-man domination. He was, rather, just the most important single individual in a group of very talented leaders, who managed to work together in remarkable harmony for many years. The mutual trust between them would vanish in the 1950s and the 1960s, but while it lasted it was a huge asset. They worked for common goals, even when scattered in separate base areas divided from one another by enemy armies, while the Guomindang wasted much of its energy on internal rivalries. Those who became most important in the later history of Chinese Communism included the following:

- **Deng Xiaoping** (Teng Hsiao-p'ing) had first joined the CCP while in France in 1924. He played a major role in efforts to establish a Communist base area in Guangxi province in 1929 and 1930, but when this failed he marched east to Jiangxi. Deng worked in the Jiangxi Soviet (not getting along well with the 28 Bolsheviks) until the Long March.

- **Lin Biao** (Lin Plao), a brilliant general, had been trained at the Guomindang's Huangpu Military Academy in 1925 and 1926. He participated in the Northern Expedition of 1926–27 and won rapid promotion, becoming commander of a battalion before the age of twenty. When the CCP and the Guomindang split in 1927, Lin participated in the Nanchang uprising. The force in which he served, commanded by Zhu De, joined with Mao Zedong's group in early 1928. By the time of the Long March, Lin (in his mid twenties) commanded an army corps.

- **Liu Shaoqi** (Liu Shao-ch'i) had been one of the first Chinese Communists to receive training in Moscow; he joined the CCP while in Moscow in 1921. He specialized in labour organization and the operation of underground organizations in areas under enemy control. He was in the Jiangxi Soviet in 1934, and started out on the Long March, but he seems to have dropped out before the end of the march, in order to take up an underground assignment behind Guomindang lines in North China. He rejoined the other Communist leaders in the northwest in 1937.

- **Peng Dehuai** (P'eng Teh-huai) had been an officer in the army of a Hunan warlord whose forces were amalgamated into those of the Guomindang in 1926. Peng led his men in rebellion against the Guomindang in 1928, and became one of the most important military commanders of the Jiangxi Soviet.

- **Zhou Enlai** (Chou En-lai) was the most cosmopolitan of the major CCP leaders. He had studied in Japan as a young man, and travelled to several European countries in the early 1920s. As director of the Political Department of the Huangpu Military Academy (of which Chiang Kai-shek was Commandant) from 1925 to 1926, Zhou was one of the few Communists to have much influence in the Guomindang armed forces during the First United Front. He helped plan the Nanchang uprising in 1927, but he spent most of the next few years in Shanghai and Moscow, occupying high positions in the Party hierarchy, instead of going into the hills. He finally moved to the Jiangxi Soviet in 1931, and was near the top of the Party hierarchy at the time of the Long March. He was an excellent negotiator and diplomat. He mediated disputes within the Party, and in his later years he played a very important role in handling the Communist Party's relations both with non-Communist Chinese and with foreign countries.

- **Zhu De**, Mao's partner since 1928, was officially commander-in-chief of the entire Chinese Red Army.

The CCP became a more nationalist organization under Mao. In part this was a simple matter of reduced foreign influence. The 28 Bolsheviks had been trained in the Soviet Union, had risen to the top largely through Stalin's backing, and had been highly responsive to Russian ideas and advice. Mao had never been outside of China and had frequently disagreed with Russian advice. Stalin probably would have blocked his promotion if he had been consulted, and indeed would quite possibly have ordered his death had Mao been so unwise as to visit Moscow during the next few years. But beyond the question of sheer independence, there was a more general sense in which Mao was more of a nationalist than the 28 Bolsheviks. He placed a great emphasis on issues such as economic development and effective administration, which concerned Chinese of all political persuasions. The 28 Bolsheviks, while of course supporting such things, were primarily interested in issues of class struggle, which were specifically Communist policies. Under Mao the CCP struggled for nationalist goals more vigorously, and often more competently, than the 'Nationalist Party', the Guomindang. Had it not done so it certainly would not have risen to control the nation as fast as it did, and might not have done so at all.

The relationship between the two types of goal – strengthening the nation as a whole, and promoting the interests of the poor against those of the rich – was not a simple one. Certainly the two could reinforce one another. In its first twenty years under Mao's leadership, combining the two types of activity, the CCP accomplished far more in the way of class struggle than it had under the 28 Bolsheviks. At the same time it was a more effective nationalist instrument than the Guomindang, which had tried to achieve nationalist goals without class struggle. However, there were also conflicts between the two, eventually very acute conflicts. By the last years of his life Mao, who had done more than any other man to make the CCP a nationalist organization, would find himself engaged in a desperate struggle against Party leaders who put their main emphasis on nationalist goals and were losing interest in class-centred issues.

The Japanese threat

China had been subject to various forms of outside interference for decades. There were foreign troops in Beiping and foreign warships on the Yangzi River; portions of Shanghai and Tianjin were under foreign rule. By the 1930s most of the Western nations were becoming less threatening; once Chiang Kai-shek had unified large portions of China and built something approaching a national government, he was able to persuade the British, French, and Americans to cease further encroachments on Chinese sovereignty and even abandon some of what they had acquired in the past. Japan, however, reacted differently; it refused to tolerate any threat to its position in China.

The Japanese had begun moving into Manchuria – the northeastern section of China – in the 1890s. By the late 1920s they controlled the tip of the Liaodong Peninsula on the south coast of Manchuria, which included the two major seaports of Dalian and Port Arthur. They also had the South Manchurian Railway running north from Dalian through most of the major cities of Manchuria. They had substantial investments in branch railway lines, mines, factories, and so on. Japanese troops guarded these possessions. There were also Japanese investments and commercial activities in Shandong, Shanghai, and elsewhere. Japanese troops began to withdraw from Shandong in 1923, but returned in 1927 and 1928, and clashed bloodily with Guomindang forces in Jinan (Tsinan), the province capital, in May 1928. Chinese resentment of such threats to their independence was growing; during and after the First World War there had been repeated anti-Japanese demonstrations, and boycotts of Japanese goods, protesting Japanese encroachment in Manchuria, Shandong, and elsewhere. These protests did not as yet seriously threaten the Japanese sphere of influence, but the Japanese wished to avoid the rise of any strong authority in China, and especially in Manchuria.

They had for many years coexisted with a Chinese warlord based in Manchuria, named Zhang Zuolin (Chang Tso-lin). While powerful as warlords went, he had not been a threat to their position. However, the northward expansion of the Guomindang in 1928 created the prospect that Zhang and the Guomindang together might be able seriously to oppose Japanese domination of Manchuria. Some Japanese officers assassinated Zhang Zuolin, expecting that his dissolute, drug-addicted son Zhang Xueliang (Chang Hsueh-hang) would be easier to control. They were mistaken; once the 'Young Marshal' had inherited his father's position he reformed his personal life, affiliated himself with the new Guomindang government in Nanjing, and finally became a serious opponent of Japan.

By the early 1930s Japan was beginning to fall under the domination of militarist fanatics. Both dreams of national glory and the economic pressures of the Depression pushed them to the idea of foreign conquest. Young, relatively junior officers of the army were the leaders. The high command, and the civilian politicians in the Cabinet, provided only weak opposition to the plans of the young officers. In 1931 the forces in Manchuria, defying the policies of the Japanese government, staged an incident (a supposed Chinese attack on the South Manchurian Railway), which they used as an excuse to conquer all of Manchuria. The civilians in the Cabinet opposed this action but did nothing effective to halt or reverse it, and within a few years the militarists took control of the government.

In Manchuria the Japanese established a puppet state, nominally independent, called Manzhouguo (Manchukuo), or 'land of the Manchus'. Its 'ruler' was Pu Yi, who as a boy had been the last emperor of the Qing Dynasty, overthrown in the Revolution of 1911. Behind this façade the Japanese ran Manchuria. They accelerated their efforts to develop its minerals, timber, and other resources. However, this was only the beginning of their ambitions. They began pushing southward almost immediately, and by 1936 Beiping (the traditional capital of China) existed in a sort of no man's land between Chinese and Japanese control. There seemed a real possibility that Japan would conquer all of China.

Chiang Kai-shek did his best to postpone a direct confrontation. When the open seizure of Manchuria began in 1931, he ordered Zhang Xueliang to withdraw without serious resistance. He wanted to have all of China united behind him before he fought a strong foreign foe. However, what this amounted to was that he wanted to continue fighting his Chinese enemies while leaving the Japanese unopposed. He was quoted as saying that the Japanese were only a disease of the skin, while the Communists were a disease of the heart. People who agitated too vigorously for Chinese resistance against Japan's encroachments were arrested. Indeed, the Guomindang was so eager to conciliate Japan that when a Chinese magazine published an article stating that the Emperor of Japan was basically a figurehead rather than a real ruler (fairly accurate, but profoundly insulting to Japanese sensibilities), a Guomindang court sentenced the editor to fourteen months' imprisonment. As the Japanese threat became more acute, even anti-Communist Chinese began to question the wisdom of such a stand.

The Second United Front

The Communist Party had been saying for several years that all good Chinese should unite to defend the nation. In the Jiangxi period this had been a purely verbal stance, but the Long March had brought the Party much closer to the areas under an immediate Japanese threat. The Party did not at first include Chiang Kai-shek among those being invited to join the Second United Front, whether because it doubted he wanted to fight Japan, or because he would have had to be the senior partner in any coalition. In December 1935 the CCP Central Committee resolved:

All people, all parties, all armed forces and all classes, in so far as they are opposed to Japanese imperialism and the traitor Chiang Kai-shek, should unite and wage the sacred national revolutionary war . . . Only by establishing the broadest anti-Japanese national united front (embracing the lower and upper strata) can we defeat Japanese imperialism and its running dog, Chiang Kai-shek.

The CCP was willing, however, to negotiate with Chiang's generals. Chiang had assigned two men to command the forces attacking the new Communist base area in Shaanxi: an ex-bandit and Shaanxi warlord named Yang Hucheng (Yang Hu-ch'eng), and the 'Young Marshal' Zhang Xueliang, who had been driven out of Manchuria by the Japanese in 1931. Both men listened to Communist appeals that it was foolish for Chinese to fight one another when the nation was being invaded. Zhang Xueliang, who wanted revenge for his murdered father and lost territory, had special reasons to be receptive. In the summer of 1936, Zhang and Yang reached a covert accommodation with the Communists, and from then on their forces staged only mock battles with the Red Army. This did not lead to total peace, since some troops not under the command of the two generals continued to make genuine attacks on Communist territory, but it reduced the pressure on the Communists to a low level while the CCP and the two generals considered their next moves.

In December 1936 Chiang Kai-shek, suspicious of the lack of progress in this phony war, flew up to Shaanxi to urge on the two generals; they responded by taking him prisoner. They then had to decide, in consultation with the Communists and the Russian government, what to do with him. In the end everyone involved agreed that China needed Chiang. If he were executed the country would be left with no true national leader, and the resulting struggles for power would be disastrous. If there were to be any effective resistance to Japan, Chiang would have to lead it. While Chiang did not humiliate himself by offering public concessions in return for his release, an implicit accommodation was worked out, Chiang was allowed to return to Nanjing, and a few months later the Communist Party formally joined in a new united front with the Guomindang. The Soviet Union also briefly resumed military aid to Chiang Kai-shek at this time.

In form, the CCP recognized the Guomindang as the legitimate government of China, while Chiang recognized the Communists as local authorities with a certain degree of autonomy. The main body of the Red Army, in the northwest, was renamed the Eighth Route Army, placed nominally under Chiang's authority, and granted a subsidy. Smaller Communist forces in East-central China were gathered together as the New Fourth Army. In fact, both sides well remembered that the First United Front between the CCP and the Guomindang had ended in the bloody conflicts of 1927, and both understood that the same thing was likely to happen again once the Japanese threat had abated.

Study questions

What did 'Communism' mean in China, in the 1930s?

What were Chiang Kai-shek's most important successes, and his most important failures?

Why was Chiang Kai-shek unable to destroy the Chinese Communist Party?

CHAPTER 5

World war and Communist victory

The Second World War provided the CCP with its great opportunity. Japan's invasion of China disrupted and demoralized the Guomindang, and at the same time provided the CCP with a cause by means of which it could rally millions of supporters to itself. By 1945 the Communist Party was not only larger and stronger than it had ever been before, but also more unified internally. Its relations with the population of the area it ruled were excellent. Meanwhile the Guomindang, never the world's model of efficient and honest government, had sunk to a level of corruption and decay that could hardly have been predicted in 1937. A relatively short civil war, from 1946 to 1949, sufficed for the CCP to expel the Guomindang from the Chinese mainland and establish a Communist regime.

The war begins

War between China and Japan broke out in July 1937. The shooting started over a minor incident, when a Japanese army unit on manoeuvres near Beiping was refused entry at the gate of a walled town, but it quickly escalated into a full-scale invasion of China. At first the Japanese seemed unstoppable. They pushed south from Manchuria, and also made landings on the coast. The heartland of Chiang's power, the developed areas near the mouth of the Yangzi, were highly vulnerable to Japanese attack. The Guomindang armies fought bravely for these areas, but overwhelming Japanese superiority in leadership and in armaments prevailed. Furthermore, the weaknesses of the Guomindang forces in command, coordination, and communications made it very difficult for them to conduct an orderly retreat when Japanese pressure became too much for them, and they suffered very severely. Chiang lost Shanghai in November 1937, and his capital of Nanjing in December. In 1938, Chiang opened the dikes that controlled the Yellow River. The river shifted its course by hundreds of miles, flowing into the sea south of the Shandong Peninsula rather than north of it. The flood, which destroyed thousands of villages, significantly delayed Japanese advances in North-central China, but could not halt them. Japan took Wuhan (and also Guangzhou on the south coast) in October 1938. Chiang was forced back into the interior of China, behind the mountain barriers of Sichuan province, where he established a wartime capital at Chongqing (Chungking).

Morale in Chongqing was initially high. Millions of Chinese had been wanting for years to make some effective resistance to Japanese incursions. Most of them remained enthusiastic despite the defeats of the opening months of the war, and the bombing raids to which Chongqing was soon subjected.

The Japanese found themselves in a quandary. They had been able to defeat the Guomindang armies even at their strongest, and by 1939 the Guomindang had lost most of its industry and many of its best troops. The Japanese could take any particular place on which they set their sights. They had supposed this meant that they could end the war by defeating the enemy and taking his capital city. The Chinese, however, when they lost a capital simply withdrew and established another one. Japan was a small country attacking a large one; it did not have the manpower to occupy the whole of China. Once the Japanese had occupied all the major cities on or near the coast, the key communication lines between them, and some of the surrounding countryside, they had taken on nearly as much as they could handle. This left a large hinterland in which their Chinese opponents could continue to operate.

The Japanese could perhaps have found enough Chinese collaborators to make up for their own numerical weakness. China's lack of internal unity offered fertile ground for such a strategy. Japan recruited a considerable number of Chinese auxiliary troops, and eventually set up a puppet regime in China headed by Wang Jingwei (who had at one point seemed to be Sun Yat-sen's heir as head of the Guomindang). However, the extent of the collaboration they received was limited. Partly this was because, like the German troops who invaded the Soviet Union a few years later, they alienated potential supporters by their extraordinary brutality. The atrocities that followed the Japanese seizure of Nanjing have become especially famous, partly because they concentrated an extraordinary number of murders and rapes in a single episode, and partly because there were

European and American witnesses to report what became known as the 'Rape of Nanjing'. But the same sorts of things happened on a smaller scale across large parts of China. Some units actually elaborated this into a slogan of the 'Three Alls': kill all, burn all, destroy all. Chinese were naturally reluctant to collaborate with such an occupier. Also, the Japanese were not really very generous with collaborators; they wanted so much out of China for themselves that there was not much left as a reward for Chinese who supported them. The result was that they got much less cooperation from the Chinese than they might have, less than the Manchus had received while conquering the country 300 years before. It is a measure of China's decay that they received as much as they did.

The numerical weakness of the Japanese offered opportunities to both the Guomindang and the CCP, but the response of the two parties was very different. Chiang Kai-shek's was essentially defensive; after putting up a stubborn fight for the lower Yangzi Valley, he retreated to the southwest beyond the reach of the enemy. Some modern institutions came with him. Whole factories were dismantled and moved up the Yangzi to Sichuan, with the workers carrying their machines. Universities moved, with the professors and students carrying their books. But these were mainly independent initiatives; the government provided little aid or leadership, and the amount that reached the interior was tiny compared with what had been needed. Cut off from the relatively westernized areas and the industry on which it had depended, Chiang's government was also cut off from the kind of environment in which it knew how to take constructive action. A disastrous inflation wracked the economy. Chiang was not even able to eliminate warlordism in the province of Sichuan, where his new capital was located. His government decayed, both in the sense that corruption ran rampant, and in the sense that many officials were struggling for personal power more than for national goals.

The Communists interpreted Japanese weakness not as an opportunity to avoid battle, but as an invitation to expand their territory very aggressively. The Fascist rulers of Japan were intensely anti-Communist, and had made propaganda claims that they were invading China in order to save it from the Communists, but in fact they almost ignored the small Communist Party for several years. The far larger and better equipped armies of the Guomindang seemed the main obstacles to their ambitions, so instead of moving west against the Communist base area in Shaanxi, they drove southward trying to destroy Chiang Kai-shek. This opened a fabulous opportunity for the Communists in the North China countryside. The Japanese had first driven away the Guomindang forces, which formerly held most of this area, and then moved on themselves in pursuit of the Guomindang. Behind their advance the Japanese left a power vacuum, in which large areas were almost empty of armed forces. The Communist Party moved into such areas and began to organize the peasants. By 1940, without even having had to do a great deal of fighting, the CCP had made itself the ruler of perhaps 100 million people scattered across the North China Plain. At this point it began causing real trouble for the Japanese, attacking garrisons and communication lines in many areas. The Japanese brought in reinforcements and counter-attacked, but they had waited too long and allowed the CCP to become too firmly entrenched. Despite extensive fighting, which caused heavy casualties among both the Communist troops and the Chinese peasants, and seriously reduced the area under CCP control, the Communists were able to hold onto an area with a population that has been variously estimated between 25 million and 50 million, in any case far more than they had ruled before 1937.

This is the period when the CCP really came into its own. The Shaanxi–Gansu–Ningxia base area, centring on Yanan (Yenan) in Shaanxi province, was the first area where the CCP had ever been able to establish a reasonably secure and stable government. The Party's relations with the peasants were good, and it was not troubled by serious internal conflict. A significant number of students and intellectuals, when the Japanese threatened the cities along the coast, went to Yanan instead of Chongqing; their education and skills proved very valuable to the CCP. There were no ostentatious personal luxuries, even for the top leaders; unselfish dedication to the cause seemed the general rule. The period when the CCP had its capital at Yanan, from 1937 to 1947, came to seem a sort of golden age; the 'Yanan spirit and style' remained a byword of revolutionary virtue for decades after.

Yanan, in the northwest, was for the CCP a secure base out of the way of major fighting. Most of the Eighth Route Army was further east, behind Japanese lines, spreading across the countryside in small bands. Peasant militiamen, who were farmers most of the time and only fought if the Japanese came into their immediate area, provided local support for the regular troops. The Japanese found themselves trying to destroy forces that they simply could not find.

Special tactics were part of the reason the Eighth Route Army could evade the Japanese. There was a trick called 'the segmented worm', which could be used if a guerrilla unit were being tracked by the Japanese. The guerrillas marched as a group, but every so often two men dropped out of the column and hid. The result was a nice clear trail, left by the main body of guerrillas, but this trail was left by fewer and fewer men until it finally faded into nothingness. If the Japanese unit were large, this would be the end of the matter. If it were small, the guerrillas scattered behind the Japanese unit might even reassemble and try to ambush it on its way home.

Such tricks, however, were much less important to Communist success than effective organization of the peasants. The Eighth Route Army tried to build itself a base of support in every village. Troops operated under strict discipline, and were forbidden to abuse the population. Local militias and underground organizations kept the Eighth Route Army informed about enemy activities, while denying information to the Japanese. The peasants dug extensive networks of tunnels under and around many villages, in which both peasants and guerrillas could hide when necessary. In the 'liberated areas', local governments under a greater or lesser degree of Communist leadership helped guarantee material support. They enabled the Eighth Route Army to support itself through taxes collected within each village by organizations within the village, rather than having to take things from villagers on the impromptu basis, closely resembling looting, by which most Chinese armies supplemented formal taxes.

Most important was the inadequate size of the Japanese army. Man for man the Japanese were far more formidable than the Guomindang forces the CCP had previously fought, but Japan did not have enough men to garrison every area simultaneously; most villages were free of Japanese troops at any given time. Communist-ruled villages were vulnerable to patrols or raids from Japanese units, but cooperation between the Eighth Route Army forces and local guerrillas made such raids risky for small Japanese forces, and tied down enough Japanese troops guarding vital installations to make it hard for the Japanese to mount many large offensive operations into the liberated areas. Peasants could afford to flee their villages and go into the hills for a brief period, in the face of such raids, provided they did not have to do so too often. This was quite different from the situation the Communists had faced during the Jiangxi period. Then the Guomindang army had been large enough, relative to the size of the CCP base areas, so that it could seriously have contemplated garrisoning every village. Furthermore, inhabitants of the villages were much closer to being unanimous in opposition to the Japanese than they had been in earlier struggles against the Guomindang.

What developed in North China was a classic case of guerrilla warfare. Japanese posts and communication lines were harassed both by raids of the Eighth Route Army and by local guerrillas. The Communists, whether operating as individuals in villages under Japanese control or as units in areas under Communist control, were very hard to find. Widespread popular support ensured that they had recruits, supplies, information, and relative secrecy in their own movements.

Communism, nationalism, and the 'New Democracy'

The CCP was determined to drive out the Japanese. Besides direct military struggle, this required great effort devoted to administrative construction, building up the economy, and so on in order to support the military effort. None of these matters were specifically Communist programmes. The Party was functioning very much as a nationalist organization; indeed it was struggling for nationalist goals more vigorously and more competently than the Guomindang.

Traditional Marxism had treated the initial modernization of society as a task of the capitalist class. Bourgeois leaders were supposed to overthrow feudalism and establish nation-states with strong central governments, effective communications, modern industry, and a large class of industrial workers. Only then would it be time for the working class, under Marxist leadership, to carry out a socialist revolution. When a Marxist revolution actually came, however, it was in the rather primitive society of Russia where the bourgeoisie had not yet got very far with this process of development. Lenin and his followers had therefore had to develop a variant theory, according to which the bourgeoisie of some societies was too weak and inept to carry out the role which traditional Marxism had assigned to it. The Communist Party would have to carry out the actual tasks of what it called the 'bourgeois', 'bourgeois-democratic', or 'national-democratic' revolution. These are tasks that non-Marxists usually describe as 'nationalist'.

The CCP, by 1940, had carried this shift in ideas even further than the Russian Communists. Tasks traditionally regarded as part of the 'bourgeois-democratic' revolution – national independence, strong government, and the abolition of 'feudalism' – had become its central preoccupations. Mao said: 'Today, whoever can lead the people in driving out Japanese imperialism and introducing democratic government will be the saviours of the people. History has proved that the Chinese bourgeoisie cannot fulfil this responsibility.'

'The proletariat', or in practical terms the Communist Party, which theoretically represented the proletariat, would have to take the lead. The

CCP said that China needed a 'New Democratic Revolution'. Its two great tasks would be to beat off the foreign invaders and to abolish the 'feudal' structure of landlord rule in the countryside, distributing land to the tillers. It would also have to undertake more general tasks of national development – economic growth, education, and so on. The weakness and vacillation of the bourgeoisie required that the proletariat take the lead, but there was nothing specifically proletarian about the goals of the New Democratic Revolution as Mao defined them, and in any case the Chinese proletariat was far too small to accomplish them alone. The revolution, therefore, would be a joint action by four classes: the proletariat, the peasantry, the petite bourgeoisie (intellectuals, white-collar workers, shopkeepers, etc.), and the 'national bourgeoisie' (those among the capitalists who were not considered to have tainted themselves too badly by close association with the foreigners or the landlords). The statement that the revolution would be 'democratic' did not mean that individuals would have the right to oppose its policies, only that members of the four 'revolutionary classes' listed above would have the right to help shape the policies of the revolution. Some positions in local governments were even filled through contested elections. Private property would be the norm under the New Democracy; only at a later stage, when China had reached a far higher economic level, would the establishment of a socialist economy become appropriate.

At the time he wrote this, Mao was in fact compromising the class struggle even more than was required by his theory. The anti-Japanese resistance required the participation of all Chinese who could be persuaded to join, including not only people who carried out forms of 'exploitation' that the Communists considered fairly respectable, like capitalists who used wage-labour in their factories, but even the 'feudal' landlords. Mao's writings on the New Democracy included the slogan of 'land to the tillers', but for the duration of the war, landlords who opposed the Japanese were confirmed in the ownership of their land, and tenants were supposed to go on paying rent. The CCP enforced reduction of rent and of the interest rate on debts, but it did not reduce either rent or interest to negligible levels. Landlords and rich peasants could serve in local administrations, especially after the 'three-thirds' system was introduced in 1940. This was a policy under which the Communist Party limited itself to about one-third of the positions in local administrations. This was enough to let Party members dominate these organizations, but only if they could apply effective persuasion; they could not simply occupy all top posts and give orders. Landlords and rich peasants even joined the Communist Party in significant numbers.

Such practices raised the obvious questions of whether the CCP was transforming itself from a Communist Party, an instrument for class struggle, into a simple nationalist movement. Consideration of the actual progress of the class struggle, both before and after the formation of the Second United Front, will show that this was not the case. Certainly the Party had become more nationalist than before, but the real cost to the class struggle had been rather small. When the Eighth Route Army arrived in a North China village, it did not truly have the option of immediately over-throwing the landlords and rich peasants, distributing their land to the peasants, and placing the village under the political control of the poor. Experience had shown that involving the broad mass of the peasants in class struggle, and really freeing them from landlord and rich peasant con-trol, took years to accomplish. In the Jiangxi period the landlords and rich peasants had often been able to infiltrate the Party and block or distort the effects of land reform for a considerable time, despite the best efforts of the CCP. An attempt quickly and radically to restructure North China villages in 1938 would have been dubious not only on the grounds that it would have forced the Party to put resources into the class struggle that were desperately needed in the struggle against Japan, but also on the grounds that the attempt would have failed.

After a few years in power in a given area the Party was in a much better position to lead a genuine class struggle. Its military control was firmer. It had a more extensive knowledge of local society. It could draw on the services of some poor peasants who had been mobilized politically, who could identify landlord and rich peasant elements within the Party and within local administrations, and could become replacements for these elements if the leadership decided to carry out a purge. Had the Party, in this situation, still remained as lax in the class struggle as it had seemed in the beginning, then one could really conclude that it had, temporarily or permanently, abandoned its commitment to class struggle.

Such was not the case. As the war progressed, some of the landlords and rich peasants within the Party were weeded out. Rent reduction laws, once loosely enforced, not only became more effective but were applied retroactively. Landlords who had not reduced rents when the laws were first announced were made to cough up the surplus rent they had collected. The laws themselves were stiffened; in some areas the limitation of rents to 37.5 per cent of the crop, set early in the war, was reduced to 30 per cent and then to 22.5 per cent before its end. Landlords and rich peasants, long in the habit of shifting the tax burden onto the poor, had to pay graduated land taxes, plus retroactive payments for taxes evaded in the past. Without an overt land reform, the Party had weakened the economic position of the landlords and rich peasants very drastically. Many of them had to sell part of their land, for considerably less than its real value, in order to make the payments demanded of them. Land was also confiscated from those accused of collaboration with the enemy.

If one looked only at Party rhetoric, one might think that the CCP had made, temporarily, a drastic shift in its nature when it entered the Second United Front in 1937. In actual fact, however, it was continuing to carry out egalitarian reforms that constituted a large fraction of what it would have been able to accomplish if not involved in a united front. If one considers in addition that a certain amount of class compromise was vital if the Party were to expand its territorial base rapidly, one will note that the United Front was enabling the Party to implement mildly egalitarian policies in areas where it would not otherwise have been doing anything at all. United front and egalitarian reform were not incompatible at this time.

Chiang and the United States

Japan had originally envisaged a fairly short and simple campaign. However, the Guomindang proved unwilling to surrender, even after repeated defeats. Furthermore, there were increasing problems with third countries. Japan was attempting to displace the major Western powers from the spheres of influence they had long enjoyed in China. Britain and France were too preoccupied with their impending war against Germany to offer direct opposition, but they allowed supplies to move through their respective colonies, Burma and Vietnam, to reach the beleaguered government of Chiang Kai-shek. Japan began moving into Southeast Asia, partly in an effort to choke off some of these supply routes.

The United States had likewise been distressed by the Japanese invasion of China, was more distressed by Japanese penetration of Southeast Asia, and, unlike the preoccupied European powers, had the ability to make its displeasure felt. Despite the generally isolationist temper of the country, President Roosevelt favoured resistance against German and Japanese aggression. By 1940 his administration was providing Chiang Kai-shek with significant material aid. In 1941, the US army even began unofficially supplying pilots to fight in Chiang's forces. These men became known as the 'Flying Tigers'.

More important, by 1940 the USA was beginning to reduce its trade with Japan. This forced Tokyo to choose between retreating and expanding the war. The Japanese economy could not survive without imported raw materials, much of which had been coming from the USA. Persuading the USA to continue or resume trade in petroleum and other vital goods would require Japan to abandon its effort to conquer China; Japan's military rulers could not have remained in power after such a humiliation. The alternative was to obtain another source, by conquering sections of Southeast Asia in which many vital raw materials, especially rubber and petroleum, could be found. Once the decision had been taken to go forward rather than back, the logical consequence was war between Japan and the USA, which began at Pearl Harbor in December 1941. In the following months the Japanese were astonishingly successful, taking the Philippines, Malaya, Indonesia, and Burma. This not only won them the petroleum, rubber, and other raw materials they needed, but it also cut the last land route for US aid coming into China. For the time being the only supplies that could reach China were those flown over 'the Hump', an air route across the Himalayas that was tremendously dangerous and expensive for the relatively low-flying aircraft of this period.

As soon as the United States entered the war it sent General Joseph Stilwell to coordinate aid to Chiang Kai-shek, and US military activities in the area of China. He quickly found himself on very hostile terms with Chiang. Stilwell, an aggressive military commander, felt that his mission was to make the Chinese as effective as possible in the war against Japan. This required drastic improvements in the Chinese Army, whose men were not adequately armed, trained, paid, clothed, or fed, and whose officers were often incompetent and corrupt. It also required that Chiang Kai-shek use his forces aggressively, especially to expel the Japanese from Burma and reopen a transport route by which large amounts of US supplies could reach China.

Chiang showed no enthusiasm for any of this. During his rise to power in the 1920s he had been willing to take risks, but years of struggle to defend his position against external opponents and disloyal subordinates had given him a miser's attitude to power. He hoarded guns, ammunition, and troops. He knew he would be fighting for many years – against the Japanese, perhaps against competing non-Communist leaders within China, and surely against the Communists. The United States was going to defeat Japan regardless of what he did; why should he launch vigorous campaigns against the Japanese now, which would use up supplies he might need desperately in some future war?

The idea of letting Stilwell train his officer corps seemed equally undesirable. Like many emperors of previous centuries, Chiang felt that it was better to be poorly served by weak subordinates than to be overthrown by

PLATE 5.1 *Madam Chiang Kai-shek stands arm-in-arm behind her husband (left) and General Joseph Stilwell (right). Chiang Kai-shek and Stilwell despised one another, but had to maintain a public pretence of friendship and cooperation. (© AP/PA Photos.)*

strong ones. He was not likely to forget how two of his generals had taken him prisoner and almost executed him in 1936. If Stilwell had been able to train and select officers he would have increased the effectiveness of the Guomindang army tremendously, but he also would have replaced a venal and passive group, which Chiang could control, with just the sort of alert young men who have carried out innumerable military coups, in Asia, Africa, and Latin America, during the past half-century. Chiang preferred to listen to the advocates of air power. General Claire Chennault (commander of the Flying Tigers before Pearl Harbor, commander of the US army's 14th Air Force in China from 1942 onward) offered the hope that bombing planes could do most of the fighting against Japan, without the need for dangerous reforms in the army.

Stilwell quickly came to dislike Chiang and eventually to hate him. It has often been said that Chiang was concerned with the long-range problem of fighting the Communists, and that Stilwell objected because he wanted to concentrate on the immediate problem of the Japanese. This is true only in part. If Chiang had followed a rational policy of strengthening his army as much as possible for a future war against the Communists, and this had prevented him from doing much against the Japanese, Stilwell would certainly have objected, but it is not likely that he would have come to despise Chiang so totally. In fact much of Chiang's miserliness made no sense in terms of *any* military objective. His chances of defeating the Communists would have been higher – much higher – if he had fought the Japanese vigorously, accepting Stilwell's advice, instead of acting the way he did. By abandoning the idea of vigorous resistance to the Japanese he was throwing away the morale of his army and his prestige among the population, both of which had been fairly high in 1937 when he had seemed a symbol of nationalist resistance. If he had distributed equipment and supplies to his troops more freely this would not have been mere expenditure; it would have been investment, enabling the army to hold or retake territory the possession of which would have strengthened Chiang considerably. This was most conspicuous in regard to Burma. The expense of expelling the Japanese from Burma, when Chiang finally (with great reluctance) was persuaded to participate in a Burmese campaign, was far more than compensated for by the great increase in the amount of supplies that could be brought into China once a Burmese route was opened. Chiang did not really think in such terms. Stockpiles containing thousands of tons of ammunition and supplies, brought over 'the Hump' at great cost in money and lives, were destroyed when Chinese troops, who had not been issued adequate ammunition, were unable to defend the stockpiles against Japanese advances.

At first, when all Chiang had against Stilwell was that he was a brash and insufficiently respectful foreigner with dubious ideas, cooperation had been difficult. Eventually, the mutual hatred of the two men made it impossible.

Stilwell wrote poetry referring to Chiang as 'the little bastard' and 'the Peanut'. He even got to the point of drafting some preliminary plans for a military coup against Chiang, although he never developed a serious plot. Chiang might tolerate the presence of such a man for the supplies he provided, but at all costs would prevent him from becoming too influential in the Chinese officer corps. Stilwell continuously tried to use American aid as a source of leverage, to persuade Washington to make such aid contingent on Chiang's willingness to reform his army or even place it under Stilwell's command, and sometimes he seemed to be succeeding. In the end, however, President Roosevelt decided that if Stilwell and Chiang could not work together it was Stilwell who would have to go. Stilwell's successor, General Albert Wedemeyer, developed a better relationship with Chiang and accomplished more.

The 'Dixie Mission'

As the war went on, the Americans grew interested in another Chinese group: the Communists. They knew that the CCP was conducting some kind of resistance against the Japanese in northern China, and wanted, at the very least, to have the Communist forces rescue American fliers shot down in the area. Some Americans suggested going much further, to engage in joint operations and supply the CCP with US arms and ammunition. This was not as startling a proposal at the time as it would have appeared a few years later. In the European theatre of the war the USA was supplying the Soviet Union, and Tito's Communist partisans in Yugoslavia. In the struggle against Japan, the USA cooperated to some extent with Ho Chi Minh's organization in Vietnam, the Viet Minh. However, in Vietnam, and even more in China, the USA had to deal with important allies who opposed aid to local Communists. Chiang Kai-shek was able to prevent US aid from being given to the CCP, and not much US equipment was given to the Viet Minh.

Mao was eager to develop a cooperative relationship. In the short run, he had many men but few modern weapons; even a very modest quantity of US equipment would have strengthened his army tremendously. Looking a little further ahead he could see that the civil war between Communists and Guomindang was likely to resume before long, and he wished to avoid having the US support the Guomindang if and when such a thing occurred. He also wished to avoid excessive dependence on the Soviet Union. His past experiences with Stalin had not been pleasant, and in any case the Soviet Union had been too devastated by the war to be capable of helping much in the reconstruction of China. A friendly relationship with the USA seemed overwhelmingly desirable, and the main thing the USA was likely to demand in return for any aid it provided – vigorous action against the Japanese – was something the CCP was doing anyway.

The USA finally defied Chiang to the extent of sending some diplomats and officers to Mao Zedong's headquarters in Yanan. The US Observer Group (sometimes referred to as the 'Dixie Mission' because it was going into rebel territory), commanded by Colonel David Barrett, arrived there in July 1944. Most of the Americans were favourably impressed. The CCP seemed less corrupt, more unified, and more vigorous in its resistance to Japan than the Guomindang. United States fliers shot down over North China, and smuggled across hundreds of miles of territory where the Communists either ruled outright or operated as guerrillas, confirmed to their superiors that the CCP was both strong and popular over a broad area. The more dictatorial aspects of Communist policy were not conspicuously visible to Americans whose stays in Communist-ruled areas tended to be relatively brief.

In the end, the contacts that the USA developed with the CCP led to very little. Allying with the CCP would have been tantamount to abandoning Chiang Kai-shek, and for a whole range of reasons the USA could not do this. Turning against what it recognized as the legitimate government of China, the government it had come to aid, would have seemed dubious on moral grounds. In practical terms, Chiang Kai-shek had an army that was far larger and better equipped than Mao's, so for all its problems this army seemed likely to be the more useful as an ally against Japan. Finally there were political considerations. Both Chiang and his American-educated wife were extremely popular in the USA. Wartime propaganda usually tends to exaggerate the merits of any ally. Chiang had been built up in the American press as a strong and popular ruler, leading a vigorous resistance against the Japanese invaders. Reports by American diplomats in China, showing the real situation, were not available to the general public. Some of the diplomats in question would later see their careers destroyed as punishment for their having questioned Chiang's virtue.

The Japanese surrender

The end of the war caught everyone by surprise. On 6 August 1945, the United States used an atomic bomb to obliterate Hiroshima, one of the few Japanese cities that had not already been destroyed by conventional bombing. On the night of 8/9 August, in accord with promises made at the Yalta

Conference six months before, the Soviet Union declared war on Japan and invaded Manchuria. On 9 August a second atomic bomb fell on Nagasaki. Japan capitulated within a few days. This led to an immediate and drastic intensification of the competition between the CCP and the Guomindang. Japanese troops would be surrendering; which side would obtain their weapons? Which side would take over the cities Japan had held, which included almost all of China's industries?

General George C. Marshall went to China in December 1945, as President Truman's personal representative, with instructions to prevent civil war and achieve the 'unification of China by peaceful, democratic methods'. President Truman (like President Roosevelt before him) wanted a strong China, allied with the USA, to form the linchpin of post-war US policy for Asia. A war between the Guomindang and the CCP would weaken China and therefore had to be prevented. Roosevelt and Truman tried to make the wartime United Front permanent; to make the Guomindang and the CCP compromise their differences peacefully. Neither the CCP nor the Guomindang expected this to work, but neither side wanted the onus of starting a new war, so for about a year they manoeuvred for advantage, while the USA tried to keep them from one another's throats and arrange for a coalition government.

Unfortunately for Marshall, US policy was fundamentally inconsistent. He was supposed to mediate between Chiang Kai-shek and with Communists, to help them settle their differences without civil war. His success in this role depended on convincing both sides that the USA was strictly impartial in this dispute. At the same time the USA was treating the Republic of China (in other words Chiang Kai-shek) as a US ally, and providing it with very important military assistance. The United States tried to prevent Japanese troops from surrendering to the Communist forces; the USA told the Japanese to keep their weapons until Guomindang forces could come up from the southwest to accept their surrender. It provided sea and air transport for Guomindang forces to come up from the distant southwest to take over the cities of North and Central China. This helped to overcome the advantage of the Communists, who had a much shorter distance to travel but had to move on foot. United States Marines landed at some key points in North China to hold them against the Communists until the Guomindang forces could arrive. By the time Marshall reached China at the end of 1945, the US role in Chiang's manoeuvring against the CCP was no longer quite so massive as it had been in the first months after the Japanese surrender, but it was still substantial. The Marines were still in North China, US advisers were assisting the Guomindang armed forces in a variety of ways, and US equipment continued to arrive. In this light, Marshall's attempts to convince CCP negotiators of his impartiality in the developing conflict appear rather naïve.

The Russians formed a complicating factor. Earlier in 1945, before the USA was sure that the atomic bomb would really work, it had asked the Soviet Union for a promise that Russian troops would help in the final stage of the war against Japan. The Soviet Union declared war on Japan on 8 August. This was approximately the date that had been agreed between Stalin and the Americans, but by this time the atomic bomb, first used two days before, had reduced the need for Russian troops. Instead of facing a difficult and bloody battle to subdue a fanatical enemy, the Russian troops were able to conquer Manchuria, the most industrialized area of China, quickly and without much loss.

This was a boon to the CCP, but not an unlimited one. The Russian troops allowed their Chinese comrades into Manchuria, and CCP forces under General Lin Biao spread over the Manchurian countryside and began to propagandize and recruit among the villages. Stalin, however, was far more interested in his own welfare than in that of non-Russian Communists. Manchuria was important to him mainly as a source of industrial equipment, which could be hauled back and used in the reconstruction of the war-ravaged Soviet Union, and as a bargaining chip for the extraction of concessions from the Guomindang government. He was willing to aid the Chinese Communists to a certain extent, allowing them to operate in Manchuria and giving them a portion of the equipment taken from surrendering Japanese forces. However, he did not expect them to take control of China in the immediate future, so he did not feel the need to win their goodwill by really generous aid; on the contrary the CCP was long to remember the way the Soviet forces looted the factories of Manchuria during the winter of 1945–46.

On 14 August 1945 the Soviet Union signed a set of agreements with Chiang Kai-shek, including a Treaty of Friendship and Alliance. Chiang gave Stalin the naval base at Port Arthur, at the tip of the Liaodong Peninsula in southern Manchuria, and partial control (which soon became in practice full control) of the adjacent commercial port of Dalian. The Soviet Union also got partial control of major rail lines in Manchuria. In return Stalin recognized Chiang's government as the government of China, and promised that Russian aid and support would go to Chiang and to no one else.

Within a few months after the Japanese surrender, the first stage of the contest between the Guomindang and the CCP had been completed. It did not involve much violence; it was mainly a matter of which side reached and occupied any given area first. The rich provinces along the Yangzi River went mostly to the Guomindang, which took not only the major cities and communication lines, but much of the countryside in between. In the North China Plain, especially north of the Yellow River, the Guomindang got some of the cities but the Communists got most of the countryside. Finally, in Manchuria the Russians held the cities and the CCP the countryside. Here the Guomindang and the CCP manoeuvred to determine which would be able to occupy the cities when the Russians withdrew. Each side obtained some Japanese arms and even got some Japanese soldiers to join its forces.

The Soviet Union had originally promised to withdraw from all of Manchuria by 3 December 1945. However, Chiang found the Russians not cooperative about letting Guomindang armies into Russian-held areas before Russian withdrawals, so they would be in position to take over as the Russians moved out. By the time the Guomindang could arrive in evacuated positions, it often found them in the hands of the CCP. Stalin offered to postpone his withdrawal if Chiang asked him to do so, to give the Guomindang time to organize itself so it would at least be ready to move into evacuated positions immediately after the Russians left them. Chiang did indeed ask for postponements of the Russian evacuation, first to 3 January 1946, and then to 1 February.

Chiang clearly felt that the presence of Russian troops in Manchurian cities would hinder rather than aid the efforts of the CCP to take these cities. Chiang assumed, and seems to have been correct in assuming, that CCP forces would not be able to get into key positions until the Russians left them. Furthermore, he thought there was a reasonable chance that when the Russians withdrew they would do so in such a fashion that Guomindang forces would be able to replace them before the CCP could occupy the positions being evacuated. This reveals an extraordinary awareness, on Chiang's part and that of the Americans who were advising him, of the differences that could exist between Russian and Chinese Communists. This was a period when Communism was often regarded as a monolithic worldwide movement, and historians have taken too little note of the way Chiang Kai-shek, in 1945, treated the Russian and Chinese Communists parties as separate organizations with divergent interests.

The Russians did not, in the end, prove as cooperative as Chiang had hoped. They eventually allowed Guomindang units to enter some key Russian-held cities before the Russian troops pulled out, but not on the scale that Chiang needed, and to the delays in evacuation which Chiang had requested they added further delays of their own. The pull-out of Russian troops was not completed until 3 May 1946, and it was handled in such a manner that the CCP was able to reach many important positions before the Guomindang. The departure of Soviet forces, except for their continued presence in Port Arthur and Dalian, left no significant armed force separating the Guomindang and the CCP.

A truce existed, but it was never very firm. Aside from an absence of genuine goodwill on either side, the truce suffered from the tension between two principles. It was supposed to protect the territory held by the CCP from efforts at armed seizure by the Guomindang. At the same time it recognized Chiang Kai-shek's government as the legal government of China, and forbade CCP interference with Guomindang communication routes. Even given far more goodwill than actually existed, it would have been difficult to avoid trouble over Chiang's desire to open communication routes through the Communist territory which often separated the Guomindang-held cities.

Both the CCP and the Guomindang sometimes made promises, to please General Marshall, which they had no intention of keeping. Thus in late February of 1946 the two sides signed an agreement on mutual reduction of armed forces, under which the Guomindang army was to be reduced to ninety divisions of not more than 14,000 men each, while the Communist forces would be cut to eighteen divisions. This would have been tremendously advantageous to Chiang, and not simply because the numbers were loaded in his favour. Many of the units nominally under his command were in fact so unreliable that if, with American backing, he managed to disband them, his position would be strengthened rather than weakened. The CCP, on the other hand, really needed all the forces it had and was vigorously expanding them. It signed the agreement, but thereafter did not make even the most preliminary gestures towards implementing it.

The Guomindang, on the other hand, took just as cavalier an attitude to the cease-fire agreement it signed in January 1946. The implementation of this agreement was supposed to be supervised in the field by joint teams of US, Guomindang, and CCP representatives. The Guomindang signed, but then simply refused for an extended period to allow any joint teams to enter Manchuria, the area of greatest conflict. The problem in this case was that peace seemed likely to be far more beneficial to the CCP than to the Guomindang. The Japanese surrender had allowed the CCP to take over an area out of proportion to its military strength. Given a few years, Communist cadres would win the allegiance of the peasants, reform village politics on revolutionary lines, and build for themselves a tremendously powerful organizational base. The longer Chiang waited before attacking the Communists in these areas, the stronger the opposition he would face when he finally did so. In the areas that had recently come under Guomindang rule, on the other hand, Chiang's government was utterly incapable of carrying out programmes analogous to those of the Communists, to win the allegiance of the mass population. It could not expect its strength to grow spectacularly with the passage of time. In July 1947 the US ambassador commented on the rapacity of the men who had come up from the south to represent Chiang in Manchuria, and the hatred that had grown up between them and the people they were trying to rule:

Nationalist southern military forces and civil administrators conduct themselves in Manchuria as conquerors, not as fellow countrymen, and have imposed a 'carpet-bag' regime of unbridled exploitation upon areas under their control. If military and civil authorities of local origin were in control, they too would probably exploit the populace, but experience has shown that Chinese authorities of local origin, in general, never quite strangle a goose laying golden eggs, and furthermore, it is a human trait to be less resentful toward exploitation by one's own than towards that by outsiders. The result of this is that the countryside is so antagonistic toward outsiders as to affect the morale of non-Manchurian troops and at the same time arouse vindictiveness in southern military officers and civil administrators.

The Communist forces under Lin Biao had of course also been outsiders when they entered Manchuria in 1945, but they had established good relations with the people, and by 1947 local recruits made up a large proportion of their troops there.

The result of this difference in situations was that while both sides expected war, and probably both sides wanted war, it was to Chiang's advantage to hasten it, and to the advantage of the CCP to postpone it. There were serious violations of the truce on both sides, but the Guomindang was the side that launched such systematic and such massive offensives as to give the impression that it had no desire for a peaceful settlement.

The spring and summer of 1946 saw repeated armed clashes, after which American mediators had increasing difficulty restoring even a temporary truce. Finally, in November 1946, negotiations broke down completely. The pattern of the fighting at first seemed similar to that which had followed Japan's attack on China in 1937, but this time it was the Guomindang that spread along the roads and railroads. It took most major cities, but it did not have the troops to spread over the whole of the country-side as it advanced through North China and Manchuria. Chiang's men took the Communist capital at Yanan in February 1947, but the Communist leaders simply evacuated it and managed their war from mobile bases.

Some Guomindang leaders said they expected to destroy the CCP within a few months; most Americans expected a long and inconclusive struggle. However, CCP strength and Guomindang weakness soon began to show. On paper Chiang's army was perhaps three times as large as that of the Communists, and better armed, but much of this army was either of very low quality or not available for actual use. Chiang had to play off his various generals against one another, and many of the troops nominally under his control were either commanded by men he did not trust, or needed for the task of watching men he did not trust, far from the areas of combat against the Communists. Chiang no longer had anything like the advantage he had enjoyed against the Jiangxi Soviet; he could not even occupy all of the cities and major transportation lines. His troops pushing up the South Manchurian Railway were stopped well short of Harbin, an important industrial centre and the capital of Heilongjiang province. At the same time the low quality of the Guomindang troops guaranteed that the Communists would be able to capture considerable quantities of weapons to equip their new recruits.

In late 1946 and early 1947 Chiang Kai-shek stretched his forces to the limit, whether because he wanted to knock out the Communists before they got any stronger, or simply because he wanted to take as much territory, and especially as many of the relatively industrialized cities, as he could. He put hundreds of thousands of his best troops into Manchuria. His armies in the north, far from their bases of supply, were threatened by steadily growing Communist armies in the countryside around them.

The United States found it difficult to work out a clear policy. Chiang Kai-shek had been a US ally for several years, and was popular with the American public. The USA was also distrustful, to say the least, of any Communist Party. However, American policy-makers were reluctant to get involved in a civil war which Chiang had started against American advice, and which he was conducting in a manner very unlikely to lead to victory. Chiang was launching over-optimistic offensives against a powerful enemy, while American advisers were pleading with him to make the kind of reforms that could give him a really firm grip on the territory he already held. The USA was reluctant to give him much aid as long as he ignored this advice, and was determined not to allow aid to escalate to the point where it would imply a guarantee to preserve Chiang's government.

In August 1946, wanting to disengage the US a little further from the growing conflict, General Marshall instituted an embargo on the sale of US weapons to Chiang. He also withdrew US advisers from some Guomindang units actually involved in combat against the Communists. The US Marine Corps, which had been guarding coal mines and some important transportation lines in North China, freeing Guomindang troops for service elsewhere, handed these responsibilities over to the Guomindang in September 1946. Most of the Marines withdrew from China late in 1946, though a small force remained in Qingdao until 1949. However, the effect of such steps was blurred by the continuation of several forms of US aid to Chiang Kai-shek. Military advisers remained in some sections of Guomindang armed forces. Also, the embargo only prevented the United States from selling weapons and ammunition to the Guomindang. It did not prevent the sale of some other types of military equipment, and it did not prevent Marine units departing in the first half of 1947 from *giving* surplus artillery ammunition to the Guomindang. The USA, despite Marshall's wishes, was involved.

The embargo was lifted in May 1947, and the Guomindang was able to resume buying ammunition and equipment, no longer needed by the US armed forces after the end of the Second World War, at a small fraction of its original cost. In 1948, the US resumed outright military aid – sending equipment for which China was not asked to pay even at discounted prices.

The return to land reform

At the same time it resumed civil war against the Guomindang, the CCP also resumed violent class struggle against the landlords and rich peasants. This was a gradual and unplanned development. Party leaders were not sure how radical they were going to become, and indeed they did not always define their policies of the moment very clearly.

As has been remarked above, the CCP had not abandoned the class struggle totally during the war against Japan. Rent reduction, graduated taxation, and the promotion of some peasants to leadership positions in the villages had weakened the traditional élite considerably. However, this élite was far from having been destroyed. Many landlords and rich peasants retained most of their land, and retained either general prestige or actual positions of leadership in their villages. In the second half of 1945, and in 1946, the CCP made increasingly radical attacks on these people. The Party first directed the peasants against people who had supported the Japanese, but then turned the attack against those guilty only of collecting rent or making high-interest loans. Before the end of 1946 there were many areas in which all conspicuously large landholdings had been eliminated.

The land reform campaign soon became very radical indeed. It led to attacks on middle peasants who did not really have much more than an average amount of wealth, and even on some people whose wealth was average or a shade below average. It also led to damaging purges within the Communist Party. There are a variety of reasons for these excesses, which the Party later realized to have been mistakes. One was that the Party had unrealistic expectations of what land reform could accomplish. The Party liked to blame the exploitation of the landlords for all or almost all of the peasants' problems. It was far too quick to assume that the peasants could all have a decent life if only the landlords' wealth were properly distributed. Chinese Communist Party publications often stated that the landlords and rich peasants, who together amounted to not more than 10 per cent of the rural population, owned 70 to 80 per cent of the land in China. Unfortunately for the CCP, the actual landholdings of the landlords and rich peasants were nowhere near this level. Landlord and rich peasant holdings were particularly small in North and Northwest China. Redistribution of wealth could at best partially alleviate the peasants' problems in these provinces; the real problem was that there was not enough wealth to go around.

When the landlords' wealth had been divided and many peasants were still unpleasantly close to the edge of starvation, the Party began spreading its nets further and further to find additional people from whom land and other wealth could be confiscated. The victims included rich peasants, and then middle peasants who owned more than the average amount of land and farm equipment, and finally some people who were actually at or below the average level of wealth, but whose parents or grandparents had been landlords or rich peasants, so it could be claimed that their inherited land and goods had come originally from their ancestors' exploitation of the poor.

Party leaders became increasingly suspicious of their own village-level organizations. If redistribution of wealth had not resolved the plight of the poor, suspicion naturally fell on those who had managed the programme. The suspicion was partially justified. Some cadres had taken for themselves part of the wealth confiscated from the rich. Some had protected landlords or rich peasants from full redistribution of their property. But Party leaders, who had exaggerated ideas of what a full and correct redistribution could have done for the poor, thought the village cadres must be far worse than they actually were.

By the second half of 1947 the Party was pushing a remarkably extremist policy in the villages of northern China, to bring the poor peasants and agricultural labourers up to full equality with all the other elements in society. Landholdings were to be equalized in each area, and there was also to be significant redistribution of agricultural tools, draft animals, seed grain, money, and other forms of wealth. Landlords and rich peasants were in theory to be cut down to equality with the poor; in practice many landlords were stripped of everything they had, and some were killed. More startlingly, the ordinary poor peasants were also promoted relative to the veteran cadres of the Communist Party. Top leaders decided that local cadres had been abusing their positions to the detriment of the Party. They invited the poor peasants to stand in judgement over the cadres and Party members, to take from them any excess land and goods that might have stuck to their fingers during previous redistribution of wealth, and to criticize and punish them if they had been arrogant or abusive to those below them.

The ensuing turmoil involved the collision of two very different views of the nature of society and politics. Traditional China had been a very hierarchical society. All understood that some members of society were wealthy and powerful, and could do almost as they pleased, while others were poor and weak. Many peasants who had risen to positions of village leadership in the early stages of the revolution assumed as a matter of course that they would enjoy what they regarded as the normal perquisites of leadership – the rights to make decisions and command obedience. They were the ones who had made possible the redistribution of landlord wealth; to many of them, and to many of the ordinary peasants, it seemed only fair that they should be rewarded by being given an extra share in the distribution. Some of them had acquired valuable objects simply by default. Everyone knew that if the Communist Party were ever defeated, peasants who had taken large and valuable objects would be in danger of their lives. If landlord property were distributed while the village was still not sure which way the civil war was going, a revolutionary cadre could sometimes get a wagon or a team of mules simply by being the only person who dared accept them. For such reasons, peasants who had led in the early stages of the revolution in any particular village were likely to have profited from it more than their neighbours.

To Party leaders, on the other hand, such phenomena represented serious corruption. Communism was supposed to be an egalitarian doctrine, and real egalitarianism required a total break from the hierarchical traditions of Chinese society. The Party decided that infiltration by the traditional élite, and the tendency of peasants who rose to positions of leadership to differentiate themselves from the people, enrich themselves beyond the level of the common peasants, and take on the arrogance and self-importance of the traditional élite, threatened the very soul of the revolution.

Given such a climate of opinion, Party leaders exaggerated the magnitude of the problem they faced. As has been mentioned above, they exaggerated the extent to which redistribution of landlord wealth could improve the lives of the peasants, so when they saw the peasants still in difficulties they thought that some very large proportion of the wealth formerly held by the landlords must have failed to reach the hands of the peasants. When they saw veteran cadres at the village level guilty of arrogance, minor corruption, or simply giving orders to the peasants instead of explaining programmes to them in such a fashion as to win voluntary cooperation, they reacted with a degree of shock and horror that implied not only that this behaviour was undesirable, but that it reflected an astonishing failure to meet normal and reasonable standards of behaviour. In fact, most of the cadres in question had adhered to a standard considerably higher than what they had grown up thinking of as normal élite behaviour. If Party leaders wanted to set a still higher standard, they should have understood that they would need to conduct a long, slow educational campaign among the cadres.

In the early months of 1948, the Party relaxed the extremes of its drive for egalitarianism. It had always been hesitant about trying to achieve total equalization of landholdings, since this would require taking land from anyone who owned even a little more than the average amount. Complete equalization attacked the interests of well-to-do middle peasants who were not to any serious extent exploiters, who were not hated by their neighbours, and who did not own enough for their expropriation to bring all that great a benefit to the poor. It appeared threatening even to poor peasants, whose ambition after the land reform was to work hard on the land they had just acquired, save, and make themselves well-to-do middle peasants. China could not afford for the poor to think that if they worked hard and enriched themselves they would only be expropriated.

In the political sphere the extremes of anti-élitism were similarly relaxed. Those who investigated village cadres and village Party branches stopped assuming that they were likely to find massive corruption, landlord infiltration, and abuses of power. The Party stopped being so determined to get all the poor peasants involved equally in village politics; it would settle for having all of the poor involved to some extent, and those of the poor peasants who seemed to have a talent for leadership moving to the top positions.

However, one must remember that while this might be more moderate than what had been happening in the autumn of 1947, the Communist Party was still carrying out a remarkably radical programme by any other standard. In villages where a Communist apparatus existed, local Party members and cadres continued to be called to account if there was solid evidence that they had been guilty of arrogant abuses of their powers, or that they had used their positions to enrich themselves. In newly 'liberated' areas the Party did not act quite so hastily as before, but it was still determined that the destruction of the traditional village élite should be completed within two or three years. Landlords lost most of their wealth, and rich peasants lost a significant amount. Landlords continued to be imprisoned or executed, even if in smaller numbers than in earlier years. Their prestige, and their control of village affairs, were destroyed as completely as the Communist Party could manage. In their place a new ruling structure was recruited from among the peasants. Where village reforms were carried out in accord with Party policy, the bulk of the peasants not only acquired considerable wealth from the expropriation of the landlords, but also acquired a significant voice in village affairs. Even where local officials carried out the reforms in a hasty and slipshod manner, the degree of equality in village society was greater than it had ever been before.

The very radical line followed in the villages during the winter of 1947–48 provides interesting parallels, and contrasts, to the radicalism of the Cultural Revolution in the 1960s. In both cases the Party developed policies of extreme egalitarianism, which were later repudiated on the grounds that they had harmed both the Party itself, and elements of the mass population. However, from the Communist viewpoint the damage done by leftist excesses in the land reform of the late 1940s was limited, and the errors were corrected quite fast. Some of the reasons will be discussed in Chapter 6, but it is worth mentioning here that in the 1940s policy discussions were still being conducted on a rational basis. The Party was describing what it believed the situation to be, and the policies it was developing to deal with that situation, in clear, simple, and rational language. This made it relatively easy for people to notice if the description failed to match the actual situation (as with wild exaggerations of the number of landlord infiltrators in the Party), or if the arguments justifying a particular policy seemed weak (as with the expropriation of land from well-to-do middle peasants). In the Cultural Revolution, public debate was conducted in such stereotyped and inflated rhetoric as to hamper rational decision-making.

The final Communist victory

Meanwhile, the Civil War was approaching an end. Chiang had sent his best military units into North China and Manchuria. They pushed northward as far as they could go, taking the CCP capital at Yanan, and moving up the rail lines into the interior of Manchuria. They strung themselves out over long and tenuous communication lines, surrounded by Communist-held villages, until they needed to devote most of their efforts just to defending their positions and their supply lines against the harassment of CCP guerrillas. By the middle of 1947 they were losing the initiative, and starting to huddle into their garrisons. Their advantage in numbers and weapons was still great, but not as great as in the past; the CCP had been recruiting vigorously, and had acquired a considerable amount of Japanese equipment, some captured directly and some handed over by the Russians before they left Manchuria in 1946. The Guomindang forces, suffering from incompetence, corruption, and disunity, were losing such offensive spirit as they had previously had.

Civil society in the Guomindang zone was also in a state of decay. Rampant inflation undermined the economic position of the middle class. The corruption of the Guomindang administration remained a conspicuous embarrassment.

Chiang Kai-shek, who could remember when the Guomindang had been a dynamic and aggressive party, bent on a revolutionary transformation of Chinese society, was well aware of how low it had sunk (though he may not have realized the extent of his own responsibility for that decline). Desperately trying to shame his subordinates into some effort at reform, he commented: 'To tell the truth, never, in China or abroad, has there been a revolutionary party as decrepit and degenerate as we [the Guomindang] are today; not one as lacking spirit, lacking discipline, and even more, lacking standards of right and wrong as we are today.' Officers neither trained their men properly in combat skills, nor gave them adequate food, clothing, or medical care; 'since the officers treat the men in this way it must be considered very good if the men do not mutiny or desert'. Loyalty to the cause was minimal: 'Everyone nourishes the evil habit of caring only for himself and is concerned only for the advantage of his own unit; towards the perils and difficulties of other troops, or the success or failure of the whole campaign, they give almost no thought.'

During 1947 the Communist forces, which had adopted the name 'People's Liberation Army' (PLA) in 1946, definitely gained the initiative. They controlled most of Manchuria, and much of the countryside in the portion of the North China Plain lying north of the Yellow River. In April 1947, the Guomindang shifted the Yellow River back to its northerly (pre-1938) course, cutting off Communist forces in Shandong from those to the north and west. But in June the Communists sent about 100,000 more men south across the river, who soon won considerable victories in the area between the Yellow and Yangzi Rivers.

During 1948, increasing numbers of Guomindang troops defected to the CCP; this allowed the PLA to expand to an extent that might otherwise have required making unacceptable demands on its support base in the villages by aggressive mobilization of peasant manpower. The Guomindang positions in Manchuria were shrinking islands in the sea of Communist countryside, having steadily less contact with one another. The Communists probably could have begun eliminating these islands earlier than they did, but by waiting until they had powerful forces even in areas well south of the Yellow River, they were giving themselves a genuine chance of not just defeating the Guomindang armies but trapping and destroying them before they could retreat south of the Yangzi. Chiang Kai-shek's refusal to extract his troops from this situation, while he still could, allowed the Communist strategy to succeed better than even the Communist leaders had really dared to expect.

Once it became apparent that the CCP could not only isolate Guomindang garrisons from one another, but actually bring strong enough forces against individual garrisons to destroy them, the end came very quickly. Normally, a victorious army uses up supplies and equipment in the course of its advance, stretches its supply lines, and has to garrison conquered territory. The effective strength available at the front will therefore tend to shrink as the advance goes on. The Communists in North and Northeast China, however, were clearing out Guomindang bases from between Communist bases. With each victory they captured large quantities of equipment and ammunition, their supply lines became shorter with the removal of an obstacle around which they had formerly had to detour, and the forces that could be concentrated against the next target became larger.

As late as 15 September 1948, just before the collapse began, the Guomindang armies still had substantially more total manpower than the CCP. Their superiority in arms and equipment was even greater, and for the most part they had adequate ammunition. However, it was a case of the sheep outnumbering the wolves. The Guomindang forces in North

China and Manchuria were scattered in garrisons far enough from one another to make supply very difficult. Chiang Kai-shek, in his determination to hold important cities, kept his men in exposed positions far to the north rather than pull them south while there was time to do so. If asked to come to one another's assistance they generally moved slowly and hesitantly or not at all, so the Communists could concentrate overwhelming force against one, and then move on to the next. Finally, when the attack began against any particular city, some units often surrendered or went over to the Communist side, opening up great gaps in the defensive line, with the result that troops who were willing to make a last-ditch resistance were unable to do so in any effective manner. Thus the Guomindang armies, first in Manchuria and then in North China, ceased to exist in a remarkably short period. The Communist forces not only suffered few losses, but actually expanded during the campaign through the absorption of troops who switched sides.

The destruction of the Guomindang forces in Manchuria, in October and November of 1948, made an eventual Communist victory certain. The destruction of Guomindang forces on the North China Plain, culminating in the Huai-Hai campaign of November 1948 to January 1949, ended the possibility that the Guomindang would even be able to mount a decent rearguard action. It had lost over a million men, including almost all of what passed in its decrepit forces for élite unit, in four and a half months. The PLA on the other hand had grown substantially in strength. It had suffered serious casualties in some battles, but not in many, and these had been more than balanced by its gains in manpower and weaponry through absorption of Guomindang units that had surrendered or defected. From this point onward the PLA swept southward against minimal resistance.

On 21 January 1949, Chiang Kai-shek officially resigned as president of the Republic of China; Vice-president Li Zongren (Li Tsung-jen) theoretically took Chiang's place. Chiang thus escaped the embarrassment of presiding officially over the collapse of his government. However, he kept real power in his own hands; he continued to issue orders to his generals and other high officials just as if he were still president. As his military position on the mainland of China became hopeless, he withdrew as many of his troops as possible to the island of Taiwan. On 1 March 1950, on Taiwan, he once more took the title of president of the Republic of China.

The PLA crossed the Yangzi River in April 1949, and reached Guangzhou on the south coast in October. At this point the civil war seemed effectively over. Before the end of 1950 the PLA had even reached Tibet in the southwest, which had been shown as part of China on maps, but where

PLATE 5.2 *Mao Zedong arrives in Beiping (soon to be restored to its old name of Beijing), March 1949. The Guomindang had about 200,000 troops in and around the city, but the general commanding this force had surrendered his men, and their weapons, without a serious fight. He was rewarded by being made minister of water conservancy in the new Communist government of China. (© Collection J.A. Fox/ Magnum Photos.)*

no Chinese government had exercised any real power for almost forty years. The only Chinese territory they did not hold was Taiwan. On 1 October 1949, in the old imperial capital of Beijing (now restored to its traditional name, after having been called Beiping for twenty-one years under the Guomindang), the nation's new rulers proclaimed the establishment of the People's Republic of China (PRC).

Study questions

Why did the United States support Chiang Kai-shek as strongly as it did? Why didn't the United States support Chiang Kai-shek more strongly than it did?

At what point did the Communist victory over the Guomindang become inevitable?

What were Chiang Kai-shek's most damaging weaknesses?

CHAPTER 6

The People's Republic of China, 1949–57

The new regime seemed at first to be in the mainstream of Communist development. The PRC, like other Communist states, was ruled by two parallel hierarchies. Each one ran from the capital in Beijing down to the village level. One was the formal government, with Mao Zedong as Chief of State and Zhou Enlai as Premier. It embraced both a structure of territorial units running from 'greater administrative regions' down through provinces and counties to village administrations, and also functional units such as the ministries of trade, justice, etc. Ultimate power, however, lay with the Communist Party apparatus, which paralleled and penetrated that of the government at every level. The relationship of Party members to non-members was not one of simple command; there were many Party members in the government whose immediate superiors, in the governmental chain of command, were non-members of the Party. However, the Party as an institution provided the leading core of the government. The Party was tightly centralized; Party members accepted the decisions of the central Committee, which in turn accepted the authority of a few top leaders who belonged to the Politburo.

Roles in this system were not highly specialized. For the first few years the PLA played a major role in most government operations. Even after the military as an organization was separated from the civilian government, almost everyone of real importance held more than one position, and it was not unusual for a single individual to hold simultaneous positions in the civil administration, the PLA, and the Party.

The very rapid advances of 1948 and 1949 had given the CCP control of very extensive areas where it had no real organizational base. Great cities like Shanghai and Wuhan were a serious challenge for a party most of whose past experience had been in the countryside, and indeed in the more primitive and backward parts of the countryside.

The CCP did not have deep roots even in all of the countryside. It had operated mainly north of the Yangzi for the past fifteen years; most of its activities in the south had been restricted to a few guerrilla zones. It did not have many members who spoke the southern dialects. Under such conditions plans for the rapid collectivization of agriculture, or the replacement of private ownership by socialist control in industry, would have been absurd. The Party might 'control' the newly conquered areas, in the sense that the PLA had driven out the Guomindang forces, but it had to do a great deal of work just to establish an effective administration in central and southern China, much less carry out its long-term goals of social transformation.

The Communist Party's policy was strictly pragmatic in the early years. It needed to maintain public services, maintain or establish law and order, and get an administration running. It did not have half the number of ideologically reliable people it would have needed to do these jobs, so it quite calmly set about recruiting thousands and thousands of unreliable ones. Before long standards would be raised, and these people would either have to be reindoctrinated in a satisfactory fashion or lose their positions, but for the moment the main priority was seeing that necessary tasks got done. The CCP did not merely ask technical personnel like railway maintenance men and power plant supervisors to stay on their jobs; it did the same with many of the people who had staffed the tax-collection bureaux, police agencies, and criminal courts of the old regime.

This was a remarkable demonstration of self-confidence, in a situation where many Communists might have felt that their power and their revolutionary purity were at risk. The Party knew that it was taking on people, in politically sensitive jobs, many of whom had no understanding of Communism and some of whom actively disliked it. It had seen how the opportunists had swarmed into the Guomindang after 1927, and had helped to convert a revolutionary movement into a corrupt and stagnant bureaucracy. However, the CCP had no doubt that it could guide and supervise its own new recruits, so they could neither take over the new government and subvert its revolutionary goals, nor conspire against it and overthrow it.

The Communists had by no means turned into a group of moderates. One reason for their confidence that they could keep control of the situation was the ruthlessness with which they dealt with those they considered not just unreliable but outright enemies. In their first few years in power they executed hundreds of thousands of people. The victims included 'counter-revolutionaries', bandits, landlords considered to have been exceptionally vicious, and so forth.

Reform in the countryside

In the villages of southern China, the first years of Communist rule were a period of continual turmoil and change. The CCP wanted to destroy the existing rural élite, and break up concentrations of wealth in the country-side. There were precedents for such a policy in Chinese tradition, both in ancient documents and in the actual policies of past dynasties. The found-ing of a dynasty in pre-modern China had usually been accompanied by an effort to break up at least some large landholdings, since large land-holders tended to take for themselves the share of the land's production that might otherwise have gone to the government through taxation. However, the egalitarian policies of the CCP went far beyond those of past dynasties.

The Party was determined to destroy the traditional ruling order in the countryside, which meant stripping the old élite of its power, its prestige, and most of its wealth. Merely redistributing the land would not have achieved the Communists' goal. The landlords' influence was far too deeply ingrained in village culture for Communist cadres simply to tell the peasants they did not have to serve and obey the landlords any more; the only way to eliminate the landlords' control was to destroy them as a class.

While the old power structure was being destroyed, a new one was being created. Part of the new structure was introduced from outside the villages: organizational networks made up of veteran Communists, and new recruits coming mostly from the educated population of the cities, spread out into the countryside from province capitals and county seats. Part grew up from the base level, as village peasant associations began to produce people with a talent for leadership, who could become village leaders and then move up to higher levels.

In each village the transformation was supervised, on a sporadic basis, by travelling work teams usually sent out by authorities in the county seat. Every few months a team would come, and stay for a few days or weeks. It might have some specific job to do, such as tax-collection, or it might have come simply to supervise social transformation, but in either case it would propagandize the poor peasants, to persuade them both to support the new government and to rise up to defend their own interests against the rich and take control of village society. The work teams sponsored the organization of peasant associations, and the most active and enthusiastic peasants became the new leaders of the villages.

There were a hundred things that could go wrong in the attempted transformation of the villages. Few members of the travelling work teams were experienced revolutionaries. A good many were intellectuals from the towns, from middle-class or even upper-class backgrounds. Some could not conceive of poor peasants really learning to run village affairs; others simply did not think they had the time to find and train peasant activists. All government personnel at this time had more work to do than time to do it in, and the tradition of éitism and bureaucracy in Chinese culture was so strong that it took newly recruited functionaries long enough just to learn that the new regime wanted them to politicize the poor at all; it took longer to persuade them that politicizing the poor could take precedence over other tasks. The idea that the government might use some criterion other than the successful collection of taxes, when judging tax-collectors and considering them for promotion to more important jobs, was especially startling.

The poor peasants did not automatically join in the revolution against the landlords; the idea of the poor overthrowing the rich was as alien to many peasants as it was to urban intellectuals. Some peasants felt they had been reasonably treated under the old order; they were grateful to have been able to rent land, rather than angry that part of the crop had gone to the landlord. Some simply did not believe that a group of strange people from the city, who were not even planning to remain in the village for very long, could really succeed in arranging the overthrow of the class that had ruled the village for time beyond memory. They feared that when the dust settled the landlords would still be in control, and that anyone who had been so foolish as to join in the attack on them would be in very serious trouble. Some peasants were bound to the landlords by kinship or clan ties. For any or all of these reasons, when the travelling work teams had recruited peasants into a peasant association, the peasants might still show little enthusiasm for a vigorous attack on the landlords. They might remain silent or even agree quite vocally when a landlord lied about his status, and passed himself off to the work team as a middle or poor peasant.

In many areas there were active feuds between rival villages or clans, and the 'us against them' in the peasants' minds was peasants and land-lords of their own village fighting against peasants and landlords of the neighbouring village. They could not easily be brought to believe that the peasants of both villages should unite against the landlords.

Even if power could be placed in the hands of genuine peasant activists, properly independent of the landlords and rich peasants, there was no guarantee that these activists would be the kind of leaders the CCP was looking for. Being a poor peasant did not necessarily cause one to treat other poor peasants with respect and consideration. In traditional village society, people of power and influence had been able to use their positions to command obedience from those below them, reward their friends and relatives, harass their enemies, and enrich themselves. Many poor and middle peasants now rising to positions of leadership felt entitled to behave in the same fashion, to a greater or lesser extent.

In the early stages of the transformation most landlords did not suffer too badly. The rents they collected were reduced and their taxes increased. Some debts the peasants owed them were cancelled, and the interest on others was reduced. But even where such policies were thoroughly enforced (which in many areas they were not), the typical landlord was left with a substantial income, and none of his property was confiscated outright. Only a few known as 'local despots', who were charged with exceptional crimes against the peasants, were put on trial, and had the bulk of their property confiscated.

After a year or two of these campaigns, each village had a core of peasant activists, with some leadership experience. A much larger number of peasants had achieved at least some degree of politicization through the peasant associations, and had attained enough benefits through the reduction of rents and the interest rate on debts, and refund of some rent recently collected by the landlords, to be convinced that class struggle really could be worth while. A couple of 'local despots' might have been tried before 'people's tribunals', raising the confidence of the peasants that they could actually win in a confrontation with a landlord. Once this groundwork had been laid, a full-scale land reform campaign, involving an attack on the whole landlord class and to some extent on the rich peasants, became practical.

The land reform was more thorough and more drastic than previous campaigns. Everyone classified as a landlord was subjected to expropriation; they were only allowed to keep an amount of land equivalent to what was being given to the poor peasants. This meant that they were being reduced to below the average level of wealth in the countryside, since the redistribution of their land usually left the poor peasants still owning less land than the average for the rural population as a whole. Significant amounts of money, grain stocks, tools, draught animals, and sometimes housing were also taken from the landlords. However, if they were involved in commercial or industrial enterprises these enterprises were at least partially protected from confiscation. A significant fraction of the landlords, charged with crimes more serious than mere economic exploitation, were imprisoned or executed.

The CCP was not trying to achieve total equalization of wealth in the countryside. To have taken away the surplus wealth of everyone who owned even a little more than the average would have made the Communist Party far too many enemies from a political viewpoint. It would have disrupted production in the short run by attacking the most efficient farmers, and in the long run by giving people the feeling that if they worked hard and saved to improve their position, they might end up losing everything to some future wave of redistribution. The CCP therefore gave absolute protection to middle peasants (people whose incomes came primarily from their own labour, with little or none coming from exploiting the labour of others), and partial protection to rich peasants (those whose land was worked to a substantial extent by tenants or hired labourers, but who still did a serious amount of agricultural labour themselves). The rich peasants had been among the more productive farmers; they had better tools and could sometimes use more sophisticated farming techniques than the poor. To maintain production, especially in the areas immediately around major cities, which kept the urban markets supplied, rich peasants were allowed to keep all the land they worked by their own labour and hired labour, and even some of what they rented out. This left them substantially better off than the average peasant.

The CCP was well aware of the difficulties facing outsiders coming into a village and trying to rebuild its whole political and economic structure. Even the work teams supervising land reform, which stayed in any given village longer than previous teams and had the assistance of peasant activists trained and recruited by previous teams, might have been lied to, been hasty or careless, or simply had the bad luck to rely on activists who looked good at the time but would later become corrupt or dictatorial in the way they ran village affairs. The Party therefore waited several months after the departure of the land reform work team from each village. During this time, if anything had gone seriously wrong, the fact usually became apparent to the peasants of the village in question. Then another team of cadres came to investigate. Only after this final team had given its seal of approval did the changes wrought during the land reform become final.

Leaders of the CCP had little trouble deciding how to manage class struggle in the villages, from 1950 to 1953, because their egalitarian ideology meshed so well with their own self-interest. When they handed landlord

land over to the peasants, they were creating a tremedous reservoir of peasant gratitude and loyalty. (Fifteen years later, peasants who had no understanding of Mao Zedong's current policies still venerated him as the
person who had given them the land.) The CCP emerged from the land
reform with a village-level organization far stronger than the Guomindang
had ever had, and stronger than the Soviet Communist Party had ever had
in the villages of the Soviet Union.

After the land reform things would seldom be so simple. The CCP
would find, more and more, that it had to choose between its egalitarian
ideals on the one hand, and its pragmatic economic and political interests
on the other.

Into the cities

Chinese Communism had been born in the cities, but it had been essentially a rural movement since 1927. The Party that marched into Beijing,
Shanghai, Wuhan, and Guangzhou in 1949 found itself in an essentially
alien environment. If the CCP leaders were to run the urban economy, and
then expand and develop it, they would have to gain the support not only
of workers, but also of people with vital skills – technicians, managers,
and administrators – and at the same time acquire some of those skills
themselves.

This challenged the Communists, as Communists, in a way the problem
of transforming the countryside had not. Few members of the traditional
rural élite had skills vital to the economy; indeed many of them had constituted an actual impediment to a more efficient agricultural economy.
There were only a few manager-landlords, and so on; they could be given
special treatment, so their skills would not be lost to the economy, without
compromising the overall pattern of the class struggle. But in the cities
most of the élite made some genuine contribution to society. There were
educated people of all sorts, desperately needed in a country as backward
as China. There were technicians and skilled workers. There were industrial capitalists, who might be classed as exploiters but who had manage-
rial expertise without which the country would be crippled. Even the
merchants, treated as parasites by both Marxist and Confucian theory
because they did not create goods, but made a profit simply by moving
them about, would be indispensable until socialist networks of distribution
could be organized.

In the short run, the Party had to prevent any breakdown in urban society;
to maintain services and production. In the long run it was determined to

PLATE 6.1 *Bicycle parking area, Beijing.* (*Photograph by MTI, Camera Press London.*)

how many work points it had earned, and partly on how much land, tools, and other capital it had contributed when the cooperative was formed. Finally would come a fully socialist cooperative, which might contain 100 or more families, and in which the crop would be divided strictly according to the amount of work done by each family. Delays were permitted in areas inhabited by non-Chinese minorities, but the great majority of the ethnically Chinese peasants were not only in cooperatives but in fully socialist cooperatives by the end of 1956.

In the cities capitalist businesses were either taken over outright, or converted to the status of state-private joint enterprises, in which the state had the final say in all decisions. The former owners were paid dividends for several more years, and in many cases were kept on as managers, but they had lost control. This transition was mainly completed during the winter of 1955–56.

Most Party leaders had not expected the transition to come this soon, and some disapproved of hasty changes, but once the Party had consolidated its position enough to be capable of collectivizing the major sectors of the economy, which it had by 1955, Mao Zedong saw little reason to wait. The imminent abolition of the private economy was having an inhibiting effect on production, especially in the cities. The capitalists knew that their factories were probably going to be nationalized before long. This expectation could produce ghastly results, as with the man who did not bother to lubricate valuable machinery, because he was sure that by the time it collapsed under this abuse it would no longer be his. The capitalists' access to scarce raw materials often depended on Communist cadres who thought of capitalist enterprise as something being given a last few years of toleration, and were unlikely to treat it with great favour. The information they needed to plan their operations adequately was likely to be included in the category of 'state economic secrets'; its possession had brought severe penalties under the Five-Anti campaign. Very high levels of profit became, in themselves, grounds for suspicion. In general, the operation of capitalist business under a Communist government involved such tensions that many of the capitalists themselves felt relieved when nationalization finally came.

In the countryside there had been a tendency towards economic differentiation after land reform, which bothered Communist leaders. Some peasants were gaining in wealth. There were rich peasants who still had the advantages of better tools, better land, and more draught animals than most of their neighbours, and former middle or poor peasants who were working their way up into the category of 'new rich peasants'. On the other hand, bad luck, bad management, or simply an acute land shortage in some villages, which had made it difficult to give viable farms to every poor peasant, had left some individuals in a position where they had to borrow at high interest rates, or even sell off some of their newly acquired land. This was, in principle, disturbing to a Party with the CCP's egalitarian doctrines. It also posed a practical threat to the development of socialism in the countryside. The Party wished to persuade the peasants to join cooperatives on a reasonably voluntary basis. A certain amount of pressure might be applied, but the PRC could not even consider the brute-force approach that had been used in the Soviet Union. Stalin had not concealed the fact that collectivization would reduce quite severely the incomes of the rich peasants (kulaks) in the Soviet countryside. The resulting kulak resistance, and the execution or deportation of kulaks and people accused of being kulaks, led to the deaths of many of Russia's most skilled farmers, and the destruction of tremendous amounts of livestock and other property in the late 1920s and early 1930s.

China could hope to avoid this, and persuade the peasants to join cooperatives on a voluntary or near-voluntary basis, only if it could promise that nobody's income would suffer very badly. This required that the peasants who joined cooperatives did so on something approaching an equal basis. In 1955, the differences in wealth in the countryside were small enough so that the CCP could say, even to people with more than the average land and capital, that if they joined in a cooperative with people slightly less wealthy than themselves, the efficiency of large-scale production, plus improved access to government loans and fertilizer supplies, would enable their share of the cooperative's income to match what they had had as individual farmers. Some well-to-do middle peasants believed this claim and others did not, but at least the claim was not transparently absurd. If the process of economic differentiation had been allowed to go on for another decade in the countryside, the prospects for voluntary collectivization would have worsened noticeably. When collectivization actually occurred it indeed avoided most of the costs that had accompanied it in the Soviet Union. Destruction of property, by people who felt that what was theirs would belong to themselves or to nobody, was relatively rare. Some people were shoved into cooperatives against their will, but there was hardly any outright violence.

To say that the transition to socialism was fast and smooth does not imply that there were no problems in the new socialist enterprises. In agriculture especially, once the land and tools were no longer the property of individual families, it was not easy to divide up responsibilities in such a way that necessary work, including maintenance of equipment, would get done. Some tools rusted in the fields, because nobody had been assigned the job of taking care of them, and there was no single individual who cared enough about them to look after them without being told. Much hard work and experience were required to deal with such problems, but the basic pattern of the Chinese economy seemed to be set.

There was one major question still facing the Party: how fast should it try to go in altering the psychological basis of the economic system? Could it expect people to work hard out of a sense of moral obligation to their neighbours and to society, or would it have to give material rewards for good work? Offering material rewards to those who did more work, or whose work required more training and skill, seemed necessary to keep the economy functioning smoothly. On the other hand, some CCP leaders feared that the use of such rewards would amount to institutionalizing inequality, and would perpetuate the individualistic attitudes already so deeply ingrained in Chinese culture. In the past, every man had been concerned primarily with his own interests and those of his family. Could one expect people to change their attitudes, and concern themselves with the interests of society as a whole, in a system that used the prospect of individual rewards as its major method for persuading them to work hard?

In the mid 1950s the CCP offered a substantial degree of material incentives, through wages, work points, and so on. There were even some spheres in which individuals or families still functioned as separate units in the economy. The most important of these was the private production that continued to occur in the countryside even after the peasants were grouped into cooperatives. Most households were assigned small private plots of land. They did not actually own these plots, but they could use them for whatever crops they wished. Many grew vegetables for sale in urban markets, and thus attained far greater profits than were available from grain crops. The peasants could also raise pigs or poultry. They could plant trees, the wood from which would belong to them as individuals. The extent to which such remnants of private enterprise should be tolerated remained a subject of controversy, but until the 1980s the peasants were seldom allowed to devote enough land or enough time to them to interfere seriously with the collective economy.

Chinese economic policy, in the mid 1950s, was following the pattern set by the USSR. The chief goal was to develop heavy industry – steel, machinery, and so forth – as quickly as possible. Russian technicians helped design and build large plants in many areas. Light industry and agriculture took second place, though they were not neglected to the extent they had been in the early stages of Stalinist industrialization in the Soviet Union. The people, especially the peasants, were expected to tolerate relatively slow growth in levels of living, so the government could put its main efforts into investment rather than into production of consumer goods.

Central economic planning really began to take effect in 1955. Yearly production targets for individual enterprises, and five-year plans establishing goals for investment and production increases in each sector of the economy, were set by the government in Beijing. The system was cumbersome, and inherently biased towards large enterprises because they were so much easier for central planners to keep track of than small ones, but it produced quite respectable rates of industrial growth during the First Five-Year Plan. (This plan ran nominally from 1953 to 1957, but the government did not actually finish writing it until 1955.)

Just as important as the increase in the sheer quantity of industrial production was the mastery of new technologies, expanding the range of goods produced. China began to manufacture, for example, penicillin in 1952, trucks in 1956, and aircraft in 1957.

The modern sector was developing rapidly, but it was only a small portion of the overall economy; China as a whole was still a very poor and backward nation. Most of the people lived in the countryside, trying to scrape out a living from inadequate plots of land without the chemical fertilizer, insecticides, or power machinery that might have enabled them to raise yields and compensate to some extent for the land shortage. All of the factors that could contribute to an alleviation of this situation were in short supply. Raising agricultural production to its full potential would require great quantities of industrial products, which the industrial sector was not yet capable of supplying. Rapid construction of new industry would require that a substantial portion of total output be used for investment rather than consumption, in a situation where the standard of living would have been miserably low even if the total output of the economy had been going into consumer goods. Out of China's tiny pool of technically trained personnel, some were unavailable for economic construction because they were busy training new technicians.

Ideological remoulding and the 'Hundred Flowers'

A large part of the revolution the CCP was trying to bring about had to take place within the minds of the Chinese people. The effort to achieve this has been variously described as 'criticism and self-criticism', 'thought reform', or 'brainwashing'. There was of course intensive indoctrination in loyalty to the Communist system. Everyone was urged to admire the Party, Chairman Mao, the Soviet Union, etc. But beyond such inculcation of loyalty, there was an important social content in the thought-reform campaigns. The Party was trying to build an egalitarian and collectivist society in a culture whose traditions were extremely hierarchical, and where individuals and families had long been accustomed to looking first to their own economic interests. The Party wanted the Chinese people to start thinking more about the interests of society. Most important, members of the élite had to be cured, at least partially, of the arrogance and selfishness that had formerly been hallmarks of élite status. For selfishness and contempt for the common people to have attained the same levels among the élite of the new regime as they had in Guomindang China would have destroyed the revolution.

Formal study of Marxist tracts was an important part of ideological reform. Some people were also immersed in an environment likely to alter their attitudes and perceptions, as when urban intellectuals were assigned to work on land reform as part of their re-education. But over the long run the central method of reform was 'criticism and self-criticism'. People had to present long analyses of their own past behaviour and attitudes, both written and verbal, which laid out their faults and errors. They also had to criticize the faults of those around them. Their peers, and the cadres supervising the process, pointed out any omissions or defects in their self-analyses. This was a very traumatic process; having one's faults exposed publicly, and laying bare the faults of friends and relatives, were extraordinary violations of traditional social norms. The sincerity of criticism and self-criticism varied, but it at least had a powerful effect in shaping public behaviour.

In 1956 Chairman Mao began to feel it was time to take some of the restrictions off public expression. He was becoming disturbed by the arrogance and inflexibility of some Communist bureaucrats, and he hoped that allowing the intellectuals to criticize such people might help to improve their behaviour. He seems to have expected that the criticism could be kept constructive, within the overall framework of the Communist system and Communist values. He assumed that ideological remoulding, plus the tremendous successes of the Communist Party in the past two decades, had made most intellectuals into genuine supporters of the system. Under the slogan 'Let a hundred flowers bloom, a hundred schools of thought contend' (a reference to the 'Hundred Schools' of the Zhou period), he invited them to express their true opinions.

It took a while for this invitation to be treated seriously, but in the spring of 1957 the intellectuals responded. Mao was shocked. Where he had hoped for criticism directed mainly against people who violated Communist norms, a great deal of what he got was directed against the system itself. The viewpoint was anti-revolutionary, 'bourgeois'. Mao seems to have allowed this to run on for a few weeks unchecked, to find out just how extreme the attacks would become and who would make them, but then the crackdown came in the 'Anti-Rightist' campaign. Many of the people who had spoken out ended up under arrest, or were shipped out to the countryside to reform themselves through agricultural labour. All were subjected to a severe dose of criticism and self-criticism. Many reached the conclusion (reasonable but probably mistaken) that Mao had been lying from the beginning, and had never intended that the Hundred Flowers be anything but a trap to catch the unwary.

The net was cast very broadly. Every organization employing intellectuals was expected to expose and punish as 'rightists' at least 5 per cent of its staff. An investigator who could not find enough rightists to meet this quota would at best have been accused of 'lacking vigilance'; more probably he or she would have been denounced as a rightist concealing the crimes of other rightists, and severely punished. In most organizations much less than 5 per cent of the staff had revealed hostility to the Communist system. The quotas therefore had to be filled by branding as rightists loyal supporters of the Communist system, who had said or done something that could be interpreted as evidence of hidden hostility to the CCP, or who had enemies who falsely accused them of having said or done such things.

Even those intellectuals who had not been branded as rightists – the great majority – were less trusted by the CCP than they had been before the Hundred Flowers. Many of them spent considerable time doing manual labour as a form of political indoctrination.

The Anti-Rightist campaign is remembered today mainly as a case of gross injustice, but the damage it did was by no means limited to the suffering of its direct victims. Higher education was to a significant extent impaired. And by discrediting educated people in general, the Anti-Rightist campaign helped to set the stage for the Great Leap Forward, in which economic planners, engineers, and others with technical skills were often disregarded, at great cost to the Chinese economy.

One problem the intellectuals faced was that many of them came from class backgrounds that the CCP considered undesirable; very few children of ordinary workers and peasants had been able to attain the level of education that qualified one for intellectual status. In the 1940s, the CCP had treated class status as a fairly flexible thing, and had recognized that changes in the economic circumstances of a person or family could change the class status of that family. By the mid 1950s, however, class labels were virtually frozen. People who had been labelled landlords, rich peasants, bourgeois, or petit bourgeois when class demarcation had been carried out in the late 1940s and early 1950s had virtually no chance of attaining a change in class status, no matter what their present means of earning a living might be. Their children inherited their class labels.

At this time – though there was no obvious cause-and-effect relationship – the Communist Party became less interested in promoting equality for women. Mao Zedong had shown an interest in freeing women from male domination as early as the 1920s. The Marriage Law of the People's Republic of China, in 1950, had considerably improved the position of women, making them more able choose who they married, to escape from bad marriages, and to own property in their own names. But after 1957, the CCP's concern for women's rights weakened.

The international position of the PRC

The Guomindang had not been able actually to administer all of the territory that was marked on maps of Asia as 'China' (though its claims to almost all this territory had been accepted in principle by the world). When the CCP came to power, it was able to impose effective administration over the out-lying areas inhabited mostly by ethnic minority groups. The PRC did not control as large an area as the Manchus had in 1911 – Outer Mongolia had been lost during the warlord era – but it controlled a larger area than any ethnically Chinese government in previous history. Its sheer size guaranteed it a considerable importance in international affairs.

The Communists came to power in China just as the Cold War was reaching its worst phase. The United States and the Soviet Union, together with their respective allies, confronted each other in hostility and fear. The PRC committed itself clearly to the Soviet side in this conflict, signing a treaty of alliance with the USSR in February 1950. Soon it was so deeply embroiled that the Western nations treated China as a worse enemy than the Soviet Union.

There had been a certain amount of friendly contact between the USA and the CCP in 1944 and 1945, but this had withered as the USA supported Chiang Kai-shek in the ensuing civil war. Even so, it seemed in 1949 that the USA might at least establish the sort of guarded relationship it maintained with Moscow and the East European satellite states, in which formal diplomatic relations and a certain amount of trade continued despite mutual suspicion. In 1949, Mao Zedong and Zhou Enlai indicated a desire to establish diplomatic and trade relations with the United States, though Liu Shaoqi was less than enthusiastic. In June of that year, Mao and Zhou invited John Leighton Stuart, US ambassador to China (which at that time meant ambassador to the Guomindang government), to visit Beiping in an unofficial capacity. They seemed rather bitter when, after seeming responsive at first, he rejected the invitation on orders from Washington.

The intense hostility between the United States and the Communist world made normalization of US–China relations difficult; the Korean War of 1950–53 made it impossible. After the Second World War Korea had been divided like Germany. By 1950 there was a Communist government in the north and an anti-Communist one in the south. The southern regime had a larger population, and made bellicose statements about forcible reunification, but the north was in fact stronger. In June 1950 the north, having (with some difficulty) obtained approval from the Soviet Union and China, invaded the south. The United States had not up to this time considered South Korea an area that the USA would have to defend if it were attacked. However, as North Korea pushed back the South Korean army and the small American forces in Korea, taking almost all of South Korea in a matter of weeks, President Truman decided that Communist conquest of South Korea could not be permitted. The United Nations (UN), where US influence was far greater than in the 1960s and 1970s, backed Truman's action. An American army under General Douglas MacArthur was officially designated a UN force, and was supplemented by units from Britain and several other countries. MacArthur's counter-attack was launched in September 1950, and enjoyed the same overwhelming superiority over the North Koreans that the north had enjoyed over the south. Soon it was North Korea that was on the brink of defeat.

The Chinese, who had not participated in the original North Korean attack on the south, became involved at this point. They feared to let a great capitalist power gain control of northern Korea; the last one that had done so, Japan, had used it as a stepping-stone for an invasion of China.

The Chinese tried to warn the USA verbally that they would not permit an American conquest of North Korea. They sent several thousand Chinese troops into Korea, put them into combat for long enough to be sure the Americans would know they had been fighting Chinese forces, and then pulled them back to let the Americans reconsider. The US forces took no notice, but continued to advance, and by November were approaching the Chinese border. It is a measure of American over-confidence that at this point, when the People's Liberation Army attacked in force, it took the Americans by surprise.

Chinese troops under Peng Dehuai pushed down the length of North Korea and a short distance into the south before they were stopped. Two more years of fighting resulted in only moderate US advances, and finally led to a peace settlement in 1953 which gave South Korea slightly more territory than it had held when the war began in 1950.

The war gave China little reason to love the USSR. The Soviet Union did not send ground troops to fight alongside the Chinese, and was not very generous with equipment or financial aid, as China struggled against the world's greatest industrial power. For the Chinese, whose economy was in ghastly shape after the almost continuous warfare of the 1940s, this was a disaster. At the same time, the war increased China's need for such aid as the USSR was willing to give; China in 1950 was not yet capable even of manufacturing its own trucks. All of the fighter aircraft that the Chinese used to defend their supply lines in North Korea against American bombing, and many of the pilots who flew those fighters, were provided by the Soviet Union. The Chinese had already allied themselves voluntarily with the Soviet Union, in February 1950; the Korean War reduced China's prospects for friendly contact with non-Communist countries.

The war confirmed the United States in its hostility to the People's Republic of China, and persuaded the USA to renew its backing for Chiang Kai-shek. Chiang had lost the mainland of China, but he managed to retain control of the island of Taiwan (also known as Formosa). This island had been part of China under the Qing Dynasty, until it was taken by Japan in 1895. It had been handed back to China when Japan surrendered in 1945. The Guomindang was not popular in Taiwan, since the generals Chiang sent there in 1945 had been interested in it mainly as a source of loot. Their suppression of a Taiwanese uprising in 1947 had been bloody. But in 1949 Chiang brought to Taiwan his government, many of his supporters, and as much of his army as he could get off the mainland. The numerous and well-armed mainlanders had no trouble controlling the Taiwanese population. This government in semi-exile continued to claim authority over the whole of China. It said that the 'Communist bandits' had temporarily occupied a part of the country (admittedly a large part, with 98 per cent of the population and over 99 per cent of the land area), but that the real government, with its capital now at Taibei (Taipei) on the island of Taiwan, still controlled a portion of the country and would some-day return to reconquer the mainland.

The USA was not at first inclined to support the Guomindang's preten-sions too strongly. Even during the civil war American diplomats had been alienated by the corruption and incompetence of Chiang Kai-shek's regime, its inability to make the kind of reforms that might have given it a chance for survival, and the fact that arms and equipment given to it tended to end up in the hands of the Communists. These factors had kept US aid down to a fairly low level between 1946 and 1949; they seemed to argue for termination of aid once Chiang had decisively lost the civil war. The Communists were not at the moment capable of crossing the 110 miles of the Taiwan Strait to attack the Guomindang on Taiwan, and the Taiwanese themselves were helpless against the army Chiang had brought over from the mainland, so Chiang was not in any immediate danger. However, he did not look very valuable as an ally.

The USA did not like the new government in Beijing either. It was a Communist regime publicly allied with the Soviet Union; it permitted Russian participation in the development of Manchuria and Xinjiang, and the existence of a Russian naval base at Port Arthur at the tip of the Liaodong Peninsula, in southern Manchuria; it had arrested some US diplomats in northern China on charges of espionage; it was issuing rather shrill denunciations of American imperialism. Many American officials regarded it as a puppet government of the USSR, on a par with the Soviet satellites in Eastern Europe. Secretary of State Acheson said: 'The Com-munist leaders have forsworn their Chinese heritage and have publicly announced their subservience to a foreign power, Russia.' Still, the exis-tence of this government was a fact that could be dealt with. The USA, after all, maintained diplomatic relations with countries that really were totally dominated by the Soviet Union; a mistaken belief that China was under such domination did not automatically preclude diplomatic relations.

The Korean War, and an intense burst of anti-Communism in American domestic politics, altered the situation. Shortly after the war broke out, even before China became involved, the USA announced that it would defend Taiwan against any effort at conquest from the mainland. Chiang was soon restored to his status of a few years before, as a valued ally. In 1954, the United States signed a mutual defence treaty with the Republic of China.

The United States had long regarded China as a friendly nation; Americans felt a sense of shock and betrayal when a Communist government came to power there. A group of people friendly to Chiang Kai-shek, generally known as the 'China Lobby', persuaded much of the American public that the Communist revolution had succeeded in China only because it had been assisted by pro-Communist elements within the United States government, who had prevented China's great and virtuous national leader Chiang Kai-shek from getting the aid he needed to hold his country. Many China experts in the US Diplomatic Corps had filed reports, in the 1940s, warning that the Guomindang government's weakness, corruption, and unpopularity imperiled its survival. Events had confirmed most of what they had said, but in the 1950s some of the most important of them were dismissed in disgrace on the logic that if they had criticized Chiang Kai-shek they must be pro-Communist. Lack of respect for Chiang, or any suggestion that diplomatic relations with the People's Republic would be either useful or morally permissible for the USA, came to be considered subversive.

Chiang, who had been a hopeless failure trying to rule China, was able to do very well at the more modest tasks of ruling Taiwan. The USA gave him enough aid not only to make him secure on Taiwan, but to let him hold small islands within a few miles of the Chinese coast, and occasionally raid the mainland itself. His government was a dictatorship; Taiwan was officially under martial law from 1949 until 1987. To advocate that the Taiwanese be given political control of Taiwan was to court imprisonment, and in some cases death. The government was unabashed in its lack of respect for individual freedom, as was illustrated by the case of a dissident who found concealed microphones in his house, smashed them, and was then arrested and gaoled for destroying government property. Killings and arbitrary arrests of Taiwanese, however, became less and less common after the first few years of Guomindang rule. In the old days on the mainland such things had been done both by police organizations actually working to defend Chiang's rule against real or imagined threats, and (perhaps even more frequently) by organizations nominally under the Guomindang but actually pursuing their own interests. Chiang's hold on Taiwan was too firm to require much use of such methods, and his hold on his own government had become strong enough to prevent massive police abuses from occurring against his wishes.

The economy flourished. Taiwan had been richer than the mainland even in 1949, and its continued development since that time has been one of the great success stories of modern Asia. When Chiang Kai-shek finally died in 1975, his son Chiang Ching-kuo (Jiang Jingguo) inherited a stable government and a thriving economy. The economy, furthermore, was mostly in the hands of Taiwanese; the fact that they had plenty of opportunity to become wealthy under Guomindang rule did much to mute protests about their lack of political power.

The United States recognized the Guomindang government on Taiwan as the legal government of all China, and refused to have anything to do with the Communist regime. It pressured other governments to do likewise. Britain established diplomatic relations with the PRC early in 1950, and maintained them despite the Korean War, but all other important Western countries, including even members of the British Commonwealth such as Australia and Canada, accepted the US line and refused diplomatic recognition to Beijing. The Guomindang continued to represent China in the United Nations for more than twenty years. The US attitude was symbolized by the way it called Beijing by its 1928–49 name of Beiping (Peiping); in Chinese Beijing means 'Northern Capital', and the US did not admit that this city was the capital of any genuine government. Assistant Secretary of State Dean Rusk said in 1951: 'We do not recognize the authorities in Peiping for what they pretend to be. The Peiping regime may be a colonial Russian government . . . It is not the government of China. It does not pass the first test. It is not Chinese.' This was rhetorical exaggeration. Rusk and his colleagues were well aware that the government of China was in the city that they called 'Peiping', and that it was Chinese.

More important than denial of diplomatic relations, and UN membership, was an American-organized trade embargo. To deny the Chinese access to dollars, the USA made it illegal for American citizens to buy anything whatever from China. There was also a long list of things that could not be sold to China. The list was theoretically based on the principle of denying the Chinese access to goods of strategic military importance. It was actually intended to weaken the Chinese economy as a whole – American policy-makers hoped that prolonged economic misery might lead to the overthrow of Communist rule – and to demonstrate US hostility to China. Many things that could be sold to the USSR could not be sold to China. A report of the US Congress explained the inclusion of plastic haircombs on the list of restricted items on the grounds that having such combs would strengthen the Chinese government, because it could use them as 'incentive goods'. (A proposal to include women's brassieres on the list was rejected.) The United States had considerable success in persuading other nations to join it in imposing similar restrictions on trade.

Finally, there were actual armed attacks. The Guomindang used some of its US military assistance to conduct raids into China both across the

Taiwan Strait and from northern Burma, where some Guomindang armies had established bases after they were driven out of southwestern China in 1949 and 1950.

Few countries were as hostile to China as was the United States. Some states not allied with either side in the Cold War, of which the most important was India, got on quite well with China in the early to mid 1950s. China was able to participate despite US displeasure at the Geneva Conference of 1954, which ended the First Indochina War. The PRC was even more successful at the April 1955 Conference of Asian and African Nations, held at the city of Bandung in Indonesia. The twenty-nine nations present included all of China's major non-Communist neighbours; some such as Japan and the Philippines had close ties with the USA. The fact that the PRC was invited to attend, and participated very successfully despite suspicion on the part of some of the others there, was a striking diplomatic triumph.

Even major US allies maintained a certain degree of contact with China, and were reluctant to impose as strict a trade embargo as the USA. Britain was by far the most conspicuous. The British could not realistically expect to hold Hong Kong if they were too hostile toward China. Economically, Britain was more dependent on international trade than were most countries, and was reluctant to reject any potential trading partner. Finally, British diplomats rejected the American theory that keeping China poor, backward, and isolated would encourage desirable changes in the Chinese government. For all of these reasons, Britain resisted American pressure to tighten its trade embargo even during the Korean War, and decided in 1957 to eliminate the 'China differential', making controls on exports to China no more stringent than controls on exports to the USSR. Most other Western powers (except of course the United States) soon followed suit, although some of the differential treatment seems to have been restored for a while at a later date.

Study questions

Compare the Communist government of China in the early 1950s with the Guomindang government in the early 1930s. How much stronger and more effective was the Communist government? Why?

How revolutionary was the Communist government of China? How deeply was it altering Chinese society?

Why was the United States so hostile to the People's Republic of China?

CHAPTER 7

The Great Leap and the great split

Up to 1957, China's policies in both domestic and international affairs seemed to fall within the normal limits of Communist behaviour. China's habit of carrying out 'mass campaigns' like the Five-Anti campaign, in which a particular policy was given tremendous emphasis for a limited period, made policy more an on-and-off thing than in most other Communist states. The Hundred Flowers represented an extraordinary, if brief, adventure in freedom of expression. These idiosyncrasies, however, were not major differences setting China off from the rest of the socialist camp. In the next few years everything changed; China abandoned both its alliance with the Soviet Union and its adherence to the Russian pattern of economic development. The shift in economic policies came first, starting in 1957 and becoming really extreme in the second half of 1958.

The Great Leap Forward

In the period immediately following the conversion to a socialist economy, China achieved respectable levels of industrial growth but very little increase in agricultural production. Mao Zedong decided that by taking adequate advantage of the economies of large-scale production, and especially by liberating the creative energies and enthusiasm of the masses instead of working through a bureaucratic planning structure, China could do much better. Experiments with units much larger than the existing cooperatives began in the countryside during 1958. In August the Central Committee endorsed 'People's Communes', which grouped together 2,000 or more households in an organization combining economic, political, and militia functions. Soon the whole of the Chinese countryside was organized into about 26,000 communes, containing an average of almost 5,000 house-holds each. These units tried to use all the advantages of large-scale opera-tion. They established communal mess-halls, so the number of people who had to spend time cooking meals could be reduced, and the extra hands freed for work in the fields. Many children were put in boarding-schools to free their parents for labour. Small fields were amalgamated into much larger ones. A commune contained enough people so that the limited percentage of its manpower that could be spared from the regular routine of production, at any given time, amounted to a large enough number in absolute terms to permit large construction projects: clearing waste land and bringing it under production, digging canals, and opening industrial enterprises of various sorts.

The ultimate goal of the Communist movement is a communist (small letter c) society, in which there will be no connection between the labour people do and the incomes they receive. Everyone will work because that is their obligation as members of society, and everyone will get food, cloth-ing, housing, etc. because that is their right as members of society. 'From each according to his ability, to each according to his needs.' During the Great Leap, most communes attempted to move a considerable distance towards this goal, though there was great variation between one commune and another. Most of the peasants' private plots were abolished. Most peasants were expected to do at least some work for which they were not paid. On the other hand, many communes simply gave food free to com-mune members, without regard to how much work each family had done to earn that food. The Chinese later described this equal sharing of food, without regard to how much labour each family had done, as 'eating out of a big pot'.

By late 1958 and early 1959 China had adopted an approach to econ-omic life very different from that of the First Five-Year Plan announced in 1955. The communes were only a part of this new approach. Mao was try-ing to achieve economic miracles by whipping people into a fever of enthu-siasm. Everyone was supposed to work very long hours, under difficult conditions, to achieve in a short time an economic transformation that would normally have taken years. Growth targets of 30 per cent per year were rejected as too modest; it was claimed that food production for 1958 would be double that of 1957, and that a similar rate of growth could be expected to continue in 1959. Chairman Mao even suggested to some peasants that perhaps they should de-emphasize food production, since their production seemed to be going beyond China's needs. The orderly processes of economic planning were discarded.

One characteristic of the Great Leap was faith in the intellectual powers of the masses. Mao told ordinary workers they were competent to modify complex imported machines, in order to make them run better. He encouraged the peasants to establish industries in the countryside.

The Soviet model for growth had emphasized heavy industry, and large plants in general. This necessarily implied a clear distinction between industrial and agricultural sectors of the economy. But when the organization of the communes made it possible to detach some of the peasants from the regular round of agricultural production for greater or lesser periods of time, they were not put only into projects for expansion of the agricultural infrastructure; many of them began to set up small industrial plants of various sorts. Perhaps the most extreme examples were the 'backyard steel mills', little furnaces capable of turning out a few tons of low-grade steel, which were set up not only in towns but even in villages scattered all over China.

The backyard steel mills were a miserable failure; the people operating them did not know what they were doing, and the metal they produced was for the most part worthless. The backyard uranium mines worked better. Peasants over wide areas of China were taught to identify small surface deposits of uranium, and refine the ore to a high enough level of purity to be suitable for shipping. Small-scale refining operations run by amateurs were inefficient and caused a lot of pollution, but they produced perfectly good uranium, and they produced it very quickly. Without them, the time necessary to create China's first atomic bomb would have been significantly longer.

The Great Leap began with a certain amount of genuine popular enthusiasm, and with some genuinely spectacular results. In the first eight months of 1958, agricultural production was running well above the levels of 1957, and the average monthly level of steel production was 50 per cent higher than in 1957. At this point, instead of consolidating the gains that had been achieved, Mao and other Party leaders lost all sense of reality and began demanding even higher rates of economic growth. They said, for instance, that the monthly rate of steel production in the last four months of 1958 should be double the monthly rate for the first eight months. A dangerously high proportion of the agricultural labour force was diverted into steel production and other industrial projects.

The situation soon began to deteriorate. Reports of tremendous success became obligatory, and soon everyone was making them regardless of reality. The disorganization in the systems for planning and data collection allowed these inflated figures to be accepted for a while; they were not just

PLATE 7.1 *Backyard steel mills, late 1958. (© Henri Cartier-Bresson/Magnum Photos.)*

lies intended for public consumption: they were actually believed, and used as a basis for planning. Many low-level officials persuaded themselves that their units were doing better than was actually the case, and so planning not only at the national level but even at the commune level was sometimes based on excessive expectations. (Inaccurate reporting of production figures was not just a temporary phenomenon. The habit of honest reporting, once lost, was not easy to restore, and the effects would be felt for the next twenty years.)

The total grain crop for 1957 had been about 195 million tons. In 1958, the total increased slightly, to 198 million tons. The weather was excellent, and the increase could have been still greater if part of the autumn crop had not been lost when the diversion of agricultural labour into industry left some villages without enough peasants to harvest the fields properly. At the time, however, it was officially proclaimed that the crop had been 375 million tons. Exaggerated estimates led dining-halls in some communes to offer very generous meals, and use up most of their food stocks before the 1959 harvest began coming in.

In 1959, the Great Leap began to become a disaster. Sheer fatigue was taking its toll; people were no longer capable of the fantastic exertions of late 1958, especially without material incentives. The shortage of agricultural labour was so acute that the total acreage planted in food crops was significantly below the level of 1957. Peasants all over China were urged to plough the land very deeply. The theory was that the soil deep below the surface would be exceptionally fertile. The actual result of deep ploughing was often to bury the topsoil and bring to the surface worthless clay and sand. The Party also ordered that seeds were to be planted more closely together than had traditionally been done. The result almost always was that the growing plants died or were stunted due to overcrowding. Some rural cadres, in their determination to achieve total compliance with directives from Beijing, even required peasants to plough under crops that had already been planted in the traditional fashion, in order to plant again using the methods of deep ploughing and close planting. These crops, planted too late in the season, did not have time to mature before the following winter arrived.

Bad weather accentuated the problems caused by these disastrous policies; the 1959 harvest amounted to only about 170 millions tons. It seemed for a time that the policies of the Great Leap were being abandoned (see below), but they were reaffirmed in the second half of the year, and carried on into 1960. Hunger became widespread, and some people began to starve; others went on the roads as beggars. At the time, however, the harvest for 1959 was glowingly reported as 282 million tons.

In 1957, the last year before the Great Leap, 1.08 per cent of the Chinese population, or about 7,130,000 people, had died from one cause or another. This was a relatively low death rate for a country as poor as China. The death rate was only slightly higher in 1958. Then, however, came the crop failure of 1959. Some people literally starved to death. Others died of diseases from which they would have been able to recover, or which they might not have caught at all, if their bodies had not been weakened by malnutrition. The National Statistical Bureau long afterward released figures that may well understate the death toll. They indicate that about 1.46 per cent of the population, or 9,640,000 people, died in 1959. This would not have seemed bad if compared with pre-revolutionary conditions – surely there was no year before 1949 when the death rate was as *low* as 1.46 per cent – but what seems more relevant is the comparison

- - - - - - Disputed border
(line of actual
control)

— - — - — Province border

HUNAN Province

0   500   1000 km

0   300   600 miles

• • • • • • • Border claim not
corresponding to
line of actual
control

MAP 5 *The People's Republic of China.*

with the periods immediately before the Great Leap. The number of
'excess deaths' – the people who would not have died if it had not been for
the food shortages and other problems of 1959 – was about 2,500,000.

In 1960, the policies of the Great Leap were combined with a second
consecutive year of disastrous weather, and together these factors reduced
the harvest to only about 144 million tons, 26 per cent below the level of
1957. Real famine returned to China for the first time since 1949; the
death rate reached 2.54 per cent. In other words, almost 17 million people

died in China during that year. More than 9 million of these were people who would not have died if it had not been for the food shortage of that year. The further decline of the grain harvest to 136.5 million tons in 1961 was mitigated slightly by imports of grain. The harvest made only a partial recovery in 1962, and the standard of living remained below pre-Great Leap levels until about 1965. The total number of 'excess deaths' caused by the Great Leap had been about 15 million according to the National Statistical Bureau's figures, at least 20 million according to most Western scholars.

The Chinese government was remarkably successful in concealing this disaster from the outside world. There were rumours, but most China specialists found these unconvincing. This is testimony to the extent to which China had been isolated from the world. The geographical pattern of the famine made it easier for the government to conceal – it was less serious in the south-coast provinces, and these were the provinces about which the foreigners could most easily obtain information.

While bad decisions on the part of the CCP had helped create a worse crop failure than atrocious weather by itself could have caused, the way the country got through the crisis showed some of the merits of the revolution. The central government had a far better command of the resources of China than any in the previous century, and could allocate considerable amounts of food where they were needed. One may doubt whether members of the Central Committee missed many meals, but the hunger was still shared between masses and élite to a far greater extent than could have occurred under any previous government. If the same degree of crop failure had occurred twenty-five or fifty years earlier, the death-toll would probably have been much worse.

The Sino-Soviet split

The alliance between China and the Soviet Union, apparently so firm in 1950, was cracking by 1960. Among the important reasons for the split were increasing Chinese self-confidence which made China less willing to accept a subordinate role in the Communist bloc, increasing Chinese demands on its ally, and doctrinal shifts in both China and the Soviet Union which eroded ideological unity.

The first source of public disagreement was de-Stalinization in the Soviet Union. When Stalin died in 1953 it was not clear who would succeed him, but all of his potential heirs agreed that the Stalinist system needed some degree of reform. By 1956 Nikita Khrushchev, who wanted really substantial reform of the Soviet system, was emerging as the new leader in Moscow. He decided that undoing Stalin's works required destroying Stalin's godlike image. At the Twentieth Congress of the Communist Party of the Soviet Union, in February 1956, Khrushchev delivered a speech denouncing Stalin. He did not describe the full extent of Stalin's crimes; he had been, after all, one of Stalin's lieutenants. But he said enough, about everything from the killing of innocent people in the purges to Stalin's gross incompetence at the beginning of the Second World War, to establish the psychological foundation for major reforms. Millions of prisoners were released from the forced labour camps. Some of the cruder aspects of centralized economic management were reformed and rationalized. Some of the limits on free expression were even relaxed, though they were by no means eliminated. (From this point until the final collapse of the Soviet Union, there would be conflicts between dissidents trying to maintain or expand the permitted range of free speech, and officials trying to narrow it.)

To Khrushchev the myth of Stalin, as the infinitely wise and benevolent leader of International Communism, was a prop maintaining a dangerously inefficient economic system, and a political structure under which top Communist Party leaders lived in fear for their lives. Reform of the system was vital, and the destruction of the myth a necessary prerequisite for reform. To the CCP leaders, however, the Stalin myth was a very useful thing. They had not loved Stalin – he had given them bad advice and little aid – but they had been out from under his thumb, and immune to his worst excesses, for twenty years. He had been a rather distant figure. They had been able quite safely to accept the myths ground out by the Soviet propaganda apparatus, and pass them on to the Chinese people to encourage friendship for the USSR and belief in International Communism.

The shock of Khrushchev's attack on Stalin was considerable in the CCP; it was even greater in some Communist parties that had been more under Stalin's control, such as those of Hungary, Britain, and the United States. The Chinese were outraged that Khrushchev had done this without consulting or even warning them in advance.

Aside from criticizing Stalin as an individual, Khrushchev was dismantling some of Stalin's policies. The Soviet Union became somewhat less overbearing in its treatment of other Communist countries. The Chinese benefited from this in a direct fashion; the Russians withdrew voluntarily from their naval base at Port Arthur (in southern Manchuria), and from various other operations on the fringes of China that had to some extent compromised Chinese sovereignty. However, when the apparatus of

Russian domination was relaxed in Eastern Europe, the results seemed less attractive: the Hungarians tried to break free of Soviet domination completely, and indeed seemed to be abandoning Communism. It took a direct invasion by the Soviet Red Army, in November 1956, to restore Hungary to the Soviet bloc. To the Chinese this seemed evidence of abominable Soviet incompetence. The Russians, on the other hand, resented Chinese presumption in trying to tell the Soviet Union how to run Eastern Europe.

Probably the most bitter controversy was that over peaceful coexistence. Khrushchev felt it was time to put relations with the Western democracies on a more reasonable basis, to increase trade, and to reduce the threat of war. Obviously, this would be easier if he stopped advocating the violent overthrow of the governments with which he was trying to negotiate. On the other hand, he did not wish to give up the doctrine that the whole world would one day be Communist. He therefore argued that the further expansion of Communism in the world would be by peaceful political means, rather than by war. Thermonuclear war could benefit nobody.

From the Russian viewpoint this made excellent sense. The Western countries were ready to accept some relaxation of tensions, and the potential benefits to the Soviet Union were considerable. In any case, the area of greatest interest in Russian foreign policy was Europe, and here the doctrine that Communists should choose a peaceful route to power was simple realism. A West European Communist Party that tried to take power by violent means would have been quickly obliterated by the armies of the North Atlantic Treaty Organization (NATO) powers. If the Soviet Union had tried to intervene it would have been even more quickly obliterated by the United States, which had a substantial edge in nuclear arms at this time. On the other hand, several countries of Western Europe had strong Communist Parties, which were permitted to run candidates in free elections, and had genuine grounds to hope that they could someday take power through the ballot box. Under these conditions, it must have seemed to Khrushchev that only a mental defective would choose violence as the road to power.

China, on the other hand, was more interested in Southeast Asia. Here conditions were very different. South Vietnam, for instance, had a government that seemed unlikely ever to permit the local Communists to participate in peaceful political processes; Communist activities were punishable by imprisonment or death. The army supporting this government, however, was extremely weak. Violent means could offer a reasonable hope for success, and eventually they did in fact succeed in making South Vietnam Communist. Mao Zedong must have felt that, given these circumstances, only a mental defective would expect a Communist Party to come to power by peaceful means.

The debate between China and the Soviet Union over this subject was a remarkably futile one, because both sides spent much of their time talking about how Communist Parties in general should act, in the world as a whole. The Chinese made incidental remarks to the effect that a peaceful road to power would be desirable if possible, while the Russians said that they approved of the national liberation movements in Africa and Asia, but both sides spent most of their time talking about the things that really interested them, and failing to notice that these were not the things their opponents were discussing. The result was that the Russians decided the Chinese were dangerously insane (which would have been reasonable if the Chinese policy line had been designed to apply to Europe), while the Chinese decided the Russians were cowards who were abandoning the idea of revolution (which would have been reasonable if the Russian policy line had been designed to apply to Southeast Asia).

The Chinese had the better of this argument in a purely doctrinal sense. They could muster a great deal of evidence for their charge that Khrushchev was abandoning traditional Communist theory and becoming a 'revisionist'. The Russians, however, had the greatest success in winning the sympathy of third parties. Chinese statements about not fearing war, even a war involving nuclear weapons (which China did not possess), created the image that the Chinese might be willing to provoke such a war.

Chinese annoyance over Russian policy was increased by the fact that the Russians seemed to be making not a general peace between the two great world blocs, but a separate peace between the Soviet Union and the United States, which left the USA free to continue its hostility to the PRC. By the late 1950s the Western powers had stopped infiltrating guerrillas and saboteurs into Eastern Europe, but similar activities directed against China were causing more trouble than before. When a relatively small rebellion in Tibet grew to substantial size in 1959, the US Central Intelligence Agency (CIA) greatly expanded its activities in the area, flying in arms and ammunition to the rebels, and bringing Tibetans to the United States for guerrilla warfare training (in the Rocky Mountains, so the altitude and terrain would be appropriate). The PLA put down the rebellion, destroyed many of the monasteries that had been the main centres of Tibetan culture, and imposed far tighter Chinese control over Tibet than had ever existed in the past. The Dalai Lama, who in the theocratic system of traditional Tibet had been both the most important religious leader and the head of the government, fled in 1959 and established a government in exile, subsidized by the United States. He and his campaign for Tibetan independence obtained much sympathy from foreign countries and he eventually, in 1989, won the Nobel Peace Prize. His prestige among the people of Tibet, despite Chinese efforts to erase the role of religion in Tibetan society and life, made him a serious problem for China. Armed struggle by Tibetans soon subsided, but until the early 1970s the CIA supported a military force of about 1,800 Tibetans in exile, waiting to cross back into Tibet and resume the fight if a suitable situation should arise.

When tensions between the PRC and the Guomindang flared up in the Taiwan Straits in 1958, Russian support for the PRC did not match US support for Chiang Kai-shek. In 1959 the USSR began to cut back its military aid to China, and in particular reneged on an earlier agreement to help China acquire atomic weapons. The Chinese felt they were being left to bear the hostility of the capitalists alone. The Russians, on the other hand, feared that Chinese recklessness might drag the Soviet Union into a war with the United States. By 1960 tension over such issues was becoming a matter of public dispute.

Soviet leaders had never liked the Great Leap Forward, based as it was on the rejection of the Russian model of economic development. They felt that the abandonment of orderly planning procedures was leading to a great deal of waste in the use of foreign aid. Also, the Chinese seemed to be upstaging the Russians with their claims of miraculous social and economic transformation. After other aspects of the Sino-Soviet relationship had also deteriorated, all Soviet technical advisers in China were called home in 1960. They took the blueprints of many half-completed plants with them. Construction of these plants, in the sectors of the Chinese economy with the highest levels of technology and planning, ground to a halt just as the more impromptu enterprises established in the Great Leap were also encountering difficulties.

Problems along the borders

A border dispute between China and India helped to exacerbate the Sino-Soviet dispute. In the late 1940s, when India became independent of Britain and the CCP took power in China, there were considerable areas where the border between them had never been settled by any formal treaty, and where the maps used by the two sides differed substantially. Some of the areas potentially in dispute were uninhabited. Others were occupied by groups that were not really, in an ethnic sense, either Chinese or Indian, and would constitute minority groups in whichever country finally won control. In short, there was not only no clearly agreed border between the two countries, but also not any clearly defined *de facto* border. Neither China nor India seems to have realized the danger implicit in this situation.

In 1957, the Indians discovered that the Chinese had for several years been operating a highway cutting across territory that was marked part of India on Indian maps. India protested, and discussions began between the two powers. There were two areas of significant size in dispute. At the eastern end of the Sino-Indian border was an area of over 35,000 square miles, loosely administered by India, called the North-East Frontier Agency (NEFA). During the Guomindang era it had been shown as part of China on Chinese maps, and sometimes on maps published in the West, but none of it had ever been under direct Chinese administration. Part of it had been administered by Tibet, but this had been before the PRC brought Tibet under full Chinese control. At the western end of the border was a block of about 14,000 square miles, consisting mostly of the deserts of the Aksai Chin Plateau, but stretching south and west into some thinly settled areas under Indian influence. The part of the Aksai Chin across which the Chinese highway ran had been shown as part of British India on maps of the colonial era, but had never been administered by Britain, or by India after the granting of independence in 1947. Prime Minister Nehru explained to the Indian Parliament that India had not attempted actually to administer this area because it was uninhabited and uninhabitable.

The Chinese attitude was that the border had never been formally defined, and would have to be negotiated. China seemed to be aiming at a compromise settlement that would basically ratify the existing situation on the ground. This would give to China the Aksai Chin Plateau, which was of value to China but not to India and had never been controlled by India. It would give to India the NEFA, which was of value to India but not to China and had never been controlled by China. The remainder of the areas in dispute were fairly small, and were of no genuine importance to either side, and so a settlement should have been possible. The Chinese signed a very generous border settlement with Burma at about this time.

The Indians regarded any compromise settlement as an offence against national pride. Also, on large portions of the border they rejected the Chinese assertion that the border had never been formally defined, apparently fearing that if they admitted that their own claim was less than ironclad, the Chinese would then demand the whole of the disputed area. The Indian army began pushing forward, and Indian government leaders hinted (despite the overwhelming military superiority of China) that they might eventually evict the Chinese from the whole of the disputed area by force. By the autumn of 1962, Chinese and Indian troops confronted one another at close range on the western end of the border, while on the northern edge of the NEFA the Indian government was ordering some troops to go north even of the border shown on their own maps.

The Chinese reacted with overwhelming force to these rather minor Indian advances. In a few weeks of campaigning, the Chinese expelled the Indians from the whole of the disputed area, but were careful not to venture beyond the area that China had claimed. China then handed back to India the NEFA, plus all prisoners and weapons taken in the campaign. The result was to impose roughly the compromise that China had been offering before, giving India somewhat more that two-thirds of the disputed area. Sino-Indian relations remained extremely hostile for about twenty years. Negotiations over the border dispute finally resumed in 1981, but produced no quick resolution.

The war seriously harmed China's international image. China was already known to be attacking the doctrine of 'peaceful coexistence' in its dispute with the Soviet Union, while India had a good reputation as the largest and most prestigious of the countries maintaining neutrality in the Cold War. Much of the international community accepted the Indian claim that the war had been unprovoked Chinese aggression. Many accounts published in the West contained blatant errors, such as: that the Indians had simply claimed the territory that had been under the *de facto* control of the British colonial government at the time India became independent, that the Chinese retained after the war more than 10,000 square miles of the territory they had conquered in the war, and that the Chinese retained after the war all the territory they had claimed before it. Such errors created an exaggerated image of Chinese aggressiveness.

The Sino-Indian conflict exacerbated the Sino-Soviet dispute; China's already low opinion of the Soviet Union was confirmed when the Russians maintained a neutral attitude in this war, fought between a Communist and a non-Communist power. By the middle and late 1960s, the dispute between China and the Soviet Union had hardened into savage hostility, with massive troop build-ups along the border between the two countries. There were even armed clashes along the border, though not on a very large scale.

The existence of border disputes between China and the Soviet Union was more a result than a cause of the hostility between the two countries. The areas actually in dispute were small, and of no genuine importance to either side. The most important was the uninhabited island that the Soviets called Damansky and the Chinese called Zhenbao (Chenpao). It lay in the middle of the Ussuri River, which formed the boundary between Heilongjiang province and the Soviet Union. The main channel of the river shifted from time to time, and this created disputes as to the proper ownership of the island. With reasonable goodwill the question could have been negotiated or simply ignored, but such goodwill was conspicuously lacking by the mid 1960s. There were bloody clashes over this island in March 1969, involving not only infantry but armoured vehicles and artillery.

The level of hatred that existed from the mid 1960s onward was out of proportion to the actual conflicts of interest between China and the Soviet Union. It seems to have been motivated mainly by emotional factors: racially based hostilities, and the sense of shock and betrayal felt by each side over the way the other, a Communist country that had been expected to be a political and doctrinal ally, had inexplicably turned hostile.

The escalation of the Vietnam War also posed serious dangers for China, especially after a series of incidents in the Gulf of Tonkin (the body of water between North Vietnam and the Chinese island of Hainan) in August 1964. On 2 August, there was a shooting incident between American and North Vietnamese vessels a few miles off the North Vietnamese coast. On the night of 4 August, much further out to sea, there was a panic aboard two US naval vessels; the Americans believed they were being attacked by North Vietnamese torpedo boats. Their mistaken reports were believed in Washington, and the following day the US bombed North Vietnam in retaliation for the imaginary incident. The Chinese had surprisingly good information about these events. Within weeks, Mao Zedong was aware that the Americans' false report of an attack on the two US vessels had been a genuine mistake, not a deliberate lie concocted as an excuse for the retaliatory air strikes.

The Chinese knew or guessed that the United States was drawing up plans for much larger military actions against North Vietnam. The danger that this would trigger fighting between American and Chinese military forces was obvious. And it was not obvious that the United States, which during the Korean War had kept military action largely restricted to the Korean Peninsula, would show similar restraint when the Vietnam War escalated. Indeed the danger seemed great enough to force a major shift in China's industrialization strategy. The locations where industries could be built and operated cheaply and efficiently were mostly near the coast. After the Tonkin Gulf incidents, Chinese leaders paid high economic costs to put key facilities in the mountainous interior, where they would be less vulnerable if the United States launched a major bombing campaign against China.

The successful detonation of China's first atomic bomb in October 1964 must have been most welcome in Beijing, though China's addition to the list of nuclear powers by no means guaranteed the nation's safety. (The previous month, the United States had asked whether the Soviet Union would be interested in joining the United States in an attack against China's nuclear facilities. The Soviets had replied in the negative.) China's first test of a deliverable atomic bomb, detonated after having been dropped from an airplane, was in May 1965. The first test of a missile with a nuclear warhead, which detonated as the missile came down on its target after travelling more than 800 kilometres, was in October 1966.

The beginning of systematic US bombing of North Vietnam, in 1965, increased the danger of a direct conflict between the United States and China. But the United States was eager to avoid triggering such a conflict. President Lyndon Johnson, not wanting to risk having US planes accidentally cross into Chinese airspace, permitted very few US air strikes in areas of North Vietnam close to the Chinese border. In September 1965, when a US navy jet had a navigational failure over the Gulf of Tonkin, approached the Chinese coast, and was shot down, the United States chose not to give much publicity to the incident.

Dispute in Beijing

Almost all the top leaders of the CCP accepted Mao's decision to split from the Soviet Union. The failure of the Great Leap Forward, however, raised serious questions about Mao's leadership. He did not have sole responsibility for the Great Leap – most of his colleagues had been just as unrealistic as Mao during the euphoria of late 1958 – but as the supreme leader of the CCP he bore primary responsibility for having led it on a disastrous course. Unfortunately, the first open challenge to his policies came at the worst possible time, and caused Mao to reaffirm his support for the policies of the Great Leap instead of persuading him to abandon them.

By the spring of 1959 it was already becoming apparent that some of the policies of the Great Leap were having a very bad effect on the economy, and that many claims of fantastic increases in production were gross exaggerations. At this point, the CCP began abandoning the extreme policies of the Great Leap. The policy shift was handled quietly, and Party leaders carefully avoided discussing the question of who might be responsible for the policies that were being reversed. Mao took much of the initiative in this effort to bring the Great Leap under control, just as he had taken the initiative in starting it during the previous year. However, when the top leaders of the Party met at Lushan, in July 1959, Minister of Defence Peng Dehuai presented Mao Zedong with a written statement saying, in effect, that the Great Leap had been a disaster and that Mao had caused it. This suddenly made this issue a matter of personal pride and personal power for Mao.

Peng Dehuai does not seem to have wanted or expected an open conflict at this time. He gave Mao his denunciation of the Great Leap privately, in writing, rather than standing up and speaking his mind before all the Party leaders gathered for the meeting. However, Mao immediately launched an all-out attack; he was not willing to wait for Peng perhaps to start an open conflict at some later date of his own choosing. Peng was defeated before he could even organize an effective presentation of his case. He was replaced as minister of defence by Lin Biao. For practical purposes he ceased to be a member of the Party leadership, though he nominally retained a high Party post.

To justify the purge of Peng Dehuai, Mao had to deny Peng's charges that the Great Leap was a failure. Mao vigorously reaffirmed the policies that just before the Lushan meeting he had been discarding as failures. He had built up so much credit from the spectacular successes that had marked his first twenty years as head of the CCP that even in 1959, when the true results of the Great Leap were becoming fairly clear, he was able to persuade the rest of the Party leadership to go along with him. The Great Leap continued for more than a year after the Lushan meeting, with appalling results.

The Great Leap was the first great example of the lack of realism for which Mao has been much criticized since his death. At its beginning, trying to interpret China's problems as advantages, he said:

Apart from their other characteristics, China's six hundred million people are, first of all, poor, and secondly, 'blank'. That may seem like a bad thing, but it is really a good thing. Poor people want change, want to do things, want revolution. A clean sheet of paper has no blotches and so the newest and most beautiful words can be written on it, the newest and most beautiful pictures can be painted on it.

There are two striking anomalies in this metaphor. One is that extreme poverty is not conducive to blankness; it tends to scar people. Whatever the characteristics of the Chinese people, nothing remotely resembling 'blankness' was among them. The other is that, even had they been blank, this would have been of dubious desirability. The transformation of Chinese society was not something that could be done *to* the Chinese people, it would have to be done *by* them. Blank paper may be desirable for writing; a blank-minded author is not. On both of these counts, Mao was deviating from his own usual attitudes. Most of the time he maintained a vivid awareness of the living strength of China's cultural tradition, both negative (as when he discussed the tremendous difficulty of overcoming 'feudal' attitudes) and positive (as when he drew on ancient sources for some of his military strategies, and for that matter when he wrote poetry which drew far more on classical Chinese models than on 'socialist realism'). Also he usually emphasized the active and creative role of the masses rather than talking about them as objects to be manipulated by a revolutionary leadership. However, the boundless optimism of this statement, its emphasis on will and the desire to make revolution as the most important determinants of success, and its claim that the impoverished masses of China have the will and the ability to transform their society, were all typical of Mao's thinking.

Traditional Marxists, and probably most leaders of the CCP, believed in an interpretation almost exactly opposite to Mao's. Socialism and communism were supposed to emerge from a highly developed economy. To the extent that the Chinese people were poor and blank, this would make it difficult for them either to formulate plans for a communist society, or to find the material means to carry out such plans once formulated.

The Great Leap was finally abandoned late in 1960. In place of massive increases in production and efforts to achieve a radically egalitarian society, the CCP concentrated on getting China out of the crisis it was in and restoring order to the economy.

Most of the peasants who had gone into industrial production were sent back to the fields, in a desperate effort to revive agricultural production and resolve the problem of food shortages. On the average, each of the communes created in the Great Leap was split into three smaller ones. Within each commune, the income of individual families, or of production teams (work units that might comprise twenty families), was related much more closely to the actual performance of the family or team. It became less common for members of a commune or of a subdivision within a commune to share their income equally, without regard to the relative contributions of different families ('eating out of a big pot').

Individual freedom in economic matters was increased to some extent. The peasants' private plots, which had been almost eliminated during the Great Leap, were restored. Rural markets at which individuals could sell part of their produce on a private basis were revived. However, it should not be supposed that all restrictions on individual freedom were relaxed.

Political controls remained very much in effect. In addition, serious efforts to limit the size of Chinese families were made for the first time.

Nobody knew the exact size of the Chinese population – the statistical system had collapsed – but it was huge, and growing rapidly. Even in 1960, the worst of the 'three bad years', the number of babies born had been almost as great as the number of people who died. In the years following the end of the famine, the population increased by more than 15 million every year.

There were already too many people for the available resources, especially land, to support decently with the available technology. The CCP, however, had for years been reluctant to accept that the population needed to be limited. Marxian economics, based on the labour theory of value, did not lead easily or naturally to an understanding of the dangers of having too large a labour force. Also, arguing that poverty was caused by over-population carried the implication that it should be blamed on the poor, with their tendency to have too many children. This seemed a gross insult to the egalitarian doctrines of the CCP. Mao commented in 1949:

It is a very good thing that China has a big population. Even if China's population multiplies many times, she is fully capable of finding a solution; the solution is production. The absurd argument of Western bourgeois economists like Malthus that increases in food cannot keep pace with increases in population was not only thoroughly refuted in theory by Marxists long ago, but has also been completely exploded by the realities in the Soviet Union and the Liberated Areas of China after their revolutions . . .

Of all things in the world, people are the most precious. Under the leadership of the Communist Party, as long as there are people, every kind of miracle can be performed.

Within a few years, however, the CCP began to realize the dreadful economic costs that rapid population growth could impose, and it began to advocate limitations on birth. The impact of the programme became significant in the cities of China, though not in the villages, around 1963. Requirements that young people postpone marriage well beyond the age traditional in China were among the most important tools of the population control effort. There was a general spirit of Puritanism in the Communist Party (though Chairman Mao's private life did not conform to this spirit). It was not just that things like prostitution were forbidden; even romance was treated as a distraction from a person's proper commitment to society. Such attitudes may have encouraged the decision to use abstinence as a population-control mechanism.

The Party still did not use the fundamental problem of overpopulation as the rationale for its policy. Instead, it stressed the short-term problems that would be posed by having too many children: the expense of educating them, the burdens on the mothers of large families, and so on. For a while, the world was presented with the odd spectacle of a Chinese government that enforced on its own people a population-control programme unusually vigorous by world standards of the time (the use of contraceptives was actually illegal in parts of the United States until 1965), but that at the same time rejected in theory the idea that excessively large populations could represent a problem for developing countries.

The expansion of economic freedom in the countryside was not matched in the cities. Urban workers did not have the right to choose jobs that suited them; state labour bureaux decided who would work for which enterprise. The assignments were often made without much regard for the wishes or even the exact skills of the people involved. The assignment was usually for life. (While this system had disadvantages, it did provide great job security. A reasonably well-paid job that one could depend on retaining for one's entire working career was referred to as an 'iron rice bowl'.)

A system of residence permits prevented people from moving from one city to another, or especially from the countryside into the cities, without permission. It was possible for some peasants to work on contracts in the cities, as short-term labour, without job security or the medical and retirement benefits received by regular city workers. However, it was extremely difficult for peasants actually to obtain residence permits for the cities, which would allow them to remain permanently. The CCP had partially recreated a phenomenon usually considered a relic of feudalism: a peasantry bound to the soil.

Economic plans based on very modest goals, a revival of free markets, and the desire of each peasant household to worry first about its own welfare, did not suit Mao's inclinations. However, in the years immediately after the Great Leap, economic policy was made mainly by a group of more moderate leaders centring on Chief of State Liu Shaoqi, Premier Zhou Enlai, and CCP Secretary-General Deng Xiaoping.

There had long been agreement among top leaders, including Mao, that he should to some extent withdraw into the background and allow others to do more of the routine work of running China. Shortly after the Great Leap began, Mao had handed over the position of chief of state to Liu

Shaoqi. At the time Mao did this on a voluntary basis. He was not being stripped of his power as a result of the failure of the Great Leap (which had not yet become obvious); he was simply shedding a job he no longer needed. Two years later, however, when CCP leaders were formulating the policies designed to pull China out of the crisis of the 'three bitter years', the group often called the 'pragmatists' pushed Mao considerably further into the background than he had expected. Mao was still Party chairman; the Chinese public continued to regard him as the incarnation of the revolution. He still had much influence in policy formation. However, when a substantial number of other leaders were united on an issue, they could and sometimes did overrule him. He later said, with some exaggeration, that he had been treated in this period like a dead ancestor – someone who is worshipped but not consulted. Mao was especially bitter about the attitude of Liu Shaoqi and Deng Xiaoping.

Study questions

What caused the split between China and the Soviet Union?

What do the very misguided policies of the Great Leap Forward tell us about the nature of the Chinese political system?

Why was the United States so committed to its alliance with Chiang Kai-shek?

CHAPTER 8

The Cultural Revolution

By the mid 1960s, the Chinese Revolution seemed to have settled down to the job of ruling China. Its main goals were essentially nationalist: a prosperous modern economy, and a government capable of maintaining national unity and upholding China's place in the world. While there continued to exist substantial economic inequalities, the distribution of wealth was probably a bit more equal than in most Western countries, and significantly more equal than in pre-revolutionary China. Almost all CCP leaders were happy with this picture. Mao Zedong was not; he felt that some fundamental goals of the revolution were being abandoned.

Education was functioning as the basis of a caste system, which to Mao seemed unpleasantly reminiscent of the system by which the Confucian scholars had dominated traditional China. He could observe that the Soviet Union was, quite literally, ruled by the graduates of advanced technical schools. This group not only managed the factories; it held an overwhelming majority of the positions on the Central Committee of the Soviet Communist Party. Despite the distrust for intellectuals that the CCP had shown so brutally in the Anti-Rightist movement of 1957–58, China seemed to be headed in the same direction. Educated people not only got the best jobs and the highest pay; they also had high prestige. They felt (and many of the non-educated agreed with them) that an educated person was fundamentally superior to an uneducated one, entitled to look down on the masses, give them orders, and avoid, *as a matter of right*, having to do any form of manual labour. China's poverty and the lack of qualified teachers restricted access to education. Even primary schooling was far from universal; graduation from secondary school, especially from one of the best schools in the major cities, marked a person destined for a position well above the average in Chinese society.

While there were great variations in income between different villages, and between different jobs in the urban sector, the overall averages showed a clear pattern: the cities were much richer than the countryside. Most capital investment was going into urban industries. The urban workers, using a considerable amount of expensive machinery, had a much higher average level of productivity per hour than the rural workers, who lived mainly by farming but did not have enough land, machinery, or fertilizer. The natural consequence was for the city people, with their greater economic power, not only to arrange for themselves an average income level about twice as high as that in the countryside but also to dominate Chinese society in other ways.

Finally, the bureaucrats of the Communist Party and the government, who dominated Chinese society more thoroughly than the Confucian scholars or the Guomindang had ever managed to do, made Mao uneasy. They formed a ruling caste, which felt entitled to make all real decisions and demand instant obedience from the people.

All three of the marks of privilege – education, urban residence, and Party or bureaucratic status – were to a considerable extent hereditary. This was not just a result of the informal social realities that exist in most societies – that the children of educated parents did better in school, that communities with prosperous and well-educated adult populations had above-average schools, and that influential parents could sometimes arrange special preference for their children. Such informal mechanisms were buttressed by very strong formal ones. The children of city people usually lived in the cities where they had grown up; the residence permit system made it very difficult for the child of a peasant to get permission to move into a city.

Family background played, in one way or another, a tremendous role in the educational careers of Chinese students. All students had an official class label, based on the status of their parents. The level of academic competence one had to show in order to win admission to a selective school depended on one's class label.

- The children of revolutionary cadres were given a strong preference in admission to good schools, and also the average educational level of their parents was somewhat higher than the average for the population as a whole. They therefore formed a large proportion of the student body at the better secondary schools and colleges.

- The children of ordinary workers and poor peasants had to meet somewhat higher academic standards to win admission, and since their parents were generally uneducated, few of them were able to do so. Partial figures are available for thirty upper middle (senior high) schools in Guangzhou; the children of ordinary workers and peasants made up, on the average, less than one-sixth of the students of these schools.

- The children of the middle class had to meet still higher standards, but thanks to the educational background of their parents, many were able to do so; they made up about half of the student body of the Guangzhou schools mentioned above.

- The children of the 'bad classes' (landlords, counter-revolutionaries, rich peasants, capitalists, and 'rightists' who had spoken out against the Communist system during the Hundred Flowers episode of 1957) had to meet the highest standard of all to win admission, but a significant number were able to do so.

The differential admissions policy led directly to differentials in the average academic competence of the students in each category. Middle-class students tended to be academically above the average in any given school, and students from the 'bad classes' very far above the average, simply because if they were not above average they would not have been allowed in the school. Students of below-average competence were generally the children of revolutionary cadres or of ordinary workers and peasants. This led to serious conflicts over the criteria to be used in choosing students for the next higher level of education, since a selection process emphasizing academic competence would clearly favour the middle class and the 'bad classes'.

The peasants of China were better off than before the revolution. They had a higher average standard of living, and more security against unexpected disasters. The élite was more solicitous of peasant interests than had been true in the old society. However, while a good many individual peasants had managed to work their way up into the élite, the peasantry as a whole was still, quite clearly, a lower class with a subordinate position in society. This was not what the revolution had been intended to accomplish.

China was having far more difficulty escaping from its past than Mao had expected. Marxist theory predicted that after the initial establishment of a socialist society, there would be a continued upward movement towards forms of society having less and less in common with pre-revolutionary patterns. Chinese tradition, however, said that the high point of each dynasty had always come shortly after it was founded; dynasties tended to decline from that point onward. Inequalities of wealth were smallest at the beginning of a dynasty, and increased later on. Mao looked at the younger generation, the people who would someday inherit power in China, and he was not reassured. Conditioned to accept substantial inequality in society, conditioned to obey authority without question, lacking experience of revolutionary turmoil or personal knowledge of what China had been like before 1949, how could they have any real understanding of the revolution? How could they be expected to preserve its ideals once the older generation was gone?

Aside from being distressed by the direction the revolution had taken, Mao felt increasingly outraged by the difficulty he sometimes had in making his beliefs felt. In some respects he seemed as powerful as ever. His picture was displayed everywhere, and the general public continued to regard him as the incarnation of the revolution. The army came increasingly under his influence after his enemy Peng Dehuai was replaced as minister of defence by his ally Lin Biao in 1959. Mao took advantage of this by initiating a campaign to 'learn from the People's Liberation Army', which increased the army's influence in the Party and the civil government. Much of the Party bureaucracy, however, did not share his fundamental attitudes and in any case did not like the way some of his mass campaigns had disrupted orderly government. On many issues, especially those involving economics, the bureaucrats had shunted him out of the main line of policy formation after the failures of the Great Leap Forward.

Mao's effort both to re-establish his personal power and to shift the overall course China was following led to the 'Great Proletarian Cultural Revolution': several years of chaotic mass struggle starting in 1966, and then a lingering aftermath lasting until Mao's death in 1976.

Most observers, both Chinese and Western, feel today that Mao had simply lost touch with reality; that in his old age he had become willing to throw away everything he had built, in his blind pursuit of Utopian dreams and personal power. Certainly Mao's optimism about the social transformation he was trying to bring about has turned out to be unjustified. Still, if he had cared to respond to the charges he knew were being made, that he was being unrealistic, he might have said: Marxist doctrine taught that in a socialist society, there would be a natural tendency for social inequalities to shrink, for greed to give way before the habit of unselfish cooperation, for the gaps separating mental from manual labour, peasants from industrial workers, cities from countryside, to fade away. More than a decade of socialism in China, and more than four decades in the Soviet Union, had provided little evidence that any such natural tendency was going to emerge. What would it be most 'realistic' for him to do? To abandon his most cherished goals without a struggle? To sit back and continue to hope that all would somehow work out for the best, despite the evidence he could see all around him? Or to fight to *make* the promises of Marxism come true, as ruthlessly as he had once fought, against odds that looked even more impossible, in the hills of South China?

Whether or not one thinks Mao's decision was so irrational as to reflect a loss of contact with reality, there can be little dispute that the results of the decision were disastrous. He failed to reach his goal, to get China off the path he called the 'capitalist road'. The country was more firmly set on that path by the 1980s than it had been in 1965. Furthermore, the cost of the unsuccessful attempt to change course was ghastly, no matter how one measures it – lives lost, students not educated, economic growth set back for years. The Chinese leadership later referred to the period from 1966 to 1976 as the 'Ten-Year Catastrophe'.

At the time the Cultural Revolution was going on, some people were puzzled that it seemed to be so much the personal creation of Mao Zedong. His name was repeated endlessly in the documents of the Cultural Revolution; it will be repeated endlessly in the account of the Cultural Revolution in this book. Great historic movements do not normally spring from the head of an individual; they arise from the logic of a situation. It seemed incredible that the social, economic, and political structure of the largest nation on earth was being drastically revised because one man willed it.

Today, after the failure of the movement, the pattern of events makes more sense. While Mao was able to find a certain natural base of support for the Cultural Revolution in Chinese society, this natural base was weak enough so that nothing remotely resembling the Cultural Revolution would have been likely to occur if Mao had not decided to make it occur. That is why it ended in failure.

1966: 'To rebel is justified!'

The conflict between Mao and his opponents came to a head in 1966. The deputy mayor of Beijing, Wu Han, was an academic who had not been a member of the Communist movement during the civil war, but who had been recruited along with many other intellectuals during the 1950s. In 1961, Wu Han wrote a play called *Hai Rui Dismissed from Office*, about a wise and virtuous official of the Ming Dynasty, devoted to the welfare of the people, who was dismissed from office by an egotistical emperor (see p. 21). It may well have been written innocently, but it looked suspiciously like a disguised criticism of Mao for the way he had purged Peng Dehuai in 1959. When Mao became disturbed by the parallel, he found that he could not even arrange for publication of an attack on the play in the major Party organs in Beijing. He had to go to Shanghai, where his own influence was greater and Wu Han's was less, to get his view into print.

Wanting to cut down the power and privileges of the ruling élite of China, Mao obviously had to find allies outside that élite. His supporters in the army would eventually play a major role, but it was students who led during the opening stages of the movement.

The Great Proletarian Cultural Revolution began as a campaign to root out 'bourgeois' influences in art and literature. By the spring of 1966 it had been broadened to deal with bourgeois influences among the intellectuals in general. Party authorities in Beijing sent out teams of cadres to conduct the movement in various schools, factories, and other organizations. Nothing suggested that this was going to become a matter of great importance; the movement seemed directed mainly against intellectuals from middle-class backgrounds, the type of people who had been attacked in the Anti-Rightist campaign of 1957. The Party bureaucracy, not Mao Zedong, controlled the teams of cadres supervising the movement.

Then, in May 1966, a woman named Nie Yuanzi (Nieh Yuan-tzu) put up a wall poster at Beijing University. She argued that the Cultural Revolution should be a vigorous mass movement, and she denounced the administration of Beijing University for restricting it and keeping it from developing properly. Mao had her poster reprinted in the *People's Daily*. In the summer of 1966 students in Beijing began, with Mao's support, to organize themselves as 'Red Guards'. They took an increasing role in the effort to root out bourgeois influences from the faculties and administrations of their universities. Wall posters attacking various professors and administrators proliferated fantastically. Before long there were far more posters than space available on the walls; rooms and courtyards had ropes strung across them like clothes-lines, from which posters could be hung. People walked along the narrow alleys between the rows of posters, reading them or putting up posters of their own.

Mao had the work teams pulled out of educational institutions in late July. With their restraining influence removed, the Red Guard movement was able to spread to institutions throughout China. The Red Guards attacked the 'Four Olds': old ideas, old culture, old customs, and old habits. They also attacked anything that they felt represented the influence either of the Soviet Union or of the Western capitalist countries. They smashed images in Buddhist temples. They raided the homes of professors and other intellectuals, confiscating or destroying Western-style clothing, books and paintings representing the Four Olds, and anything else that offended them. The owners of such materials were abused both verbally and physically. Within weeks, the first incidents in which Red Guards beat people to death began to occur. The police and the military were ordered not to interfere.

The students involved, in the first months, were mostly from backgrounds considered 'pure'. Many were the children of important Communists. They were stepping outside the bounds of behaviour normally permitted by the Communist system, and they were putting a severe strain on the system when they attacked academic administrators many of whom belonged to the Communist Party, but they regarded themselves basically as defenders of the system. They had a variety of motives for joining the Red Guards. Most were convinced that anything Chairman Mao urged them to do must be correct. Many genuinely resented the authoritarian behaviour that characterized many teachers and administrators. Many had a longstanding dislike of 'bourgeois' intellectuals, a dislike that had grown out of the competition that pitted cadres' children against students of greater academic talent who came from bourgeois backgrounds. Almost all the Red Guards were desperately eager to meet whatever criteria were currently being used to measure correct political attitude, since if their political attitude were not considered correct, their chances of further education and thus a better life would become miniscule.

On 5 August 1966, the direction of the movement began to change. Mao Zedong himself issued a statement titled 'Bombard the Headquarters', in which he charged that there were people in the CCP at all levels up to the very top who were following reactionary, essentially bourgeois policies. He did not name those he was attacking, but it soon became clear that they included both Liu Shaoqi (chief of state of the PRC) and Deng Xiaoping (general secretary of the CCP). On 15 September, Lin Biao told a mass rally in Beijing, attended by Red Guards from all over the country, that the main target for their movement should be the individuals in power who were following the capitalist road. Soon, more and more senior officials were being attacked and humiliated. Many of them, including Liu Shaoqi, eventually died as a result of the mistreatment they suffered.

At schools where the movements had at first been dominated by the children of revolutionary veterans, competing groups appeared, containing more students from middle-class backgrounds, who had long resented the special preference given to the children of cadres. They attacked the

Communist Party bureaucracy, and indeed most of the authority structure that had ruled China. Before the end of 1966, many of the original Red Guards, children of the Party bureaucracy, were rallying to the defence of that bureaucracy and struggling against the newer Red Guard units.

In September 1966, student Red Guards from colleges and even some from secondary schools were invited to go travelling through China to share information and experiences, and to learn more about revolution. They were given the right to travel free on the railroads, but tens of thousands marched on foot across the countryside, visiting Chairman Mao's birthplace, the CCP strongholds of the 1930s in Jiangxi, and other famous revolutionary sites. They hoped both to find inspiration there and to toughen themselves by enduring physical hardships along the way. About 11 million went to Beijing to attend mass rallies where they could actually glimpse Chairman Mao in person. The general right of Red Guards to travel everywhere was rescinded in December, but they continued to move about to a significant extent. They were ordered to return home in February 1967.

Organizations analogous to the Red Guards began to be formed among industrial workers. By the end of 1966, workers' organizations in Shanghai were already showing the same pattern of factional division that had appeared among the student Red Guards in many cities: there were radical organizations attacking the Party apparatus, and more conservative ones defending it.

The 'mass organizations' – student Red Guards and workers' groups – were not simply operating on their own. Shortly after Mao had pulled the Party organization's work teams out of the universities in the summer, he had begun sending in work teams of his own. However, the situation in which competing authorities issued conflicting orders to conflicting organizations of workers and students amounted to a breakdown of central control. In the confusion, many students and workers broke free of almost all organized restrictions; one or another group attacked almost every sector of the authority system that had formerly governed China. Professors probably suffered the most, but factory managers, government officials, and Party leaders also found their authority vanishing and themselves being held up to public scorn as followers of the 'capitalist road'. Many were subjected to savage physical abuse; some died.

Most Communists, once in power, become in a sense rather conservative. They place Party policy above formal law, and flout the law when their own or the Party's interests require it, but they respect the structure of Party authority. In traditional Chinese culture there was a horror of disorder, a

PLATE 8.1 *In late 1966 and early 1967, senior CCP and government members were publicly humiliated. Here, a government official is paraded through a Beijing street before Red Guards, wearing a cone-shaped hat as a sign of shame for involvement in an anti-revolutionary group. (© AP/PA Photos.)*

fear that it would lead to complete anarchy if not quickly checked. Most CCP leaders shared this attitude, but Mao seems to have been immune to it. He had once said, 'In the last analysis, all the truths of Marxism can be summed up in one sentence: "To rebel is justified." ' In the Cultural Revolution he showed utter contempt not only for formal law but for the authority of the Party, and for the normal rules governing politics within the Party. The only rule he respected in the game of politics was that the true revolutionaries must win.

With hindsight it is possible to discern approximately what Mao was after, but he did not explain his goals clearly at the time. Indeed, despite the way the Cultural Revolution lifted him almost to the status of a god, he was hardly presenting his ideas in public at all. The official edition of his *Selected Works* only covered the period up to 1949. *Quotations from Chairman Mao*, a collection of short excerpts from his writings, which in a pocket edition known as the 'Little Red Book' became almost a bible for the Red Guards, contained very little written after 1959; most of it dated from before 1949. The man who during the 1930s and 1940s had been writing long and informative analyses of major problems was by the 1960s allowing his views to be represented, for the most part, either by things he had written many years before or by the frenzied and often absurd statements of his followers.

His actions make it unmistakable that he was vitally interested in a wide range of policy questions. He cannot have believed that the Chinese people already understood his beliefs well enough so that he had no need to write about them further; there were too many conflicting interpretations of his ideas in circulation. Despite the effects of age and illness, he retained enough vigour and alertness to fight and win major political power struggles; surely he was still capable of the much easier task of writing out his views, or at least of allowing some assistant to edit into publishable form the texts of the speeches he was giving. It is difficult to escape the conclusion that, for a whole range of reasons, he had made a conscious and deliberate decision not to explain his thinking in print. Probably he wanted to let his followers experiment, and find their own way without the inhibition of too much guidance from him. Probably he was to some extent being Machiavellian, and was hoping to win the support of some people who would have opposed him if they had understood his real goals. Probably, feeling his way by trial and error through very difficult questions, and knowing his enemies would seize upon any error, he was reluctant to commit himself too publicly to answers that were still tentative. In earlier years he had been more confident; the tide of history had been running his way. He had been prepared to explain his views and the logic behind them; to be reasonable, even generous, with opponents whom he had defeated by proving that his own policies were superior. In the late 1960s, driven to increasingly desperate expedients in his efforts to regain control of a revolution that had slipped from his grasp, he discarded both civility and candour.

The Maoists presented the Cultural Revolution not as a conflict between two conceptions of the revolution, one more egalitarian than the other, but as a conflict between revolutionaries and enemies of the revolution. This was necessary in a propagandistic sense; they needed to present an almost apocalyptic vision if they wished to persuade loyal Communists to attack the Party apparatus, and educated young people whose own self-interest lay in the existing system, to attack that system. But Mao was spreading fear that the revolution was endangered, and unleashing a mass struggle to defend the purity of the revolution, without having either a coherent organization he could trust to guide it, or a clear and concrete definition of the enemy against which the struggle was to be conducted.

A number of passages in this book attempt to describe, as clearly and rationally as possible, what Mao was promoting and what he opposed. It is important to remember, when reading these passages, that they have had to be based to a considerable extent on reconstruction of Mao's goals from his actions. Neither Mao nor his followers were publishing any such clear, rational explanations of their goals during the Cultural Revolution. Statements by the radicals in this period often referred to the enemy as 'ghosts and monsters', 'freaks', or 'demons'. The intent of these phrases was to indicate that anyone so vile as to oppose the true revolutionary doctrines of Chairman Mao could hardly be considered human. With hindsight, however, such language looks like a symptom of the fact that some of Mao's followers, not having been told exactly who or what they were struggling against, were having to conjure pictures of the enemy out of their imaginations. The result was chaos.

The radicals tried to connect their enemies as much as possible to the old enemies of the revolution, the landlords and capitalists. There were certain elements of reality in this. Policies that offered advancement to young people with academic talent had given an advantage to the children of educated parents, many of whom were the children of the pre-revolutionary élites. The manager of a state-owned factory in China could be sufficiently similar to the manager of a factory in a capitalist country, in the nature of the problems he faced, the nature of his relations with his workers, and his conception of his role, that it was by no means nonsense to refer to the Chinese manager as following the 'capitalist road', although the way this phrase brushes aside the question of ownership is perhaps odd. The radicals, however, carried their fears of landlord, rich peasant, and bourgeois influence to remarkable extremes. Two radicals who had seized power in one production brigade in the countryside decided it was necessary to carry out a complete extermination of the 'bad classes' – landlords, rich peasants, counter-revolutionaries, bad elements, and rightists. They called a meeting of leaders of neighbouring brigades (one brigade usually meant one village), and the slaughter was carried out in ten brigades. The victims included children who had not even been born at the time their parents committed the actions that had caused their families to be labelled 'bad classes'.

To the Maoists, the essential characteristics defining the capitalist road was selfishness. All policies that either rewarded or encouraged individual selfishness were deemed capitalist. This definition, which does not seem very Marxist, combined what were in fact two very different types of people under the general heading of 'capitalist roaders'.

1 The typical Communist bureaucrat believed in an authoritarian meritocracy. People should compete with one another, in school and elsewhere, and the winners should be rewarded with top positions in a steeply hierarchical structure of privilege and power.

2 Many intellectuals and some economic planners, on the other hand, believed that individual freedom should be substantially expanded. Writers should be allowed to write as they pleased; farmers should be permitted to grow whatever crops they thought most profitable; more people should be free to search for jobs that suited them, rather than being assigned jobs by the state. Many of the common people, while not involved in theoretical debates, wished that they as individuals could have more freedom to choose how they would make a living.

Lumping the proponents of centralized bureaucracy and of individual freedom together under a single label was not conducive to clear discussion of the issues. There were only a few policy positions, such as a desire to stress academic competence in the educational system, on which the two types of 'capitalist roaders' were really in accord.

The three supreme elements of Maoist revolutionary purity became: personal selflessness, belief in 'the masses', and belief in Chairman Mao.

Everyone was supposed to be preoccupied with service to society, and care nothing for their own welfare. 'Craving for a comfortable life and continuing the revolution are as incompatible as fire and water.' In fact, selflessness was supposed to be carried to a point where people would sacrifice their own interests out of loyalty to the revolution without even thinking very much about whether their sacrifice would bring any concrete benefit to the revolution. The press gave considerable publicity to a story about a man who was carrying a message about Cultural Revolution policy to a remote village, and found his path blocked by a flooded river. He hurled himself into the waters, and (rather implausibly) died just as he delivered the message on the far side. There was nothing genuinely urgent about the message. One might think that he could have served Chairman Mao better by waiting for the waters to subside, delivering the message, and then making himself available for another assignment. This logic, however, was ignored; his readiness to die for the revolution made him a hero.

Everyone was supposed to believe that the common people had both the right and the ability to run society; the right to avoid being dominated by a few bureaucrats, and the ability to carry out any task of great importance without having to depend on highly trained experts.

On the other hand, everyone was supposed to have faith in the infallible guidance of Chairman Mao. Intensive study of the 'Little Red Book' became the official source of inspiration for almost any activity; it taught people how to grow more wheat, make better light bulbs, and heal the sick. Great crowds chanted it in unison.

The years of chaos: 1967–68

In January and February of 1967, Mao began to encourage an actual seizure of government by radicals organized in a three-way alliance: (1) 'mass organizations' (Red Guards among the students, and equivalent groups among the industrial workers); (2) the military; (3) officials of the government organs being seized who were willing to change sides and join in the overthrow of their own organizations. Such seizures began to occur in city governments, province governments, and ministries of the national government. Once in power, unfortunately, the new power-holders fought savagely among themselves. Different groups had different private interests to promote, and different conceptions of revolutionary purity.

In Beijing, the central leadership under Mao was also divided into three parts. (1) Most radical was the committee called the Cultural Revolution Group, of which Mao's wife Jiang Qing was a conspicuous member. The Cultural Revolution Group supported many of the most radical Red Guard factions. (2) Somewhat less radical was the military high command under Lin Biao. (3) Most moderate were the surviving sections of the civil government, under Premier Zhou Enlai. Mao stood above these three groups, balancing them against one another.

There was no simple relationship between the three leadership groups in Beijing and the different groups struggling for power in various parts of China. Many Red Guards accepted policy guidance from the Cultural Revolution Group, but some supported Lin Biao and some backed relatively moderate officials. The same divisions existed within the military, and among civil officials. If a provincial town were split by a fight between radical and conservative factions, there might well be some soldiers, some civil officials, and some Red Guards supporting each side. Participation of the army in actual street fighting was restrained by a policy (enforced to some extent, though not universally obeyed) that forbade the army to

PLATE 8.2 *During the Cultural Revolution, Mao's wife, Jiang Qing, dominated theatre, ballet, and the cinema in China. All the works produced under her supervision were characterized by very heavy-handed propaganda themes. This scene is taken from* The Red Detachment of Women. *(© PA Photos.)*

use armed force against Red Guards. However, if a military unit wished to weaken a certain Red Guard organization, it would often do so by issuing weapons to some competing Red Guard organization.

Chinese Communism had for years accepted three assumptions: (1) In any situation there exists a correct political line; (2) it is absolutely vital that everyone be made to conform to this political line; (3) therefore, anyone who defies the correct line must be forced into submission by whatever means are necessary. In the early 1950s, the CCP had been willing to be gradualistic in its approach to the goal of ideological conformity; it had been so confident of the eventual acceptance of its political line that it could remain fairly calm when confronted with momentary nonconformity. By the beginning of 1967, however, the future had become very uncertain. When two groups with different versions of the truth confronted one another, each dedicated to ruthless enforcement of what it regarded as correct revolutionary doctrine, then even minor differences in actual beliefs could provoke incredible explosions of violence, especially among the Red Guards. The situation would have been bad enough if the competing factions had been armed with knives and clubs, but soon they were using military weapons.

Changsha, for instance, the capital of Hunan province, was split for several months early in 1967 in a civil war between a 'conservative' Red Guard faction wanting the Cultural Revolution to be directed mainly against bourgeois intellectuals, and a more radical 'Rebel' faction wanting the movement to be directed more against Communist Party bureaucrats. Both sides conducted the fight with great brutality, sometimes torturing or beating to death prisoners taken from the opposing group. The 'Rebel' faction won decisive victory, but by the summer it in turn had split into the somewhat more moderate Workers' Alliance, which cooperated with the army, and the more radical Xiang River Wind and Thunder group. Both groups were heavily armed.

The doctrinal differences between the two types of 'Rebels' were not nearly so large as those that had separated 'Rebels' from 'Conservatives' in the spring of 1967. In hindsight, their quarrel seems to have been primarily a struggle for simple political power. At the time, however, each group was sure that it was involved in a fundamental struggle of good against evil. Most members were convinced that their cause was worth dying for, and many were as careless with their own lives as they were with the lives of their enemies or of innocent bystanders. A young man named Liang Heng, who witnessed a battle between the factions near the office of the newspaper *Hunan Daily* in the summer of 1967, later described the extraordinary fanaticism of these young people:

Suddenly, fifty or sixty men carrying machine guns ran past the gate of the Hunan Daily *toward me. A short man in black carried the flag with the words* 'Young People's Bodyguard Squad' *on it, the name of one of the groups in the Xiang River Wind and Thunder faction. I instinctively flattened myself against the wall and a number of people leaped for their bicycles in fear; when the men were almost abreast of me they opened fire, aiming off down the road into the distance, shaking with the vibrations of their guns.*

The enemy was out of sight, but it responded with force. The bullets whizzed through the air and, as if everything were in slow motion, the flagman fell in front of me and rolled over and over like a lead ball. The flag never touched the ground. Someone caught it and raised it, hardly breaking stride. Then he crumpled and rolled and someone else seized it and carried it forward. They never hesitated to take their places in the

front line, always running erect and proud, then falling and rolling. The
pool of blood widened to within a few feet of my bare toes. I thought
I would vomit.

There were soldiers present, but they adhered to the official policy
that the army was to remain neutral in fights between Red Guard factions.
Even when the Young People's Bodyguard Squad brought out cannons, the
soldiers did not interfere, but neither (despite angry demands) would they
give instructions in the use of the cannons. Lacking such instruction, the
young rebels proved capable of loading and firing their weapons but not
of aiming them; Liang Heng watched their shells strike nearby buildings
almost at random.

Violence broke out in every province of China, but the magnitude and
type varied. The most bizarre extreme, ceremonial cannibalism – frying
and eating the hearts and other organs of one's political enemies – seems to
have been restricted mainly to the province of Guangxi.

The killing did not involve only the 'mass organizations'; the army
was directly involved in some areas. In September Chairman Mao called
for students to return to their schools, and ordered that military weapons
be handed back to the military. The army, given the authority to use force
in suppressing Red Guard factional fighting, used that authority with a
heavy hand. Mao began pressing the various factions among his followers
to compromise their differences and join in unified organizations. Soon,
some of the most radical members of the Cultural Revolution Group were
arrested on charges that they had been plotting against Zhou Enlai and the
military.

These measures did not cure the problem, however. The level of armed
conflict died down for a while, but then flared up again. Street fighting in
the spring of 1968 sometimes involved tanks and artillery. As late as July
1968, a dispute among Red Guards in Beijing itself left fifteen students
dead.

At the end of that month, Mao finally agreed with the more moderate
of his supporters that the chaos had to end. 'Worker-peasant Mao Zedong
thought propaganda teams' including a large number of military personnel
began moving into educational institutions all over the country, and breaking the independent power of the Red Guards. Revolutionary committees, on
which the military was heavily represented, became the principal administrative units everywhere. Millions of Red Guards, from all factions, were
soon shipped out to the countryside and put to work on the land. Order
was restored on the surface – street fighting ended in most areas once the

PLA had suppressed the Red Guards – but the new authorities launched a wave of executions to consolidate their hold on power.

The extent to which political issues had been reduced to personalities was quite striking, and after Mao's death there would be vigorous denunciations of the 'cults of personality' practised during the Cultural Revolution. Chairman Mao, as an individual, became the incarnation of the revolution to an even greater extent than he had been before 1966. People bowed before his image after getting up and before going to bed. When a PLA soldier saw a school building on fire, his first thought was to save the portraits of Mao that hung in the classrooms. Only after he had done this did he turn his attention to saving human beings trapped in the building; he got the last of them out only seconds before the building collapsed. When the story was published, his priorities were not criticized; he was treated as a hero.

When the CCP issued a new constitution in 1969, Mao's name appeared in it eleven times; it repeated endlessly that 'Marxism–Leninism–Mao Zedong Thought' formed the guiding line of the Party. Lin Biao, who as head of the Army had been Mao's greatest supporter in the Cultural Revolution, was designated by name in this constitution as Mao's heir. The most bizarre thing, however, is that the Party constitution phrased the reasons for Lin Biao's elevation purely in terms of his relationship with Mao; this had become more important than Lin's concrete accomplishments. It said: 'Comrade Lin Biao has consistently held high the great red banner of Mao Zedong Thought and has most loyally and resolutely carried out and defended Comrade Mao Zedong's proletarian revolutionary line. Comrade Lin Biao is Comrade Mao Zedong's close comrade-in-arms and successor.'

The cost of the Cultural Revolution had been monumental. There was a general attack on intellectuals, the 'stinking ninth category'. All institutions of higher learning were closed for several years, due both to the struggles being conducted against their administrations and faculties, and to the fact that the students were busy being Red Guards. A significant number of colleges were reopening by 1970, but others did not do so until 1972, and the academic quality was far below the levels that had prevailed in 1965. For a relatively backward country trying to modernize itself, this was a hideous disaster. The disruption was less severe in primary and secondary education, and in industry, but still significant. The take-over by Red Guards of considerable portions of the railroad network had affected almost all sectors of the economy.

In more general terms, China suffered from a general breakdown of law and order, the effects of which endured long after the Red Guards had been shipped out to the countryside. Crime rates increased drastically, and street gangs appeared in many of China's cities. The enforcement of birth-control policies slackened, and took several years to restore. Corruption within governmental and economic units flourished. Most fundamental, the relationship between political discourse and reality was severely damaged. Most governments tell a certain number of lies, but the level of lying in Chinese public life reached incredible levels during and after the Cultural Revolution.

The process by which China had been breaking out of its international isolation was also set back by several years. As all aspects of revolutionary purity became crucial, foreign influences especially came under attack. The PRC, which despite its conflicts with the Soviet Union and India had won steadily greater international acceptance, and by 1965 had been approaching its longstanding goal of replacing the Guomindang as the representative of 'China' in the United Nations, withdrew into virtual isolation. Ambassadors to foreign countries were called home. After the radicals had taken over the Foreign Ministry, China's remaining foreign contacts came to be conducted in a rather strident fashion. When Chinese in various countries came into conflict with the governments of those countries, Beijing mobs sometimes invaded the embassies of the offending governments.

Probably the worst such incident was the attack on the British embassy. There existed a substantial Communist organization among the Chinese population of the British colony of Hong Kong. In 1967, the PRC began encouraging the Communists in Hong Kong to seize control of the colony. The British administration in Hong Kong resisted successfully, and with remarkably little use of physical violence. In August 1967, a mob of Red Guards protested British actions in Hong Kong by sacking the British embassy in Beijing. They gave the chargé d'affaires a severe beating, tore the clothing from female members of his staff, etc. This incident was so clearly harmful to China's interests that in its aftermath Zhou Enlai was able to reduce the radical influence on the conduct of China's foreign relations, and rein in the Red Guards somewhat. This did not undo the damage already done.

The detonation of China's first hydrogen bomb in June 1967 was complicated by the efforts of Maoist radicals among the workers and technical staff at the testing site to 'seize power' from those in authority. At facilities as vital as this, however, serious efforts were made to restrain the chaos. The radicals at the nuclear testing site had invited a group of student Red Guards to come and join them, but these had been arrested before reaching the site. China's ability to detonate a hydrogen bomb as early as 1967, and to orbit an earth satellite in 1970, reflects the respect that continued to be given to the technical experts, many of whom had been trained in the Soviet Union or the West, working on these projects.

Perhaps the most striking thing is the way, while the revolutionary frenzy was permitted to disrupt China's relations with much of the world, the crisis in Vietnam, which posed serious dangers to China during the American escalation of 1965–68, was handled calmly and rationally. The PRC put well over 100,000 military personnel in the northern section of North Vietnam, mostly construction units working to keep the railroads open, but also anti-aircraft gunners and so on. This constituted an unmistakable warning to the United States that China would if necessary fight to defend the Democratic Republic of Vietnam. However, none of this was given much publicity. The Chinese personnel were clearly visible to US reconnaisance – indeed in some cases they did not dig in against air attack as much as they might have wished, because to do so would have rendered them less visible – but the attention of the American public was not drawn to this fact, and so when the United States government limited its actions against North Vietnam it did not appear to be giving in to Chinese pressure. The careful way the PRC avoided inflammatory rhetoric on this one issue is remarkable in the context of the times.

The organizational structure of the Communist Party was destroyed in most areas. However, while many individual military officers were purged, order and discipline were at least partially preserved in the armed forces. Even the administrative structure of the government got some protection. Zhou Enlai, who as premier headed the government hierarchy, served as a sort of moderator in the Cultural Revolution, trying to limit the spread of chaos. He did not try to oppose the Cultural Revolution, but he did what he could both to preserve the government as an organization and to protect many of the individuals who were attacked as followers of the capitalist road. The most extreme radicals naturally hated him, and he later became almost a patron saint to those who wanted to repudiate the Cultural Revolution. Mao, who was well aware that China needed some of the trained people whom Zhou was trying to protect, tolerated Zhou's activities and quashed all attacks on him; indeed, Zhou remained premier until his death in 1976.

Even on less vital matters the frenzy could be moderated in practice. When the Cultural Revolution began to attack the 'Four Olds', the treasures of China's traditional art came under suspicion as 'relics of feudalism'. Any museum or private home where they were displayed was in danger of attacks by Red Guards. However, the destruction of art was not by any means all-encompassing; large quantities were trucked off to safe warehouses. Today some of this material is once again on display in Chinese museums, and other pieces have recently been sold to Westerners, at premium prices, to raise money to help pay for China's modernization.

The initial results

As comparative order was restored in 1969 and 1970, and 'Revolutionary Committees', many of whose members came from the PLA, were established to replace the administrative structures that had collapsed in the preceding years, some of the concrete goals of the Cultural Revolution became more clearly visible. The May Seventh Cadre Schools, the 'barefoot doctors', and a massive reorientation of the educational system exemplify these.

Many administrators and intellectuals were sent to May Seventh Cadre Schools, which combined prolonged and sometimes very unpleasant manual labour with intensive indoctrination. Late in 1969 a rotation scheme was proposed under which, at any given time, one-third of the personnel of leading organizations would be released from their administrative duties to engage in manual labour in farming or industry.

The 'barefoot doctors' were people who were given a few months of medical training and were then set to providing rudimentary health care at the village level. These people really did make a very substantial contribution to public health, especially by working on the prevention of common diseases. They could refer difficult cases to clinics having fully trained medical doctors.

The whole spirit of the educational system was altered to reduce gaps between the educated and the uneducated, between mental labour and manual labour. A system that had been geared to giving a fairly good education to a few people was redesigned to give a lower level of education to a great many people. Enrolment in secondary schools expanded dramatically, while enrolments in colleges and universities, when these finally reopened, remained below 1965 levels. The duration of schooling was reduced (at the college level, five-year courses of study were typically cut to three years). Even during those years the number of hours of academic learning was reduced, so the students could devote a considerable portion of their time to manual labour, enough so their labour actually had economic value. Some grew vegetables in school gardens. Others worked in school workshops, which might turn out consumer goods and other simple products, or even have a contract with some nearby factory to produce components for large machinery.

The ability to demonstrate academic competence, through written examinations, was de-emphasized; this had been a major desire of the first Red Guards, in 1966. In the early 1970s, when an attempt was made to revive written examinations as part of the selection process for college admissions, one student handed in a paper that consisted simply of a denunciation of examinations and those who did well in examinations.

To tell the truth, I have no respect for the bookworms who for many years have been taking it easy and have done nothing useful. I dislike them intensely. During the busy summer hoeing time, I just could not abandon my production task and hide myself in a small room to study. That would have been very selfish. If I had done that, I would have been guilty of being unworthy of the revolutionary cause which concerns both the poor and lower-middle peasants and myself, and I would have been condemned by my own revolutionary conscience.

His statement was given national publicity, and he became a hero for having expressed such a correct revolutionary attitude.

College students were no longer recruited straight from the secondary schools, and were no longer selected by primarily academic criteria. Graduates of secondary schools had to complete at least two years of manual labour in agriculture or industry before becoming eligible to be nominated by their co-workers to go to college. Proper political attitudes, and a willingness to respect manual labour and those engaged in it, were supposed to be key criteria in this selection. Beyond this, when the colleges and universities began to reopen in 1970, many of the students selected for admission were not secondary graduates at all. Some had never even graduated from *lower* middle (junior high) school.

The fact that political criteria were more important than academic ones ensured that politically powerful individuals would be able to arrange admission for their children, or the friends of their children, or just someone who offered them a bribe. This was known as entry through the 'back door'. Personal influence became, in fact, more important than before the Cultural Revolution; those evaluating the political attitudes of college applicants very seldom found fault with anyone favoured by a powerful official.

It was in the early 1970s that China finally began a really massive attack on population growth. The population control programme introduced in the 1960s, which had collapsed in the Cultural Revolution, had been essentially limited to the cities. The campaign that began in 1971 covered the countryside as well, and was astonishingly effective; the national birth rate dropped by about a third within five years.

Aftermath: 1969–76

In 1969 the formal apparatus of the Communist Party, which had fallen apart during the Cultural Revolution and had been replaced by the Revolutionary Committees, began to be restored. By late summer of 1971 there was, once again, a CCP provincial committee in every province. Military men still had a major role, and Lin Biao, minister of defence, was openly acknowledged as Mao Zedong's chosen successor. As public order was restored and the Party apparatus was revived, Mao felt less need for the army and its commander, and he began to cut down on Lin Biao's authority. Lin, perhaps uncertain as to how far this would go, and not willing to give up the supreme power that had seemed within his grasp, apparently began plotting against Mao.

The details are difficult to discern; most of what we know comes from statements made, after Lin Biao was dead, by the people who had sided with Mao. They include some truly preposterous slanders against Lin, ranging up to the claim that Lin had been planning to make China a colony of the Soviet Union, and also that he had been planning to abolish socialism, handing the factories over to the capitalist class and the land to the old landlords, as private property. The propaganda of Chinese power struggles had abandoned all concern for truth or even plausibility. What seems fairly clear is that a power struggle occurred, and by September 1971 Lin had lost. He and some of his followers apparently tried to flee to the Soviet Union by air, but were killed when their plane crashed in Outer Mongolia. The cause of the crash is still uncertain.

The fall of Lin Biao was not revealed at once to the Chinese people. For a while Party leaders said nothing in public. Then there was a long period during which they denounced Lin Biao in the most extravagant terms, but without mentioning his identity; their denunciations simply used the euphemism 'political swindlers like Liu Shaoqi'. By the time they were willing to attack Lin Biao by name in the press, he had been dead for almost two years.

Mao had removed a great many people from important positions on a purely temporary basis during the Cultural Revolution. It had always been assumed that most of those sent to May Seventh Cadre Schools would eventually return to their former work, once they had been subjected to intensive reindoctrination, and once radicals satisfactory to Mao were ensconced in some key positions. The defection of Lin Biao increased Mao's need to broaden his base of support by bringing non-Maoists back into the Party and the government. During the early 1970s, even people who had been charged with the most serious crimes during the Cultural Revolution, and who seemed to have been placed permanently beyond the pale, were in many cases rehabilitated and restored to positions in the Party and government. The most important of them was Deng Xiaoping, rehabilitated in 1973. By 1975, as both Mao Zedong and Premier Zhou Enlai became too ill to handle any great amount of business, Deng was given control of the day-to-day operations of the Communist Party's Central Committee. Some of the most extreme leftists, such as those responsible for attacks on foreign diplomats in Beijing in 1967, were repudiated and even put on trial. Not all leaders purged during the Cultural Revolution were rehabilitated, but even so the range of those being asked to work together was very wide.

Extreme left-wing leaders who had risen to power in the Cultural Revolution felt that the past was returning to haunt them. They had long been worried about the danger posed by old attitudes and traditions, hence the enthusiasm of their attack on the Four Olds starting in 1966. When they saw the enemies they thought thy had defeated returning to power their worry about the strength of the past increased still further.

When attacks on Lin Biao finally began to mention him by name, they did so in the context of a 'Campaign to Criticize Lin Biao and Confucius'. The CCP propaganda apparatus charged that Lin Biao had been a Confucian, that he had used the ideas of Confucius to try to turn back the clock and undo the work of the Communist Revolution. Party propagandists tried to portray Confucius, in turn, as a reactionary who in his own lifetime had been trying to defend an old, declining ruling class – the slave-owners – against the encroachment of feudalism. The CCP praised Shi Huangdi and the Legalists (previously the villains of Chinese historiography) as valiant advocates of reform and progress, who had set out to destroy Confucianism as part of their struggle to destroy the slave-holding system the Confucians defended. The curious thing is that the people who conducted the Campaign to Criticize Lin Biao and Confucius were saying both (a) that Confucianism had already been the ideology of an outmoded and declining class of exploiters even in the third century BC, and (b) that the power of Confucian ideology was still dangerously great in the 1970s.

The ideological journal *Red Flag* said that Shi Huangdi had been correct in burying alive 460 Confucian scholars to stop them from 'recounting the past to the detriment of the present'. Apparently, as the radicals watched conservative CCP leaders purged in the 1960s returning to power, they were beginning to feel that the oppressive influence of the past was almost immortal. No measures were too drastic to use in the effort to destroy this influence, and no measures could give one any confidence that one would succeed in destroying it.

Left and Right

Policy differences between the leftists and rehabilitated rightists focussed mainly on economics. The leftists emphasized the importance of egalitarian attitudes. They did not like the use of bonuses or salary differentials to reward those who did the most, or the most useful, work. A system of economic incentives would reinforce and reward the old habit of trying to obtain as much as possible for oneself, instead of inculcating the socialist idea of doing what was best for society regardless of personal profit.

Confucian social theory held that a merchant, a man who makes a living by buying things in one place and then selling them elsewhere at a higher price, is fundamentally a parasite; he has made a profit without actually having produced anything. Mao's leftist followers took a similar view, but pushed it to greater extremes. They even disliked the idea of a productive enterprise concentrating on products that were in great demand, since such goods commanded high prices and could thus allow the enterprise to make a large profit, out of proportion to the amount of work done.

The leftists wanted to build a decentralized, self-sufficient local economy. Every region and indeed every commune was urged to achieve self-sufficiency in grain, ignoring the fact that in some areas far more value could have been obtained from the land by concentrating on tea, vegetables, and so on.

There was a short-list of industrial products for which production was encouraged everywhere. These included iron and steel, chemical fertilizer, coal, cement, agricultural machinery, and agricultural implements. Many areas went well beyond the short-list, but there were risks to getting too imaginative. Making something that brought a very high price, because nobody else was making it, could open one to charges of 'putting profits in command' and 'following the capitalist road'.

The leftists tried in some ways to reduce the gap between the cities and the villages. They greatly expanded the programme, originally begun in the 1950s, of sending educated young people (usually recent secondary school graduates) out to the countryside. About 17 million were 'sent down' between 1968 and 1978, of whom about 10 million were still in the countryside in 1978. Most of them lacked skills directly relevant to farming; the villages actually had to be paid to accept them. Some of the young people 'sent down' were actually persuaded to look on this as an opportunity to 'serve the people', but for most it was agony. If they managed to grit their teeth and smile it was from fear that if they opposed the programme they might be punished by being kept in the wilderness for life. They were reluctant to marry; a settled family life would reduce their chances of getting permission to return to the city. However, the very reasons they found life in the villages so hateful – the much lower level of material and cultural life, the paucity of educational facilities, and the intellectuals' traditional lack of respect for manual labour and the people who engaged in it – were the reasons Mao and his associates felt it was so vital to break down the barriers between city and countryside, at whatever the cost. Mao felt that people who despised village life so totally were, *ipso facto*, unqualified for the leading positions in society that the young graduates were hoping to fill.

The leftists advocated putting 'politics in command'. If someone argued that a coal-mine that operated at a loss should be closed down, they said that this was putting 'profits in command', and that the national need for more coal should take precedence over the selfish desire for profit. They did not consider that if a mine operated at a loss – in other words, if the value of the coal it produced was less than the cost of operating it – this might be a sign that its continued operation was not really in the national interest. 'Politics in command' also meant that people should do their work out of a desire to build socialism, not in order to win higher incomes for themselves. Selfishness was very nearly the ultimate sin. (Note the extreme contrast with traditional Chinese values, in which accumulating wealth for oneself, in order to be able to provide security for one's family, was a virtue.)

The rightists felt that the most important task of the revolution was to build up a strong and wealthy China, and that this task required stability and hierarchy. China was an underdeveloped country; everywhere one turned there were problems that were not being solved fast enough because of the shortage of technically trained personnel. To strip a qualified engineer of the authority he needed to manage a construction project simply because he did not have the correct political attitude, or to choose for engineering training, on political grounds, someone other than the candidate who showed the greatest technical aptitude, were luxuries China could not afford. Deng Xiaoping, by the 1970s the leading spokesman for the Right, used to say that he did not care whether a cat was black or white as long as it could catch the mice. Most of China's technicians, managers, administrators, and intellectuals – the urban élite – were convinced that the work they did required more skill than the manual labour done by the common people, and was of greater benefit to society. Both pride and self-interest made them cling, despite prolonged Maoist indoctrination, to the idea that they were entitled to a higher status and a better life than that enjoyed by the bulk of the population.

The rightists, even rehabilitated ones, seldom dared express their views clearly in public. The savagery with which the Left suppressed unacceptable ideas, even in the aftermath of the Cultural Revolution, made open debate impossible. Indeed the leftists may have executed more people in 1970 and 1971, quietly in various prisons and cellars, than during the publicly visible mass struggles of 1966–68. When major leftist leaders were brought to trial in 1980, it was charged that between 1966 and 1976 their persecution of their opponents had caused the deaths of about 34,000 people. Besides outright executions, this figure apparently included people driven to suicide, and those such as Liu Shaoqi who simply died of abuse and neglect while imprisoned. It cannot have included the casualties of the Red Guards' street fights; including those deaths would have produced a figure many times higher.

The leftists had written principles of free expression into the Constitution, but they were not above surgically severing the vocal cords of a woman who expressed herself in a manner they found too objectionable. Dominating the media of public propaganda, they presented their one-sided argument with all the carelessness of people who know that if they confound logic, falsify the facts, or misrepresent the views of their opponents, nobody will dare to point out the errors.

Argument in terms of allegory, and indirect language that avoided saying outright what the author meant, had proliferated. There had been a long period during the Cultural Revolution when the press had been filled with denunciations of 'the chief person in power following the capitalist road', also known as 'China's Khrushchev'. At least in that period everyone knew that the un-named culprit was actually Liu Shaoqi. In 1973, people similarly understood that denunciations of 'swindlers like Liu Shaoqi' actually referred to Lin Biao. But in 1974, when a campaign to criticize Lin Biao and Confucius became so important that it was clearly intended to be relevant to current political struggles, it was not obvious which living persons were the real objects of this criticism nominally directed against dead ones.

The difficulties of dialogue and compromise were increased by the way the policies of each faction formed an interrelated whole. A rightist style of industrial management *required* a rightist style educational system to train the managers, and so forth.

Efforts to combine elements of rightist and leftist policies often worked out badly. In agriculture, the role of free markets in a predominantly socialist system was a source of almost perpetual trouble. The norm for China, since the collectivization of agriculture in 1955–56, had been to allow the peasants to have small private plots on which they could grow the crops they wished, and raise their own livestock. At some periods, especially during the relaxation of controls in the aftermath of the Great Leap Forward, the peasants had been allowed considerable freedom to sell their produce at local markets, for whatever they could get for it. Where there were acute shortages of many products, such free-market activities could be extremely profitable. The head of one commune discovered in the early 1960s that the peasants were selling privately raised chickens at the local market for five times the price of chickens marketed through government channels. He decided that this was a very dangerous phenomenon; it would lead the peasants to use the desire for profits as the guide to their actions, and to neglect collective production in favour of private production, where they could obtain higher incomes without having to work any harder. He applied pressure to prevent the peasants from using the local market. In the mid 1970s, some peasants on another commune decided to take some of the land on which they had been growing grain, and use it instead to grow melons, which were in great demand and were commanding high prices. This was collective production, not private, but it was following the 'capitalist' principle of 'putting profits in command', and it clearly had the potential to make these peasants much richer than those of their neighbours who were adhering to the ideologically correct course of growing grain. Local authorities responded by destroying the melon crop shortly before it would have been ready for harvest.

The leftists devoted much more attention to vilifying the followers of the 'capitalist road' than to figuring out how to make the socialist road function effectively. They emphasized spirit over material reality; they chose policies that displayed their own correct revolutionary attitudes, rather than basing their actions on the concrete results of this or that policy. This could go to preposterous extremes. Thus we have the story, supposedly true, of a man who was trying to fight a forest fire, but getting nowhere because he lacked effective tools. He finally gave a loud cry of 'Long Live Chairman Mao', lay down, and tried to put out the flames in his immediate vicinity by rolling on them. This had no significant effect on the fire, and he was quickly burned to death. His sacrifice accomplished nothing, and it rendered him unavailable for constructive action, but it demonstrated tremendous revolutionary dedication and lack of concern for self-interest. He was praised as a great hero.

The emphasis on spirit over results had some of its most important effects in policies dealing with salaries and incomes. The leftists hated the notion of material incentives – the idea that people's incomes should be linked to the amount and quality of the work they did, so as to motivate them to work better. In their view, this legitimized greed; it taught people that trying to increase their personal incomes was normal, indeed something that the government encouraged.

Inequality of incomes was more acceptable if it were not linked directly to work, because then it would not so obviously encourage greed. It was permissible for a factory to pay Mr Wang half again as much as Mr Chen during a given month on the grounds that Mr Wang had seniority, or that he was classified as a permanent rather than a temporary employee, or that he simply held a position for which a high salary was traditional. It was not permissible to pay Mr Wang more if the reason was that Mr Wang had worked harder. The result of such policies was widespread absenteeism, laziness, or simple indifference on the part of industrial workers.

Many Communists had shown a similar preoccupation with attitudes in the earliest years of the revolution, for some of the same reasons. Most people have a certain view of the way the world works. If they are presented with a single new idea or a new situation, they can usually fit it into their existing mental structure without having to discard old assumptions wholesale. However, if they try to assimilate too many new ideas in a short time, the old world view may collapse through inability to integrate the new material. The problem is that the new material will not automatically organize itself into a reasonably complete and coherent world view, capable of replacing the old. People in such a situation often find themselves unable to answer fundamental questions. In their struggle to organize a new world view they will probably have to oversimplify matters, and they may become rather inflexible. Only gradually will they acquire enough confidence in the new structure of ideas to be able to apply it flexibly and effectively in a variety of situations.

Communism in the 1920s had represented such a departure from the traditional world view that few Party members could really predict the results of a given policy. They had no mental landmarks to tell them which way to go, to tell them that one policy would work while another would not. For lack of a better option, they often chose to do whatever would show a correct revolutionary attitude. Experience gradually filled in the gaps in what had at first been a sketchy and incomplete as well as inflexible Communist world view; it taught them how to work within the new system and how to judge what the actual results of a given policy might be. The making of Party policy had begun to be based on concrete realism by 1935, and was so based to a very large extent by 1949. Mao, however, had cast his followers adrift again in 1966. He demanded that they abandon the patterns of thought and behaviour that had become standard since the Revolution of 1949, and once again they were left frantically trying to learn how to apply a totally new world view to the complexities of the world. The results were the same as they had been a generation before: confusion, bad decisions, and a tendency to mask one's own inner uncertainties by acting self-righteously and attacking one's opponents with exceptional fanaticism and ferocity.

The full extent of the leftists' failure can be seen in the fact that some of the phenomena they most detested actually became more widespread during the period of their domination. Before 1966, moderate CCP leaders had established mechanisms by which the market, and the forces of selfishness in general, were harnessed to serve CCP goals. The leftists, their sense of revolutionary purity outraged, abolished many of these mechanisms during the Cultural Revolution. Selfishness and the market did not disappear, however. What happened was that selfishness and the market were unharnessed; they no longer operated in such a way as to serve CCP goals.

In the early 1960s the market had played a significant role in the economy. It had for the most part been a rationalizing force, which rewarded those who produced needed goods, and directed goods to those who wanted them. In the early 1970s the market played an even greater role, but it was primarily a market in favours, influence, and bribes. Under the old market system one might have obtained scarce raw materials by paying for them, at so much per ton. In the new market one gave the relevant official a banquet, a hundred cartons of cigarettes, a dozen melons, or permission for his nephew to enter college. If one had *guanxi* (personal ties) with the relevant people, a tremendous range of goods and services were available through the 'back door'. Cadres and officials unselfishly dedicated to duty and the public interest were probably less common in 1972 than in 1965.

International relations

During the Cultural Revolution the Left had been highly xenophobic, but this was more a matter of the Red Guards' determination to demonstrate their revolutionary purity than a reflection of Mao's fundamental goals. Once the frenzy had died down, the Left and the Right agreed on the desirability of resuming the movement, broken off in 1966, towards broader diplomatic and trade ties with non-Communist nations including the United States. The US government, on the other hand, had realized that good relations with China would improve its position both in the Vietnam War and in its world-wide competition against the Soviet Union. In April 1971, the Chinese signalled an interest in friendlier relations by inviting an American table tennis team to tour China. The United States responded by inviting a Chinese team to tour the United States (this was called 'ping-pong diplomacy'), and, in a more substantive vein, significantly relaxed the US economic embargo against China. Henry Kissinger, President Nixon's national security adviser, visited Beijing secretly in July 1971; President Nixon went with great publicity in February 1972.

Even before Kissinger's 1971 visit to Beijing, American pressure on the international community to isolate the PRC, and treat the Guomindang leaders in Taibei as the sole legitimate government of China, had been weakening. Canada shifted diplomatic recognition from Taibei to Beijing in October 1970; other nations followed in rapid succession.

The shift was most visibly measured in the UN, where for many years a motion had come annually before the General Assembly to replace Taibei with Beijing as the representative of 'China'. The resolution had gradually gained support, and in 1965 had come fairly close to success. The Cultural Revolution interrupted the trend for four years, but in 1970 this motion actually won a majority, 51 to 49, in the General Assembly. The USA managed only to postpone the inevitable by pushing through a procedural resolution stating that this was an 'important question' that would require a two-thirds margin to pass. In 1971, realizing that the PRC might be about to win, the USA belatedly introduced a resolution that both Beijing and Taibei should be represented in the UN, as separate governments. This 'Two China' policy might have had some success if it had been tried when the United States still had the power to say that the PRC could enter the UN only at the cost of coexisting with the Taibei representatives there, but by the time the United States made the offer it had no such power; the PRC had the votes to enter the UN without having to make any concessions. Besides, Chiang Kai-shek's government vigorously denied that it was in the UN as a representative of the area it actually ruled – the island of Taiwan. It still claimed to be in the UN in its capacity as the government of China as a whole, and denounced the American 'Two China' proposal as a 'gross insult'. The US, seeing little support for the 'Two China' resolution, did not push it vigorously enough actually to bring it to a vote. In October 1971, the General Assembly voted 76 to 35 to expel the representatives from Taibei and seat those from Beijing.

When President Nixon visited Beijing a few months later, he told Zhou Enlai privately that the United States accepted that there was one China, and that Taiwan was a part of China. 'We have not and will not support any Taiwan independence movement.' But Nixon would not repeat this publicly. And since Chiang Kai-shek was firmly committed to the idea that Taiwan was part of China, Nixon did not feel his statement obliged him to abandon support for Chiang's government on Taiwan. Most of the US military forces on Taiwan were supporting the US military effort in Vietnam, and could be expected to withdraw as the US withdrew from Vietnam. But some of them were on Taiwan as part of the US alliance with the Republic of China. Nixon told Zhou that the withdrawal of these US forces would 'go forward as progress is made on the peaceful resolution of the problem.' Since there was no visible prospect of any peaceful resolution to the hostility between the PRC and the ROC, Nixon was in effect telling Zhou that US forces would remain on Taiwan, supporting Chiang Kai-shek against the PRC, for the indefinite future. This blocked the establishment of full diplomatic relations between the United States and the PRC.

Trade with the capitalist countries grew along with diplomatic contacts, so much so that China had to expand its port facilities quite substantially by the mid 1970s. In July 1971 Britain once again abandoned the discriminatory treatment of China in regard to export restrictions; from this point onward British businessmen could sell to China as freely as to the USSR. The following month, Britain signed a £20m. contract for commercial jet aircraft. In February 1972 the United States followed the British lead in allowing China to purchase as wide a range of non-military goods as the Soviet Union. Before the end of 1972 the Chinese were negotiating to buy jet airliners from France and the USA as well as Britain. For several years the United States continued to refuse to sell equipment having potential military uses, but did not try to prevent its allies from doing so. The French sold some helicopters in 1974, and Britain signed a very large contract for Rolls-Royce jet engines in 1975.

In a step with an even greater potential for subverting the purity of the Revolution, China began sending a few students to Britain to study at the end of 1972. The number of students sent to capitalist countries increased dramatically later in the decade.

The Right was more enthusiastic about very broad contacts, commercial and intellectual as well as diplomatic, than the Left. Mao and the leftists stressed that the Chinese economy should be fundamentally self-sufficient. They accused the rightists of wanting to enslave China to the foreigners physically by depending on imported goods, which would have to be paid for by the export of vital raw materials, and also mentally by depending on imported technology and scientific ideas, and by accepting foreign technologies without change where the leftists wanted to make extensive modifications in imported designs. But the difference was only one of degree; the leftists accepted the need for substantial foreign imports, and the rightists did not want as much as the leftists charged.

Study questions

What was Mao Zedong trying to achieve in the Cultural Revolution? To what extent did he achieve it?

What did the Cultural Revolution do to China's education system?

Why did the opening up of relations between the United States and China occur when it did?

CHAPTER 9

The post-Mao reforms

Mao Zedong and Zhou Enlai presided over a government that was, by the mid 1970s, an uneasy balance of Left and Right. In a sense they were the leaders of opposing factions, but they were both to some degree compromisers. Zhou Enlai, the pragmatic administrator, had done what he could to protect many of the individuals attacked for right-wing views during the Cultural Revolution, but had not defied Mao. Mao, the extreme leftist, had a lifelong faith in the ability of human beings to change. He was convinced that individuals with incorrect views could be reformed. He had tolerated the restoration of some of his most important opponents to positions of considerable power in the early 1970s, under conditions that forced them to adapt their behaviour to his views. When both Zhou and Mao died in a single year, however, their respective factions were left under the leadership of people much less disposed to compromise.

The Right soon won an overwhelming victory. Some important leftist leaders were under arrest within a month of Mao's death, and the Right consolidated its control of the government and the Communist Party over the next two years. The rightists then began a remarkable series of reforms, undoing much of the legacy of Maoism.

The deaths of Zhou and Mao

Zhou Enlai died, after a lingering illness, in January 1976. He quickly became, in death, a greater symbol of resistance to radical policies than he ever had been in life. His enemies on the Left, led by the group later known as the 'Gang of Four' (Jiang Qing, Yao Wenyuan, Zhang Chunqiao, and Wang Hongwen), cut the official ceremonies of mourning for him to only a few days. However, in late March and early April many cities saw public

PLATE 9.1 *In April 1976, thousands of Chinese crowded into Tiananmen Square to present wreaths in memory of Zhou Enlai and read the inscriptions attached to wreaths others had presented. When the authorities tried to interfere, shortly after this photograph was taken, the crowd rioted. (© AP/PA Photos.)*

demonstrations in honour of Zhou's memory, some of which involved open attacks on the leftists, and all of which were at least acts of implicit defiance after the way the leftists had cut short the formal ceremonies of mourning in January. The best publicized of these incidents was at Tiananmen, the place in the centre of Beijing where major parades and important official ceremonies were usually held. The Qing Ming (Ch'ing Ming) festival, during which the Chinese have traditionally commemorated their dead, came early in April. Thousands of people brought wreaths in memory of Zhou, many with politically oriented poems attached, and presented them at the Monument to the Heroes of the People in Tiananmen Square. When the radicals removed the wreaths the demonstration became a riot. The radicals, instead of trying to co-opt Zhou's memory, had handed it over to their enemies by acknowledging openly that any strong gesture of respect for Zhou was equivalent to a gesture of hostility against themselves. They blamed Deng Xiaoping for the Tiananmen disorders, and he was purged for a second time two days after the incident.

The position of the 'Gang of Four' was secure only as long as Mao was available to support them. They had been promoted very rapidly, on the basis of Mao's personal favour rather than any solid record of accomplishment. Wang Hongwen in particular was called 'the helicopter' for the speed with which he had risen out of a Shanghai textile mill to take, at the age of 36, the number three position in the CCP hierarchy. These people might have been adequate as representatives for a national consensus, but what they were trying to do was to maintain a policy line that, even had it been honestly applied, would have gone against both the beliefs and the personal interests of much of the Chinese élite. Intellectuals and veteran bureaucrats were united by a belief that the main purpose of the revolution was to develop and modernize China. They felt that Maoist policies were not only denying them the rewards they had earned by their work, but also denying them the conditions they needed to work effectively on national construction. Deng Xiaoping had commented bitingly on the practice of 're-educating' senior scientific personnel, to prevent them from becoming too separated from the masses, by requiring them to spend much of their time doing unskilled manual labour. 'The Academy of Sciences is an academy of sciences and not an academy of production or of education. It is not an academy of cabbage cultivation; it is not an academy of beans.'

Beyond this, the egalitarian principles of the radicals were marred by pervasive corruption; the Maoist élite that had arisen in the Cultural Revolution flagrantly failed to practise what it preached. The technocrats felt that they were being asked to give up the power and privilege they had earned by their work on national construction not in order to make everyone equal, but so that power, privilege, and illicit personal luxuries could be enjoyed by those who had 'waved the red flag' with exceptional vigour.

The moderates even manipulated the radicals into an implicit admission that radical egalitarianism was inconsistent with rapid economic growth. The moderates used public slogans calling for greater economic construction, with the implied message that there should be rewards and political promotion for the technocrats who alone were capable of leading this economic construction. The radicals, opposing the idea of rewards and promotion for the technocrats, felt impelled to attack the slogans. By doing so they implicitly accepted the notion that only the technocrats could lead economic growth, and allowed themselves to be cast in the role of opponents of growth. They also reinforced the stereotype of the moderates as a group of technically skilled people, and lost the opportunity to attack the moderates by concentrating propaganda attacks on the considerable number of important moderates who did not in fact have any conspicuous skills.

Mao died on 9 September 1976. The first stage of the ensuing power struggle was brief; the Gang of Four were under arrest within less than a month. There were two main factions among the winners of this struggle. One was made up of the less extreme Maoists, people who had risen to power during the Cultural Revolution and its aftermath, and who wished to preserve many of Mao's policies, but who (unlike the Gang of Four) were convinced of the need to cooperate with more conservative elements. Their most important leaders were Hua Guofeng (Hua Kuo-feng), an administrator from Hunan whom Mao had designated as his successor a few months before dying, and Wang Dongxing (Wang Tung-hsing), the former commander of Mao's bodyguard, whose control of military forces in the city of Beijing had played a crucial role in the arrest of the Gang of Four. Hua Guofeng came to occupy, simultaneously, the posts of premier, Communist Party chairman, and chairman of the Party's Military Affairs Commission. Even Mao had not held such a combination of offices. This group published an editorial in the *People's Daily* on 7 February 1977, saying that whatever Mao had said must be obeyed and whatever he had decided must be upheld. Critics called this slogan the 'Two Whatevers', and sometimes referred to its advocates as the 'Whatever' faction.

The other main group was made up of right-wing leaders who had been purged in the Cultural Revolution. Some of them were back in positions of power by the time Mao died, but others were still in disgrace. Deng Xiaoping, the most important member of this group, was not publicly rehabilitated until July 1977. The slogan of this group was 'Seek truth from facts'.

The balance of power appeared fairly even at first. Deng and other recently rehabilitated rightists, while they pushed to reverse much of what Mao Zedong had done during the ten years of the Cultural Revolution, had to mute their public statements to avoid antagonizing the 'Whatever' faction too badly. They blamed leftist excesses on Lin Biao and the Gang of Four, not on Mao himself. They pretended to regard the Cultural Revolution as a great and good thing, whose spirit had been violated by the vile actions of Lin Biao and the Gang of Four. However, as the months went by the Right consolidated its position, and the Left weakened. The extent to which the Cultural Revolution as a whole was being re-evaluated was suggested by the changing evaluation of the Red Guards. People began to refer to them, in public discussions of the Cultural Revolution, as the 'beating, smashing, and looting elements'.

Each rightist rehabilitated and restored to a position of influence was another voice to support the rehabilitation of further rightists, and further reductions in the influence of the Left. When the Central Committee of the Communist Party met in the famous Third Plenum[1] in December 1978, the right-wing elements led by Deng Xiaoping were able to establish effective control.

Wang Dongxing, the most radical person remaining in the top Party leadership after the arrest of the Gang of Four, had lost almost all of his real power by the time of the Third Plenum; other leftists had lost even their nominal positions. Hua Guofeng's status as Mao's chosen heir was losing its value, and perhaps even becoming a liability as veiled remarks began to appear about the foolishness of believing in the 'Two Whatevers'. He lost his major offices soon after; Zhao Ziyang replaced him as premier in September 1980, Hu Yaobang (Hu Yao-pang) replaced him as Party chairman in June 1981, and Deng Xiaoping replaced him as chairman of the Party's Military Affairs Commission in June 1981. China was increasingly dominated by those who wanted to move quickly and decisively away from Mao's policies. As they became more open in repudiating the actions of Mao's last years, they began to discuss in public his responsibility for those actions. By 1980, Mao's portraits and statues were coming down.

The Gang of Four, Mao's most fervent disciples, finally went on trial in the winter of 1980–81 along with some followers of Lin Biao. The trial was intended to complete the discrediting of their left-wing policies, but also to show China's return to the rule of law. The government said, very loudly, that the defendants were not on trial for having lost a power struggle, but for having used illegal means – committed crimes – in trying to win it. Some of the crimes were rather political in nature, such as saying terrible things about Deng Xiaoping in order to persuade Mao to purge Deng in the spring of 1976, but others were things that would be considered crimes anywhere. Several of the defendants were accused of having framed innocent people of various crimes during the Cultural Revolution, and of having used torture to extract false confessions as part of these frame-ups.

Two of the Gang, Yao Wenyuan and 'helicopter' Wang Hongwen, confessed their crimes and expressed repentance; they were given long prison terms. The other two, Zhang Chunqiao and Mao's widow Jiang Qing, refused to admit they had done anything wrong. Jiang Qing defended

---

[1] This was the third plenary meeting that the Central Committee had held since the Party Congress of August 1977.

herself vocally, denying that she had committed some of the acts attributed to her, and saying that everything she actually had done had been at Mao's orders. Zhang Chunqiao simply refused to dignify the proceedings by saying anything whatever. Both were given suspended death sentences; they were supposed to have two years to show signs of repentance, at the end of which time the decision would be made whether to execute them. (Neither was particularly repentant, but their sentences were commuted to imprisonment anyway.) Jiang Qing finally committed suicide in 1991. The other three were released from prison, without publicity, at various dates on medical grounds. All had died by 2005.

The anathema pronounced on Lin Biao and the Gang of Four, the most conspicuous leftist leaders, was reflected on the lower levels of the Chinese power structure. Deng Xiaoping could not carry out a clean sweep, but he did remove large numbers of leftists from Party and government positions.

The new leadership launched a formal reversal of the verdicts on almost all the people, whether still living or (like Peng Dehuai and Liu Shaoqi) long since dead, who had been criticized or purged by the Maoists during the previous twenty years. Deng Xiaoping is said to have reported, in January 1980, that 2,900,000 people had been rehabilitated. The most important group among those being rehabilitated was made up of Communists who had been purged in the Cultural Revolution as followers of the 'capitalist road'. The CCP as a whole was adopting large portions of their path. But beyond this, many victims of the 1957–58 'Anti-Rightist' campaign were rehabilitated, in the flesh or posthumously. Members of the pre-revolutionary capitalist class came once again to enjoy some of the respect that had been shown them, as economic managers, in the mid 1950s just after their factories came under government control. They were even to be given financial compensation for losses they had suffered during the Cultural Revolution.

Even the landlord and rich peasant classes benefited from the change of attitudes. The Communist Party expressed no regret for the harsh way these people had been treated during the land reform of the 1940s and 1950s, but the way the CCP made class status hereditary was making some class labels ridiculous by the late 1970s. Those classified as 'landlords' included increasing numbers of children whose *parents* had not even been born at the time their families' lands had been confiscated and distributed to the poor. In 1979 the CCP decided that most 'landlords' no longer needed to be categorized as such.

The fact that some members of the 'bad classes' were supposed to have their class labels removed did not eliminate discrimination against them.

Indeed, some administrators simply did not obey the decision on allowing them to change their class label. However, discrimination was significantly reduced.

The programme of the new leadership was summarized as the 'Four Modernizations' – modernization of agriculture, industry, science–technology, and national defence. These policies involved abandoning important parts both of the details and of the spirit of Maoism. Explicitly, they involved the adoption of Western-style technology, some of which had to come from foreign countries. Implicitly they involved placing much less reliance on the collective spirit of the masses.

In education there was a renewed stress on academic achievement and a downgrading of egalitarian ideals. Leftist leaders had stressed the goal of giving at least some sort of education to everyone; they had hoped to make not only primary education but also several years of secondary schooling universal as quickly as possible. The moderate leadership that came to power in 1976 did not completely abandon these goals, but it assigned them a lower priority. The main thrust after 1976 was on providing a really good education to a limited number of people. The Cultural Revolution had led to a tremendous expansion in secondary education, while college enrolments had dropped. This naturally affected the quality of secondary schooling; in Guangxi province, for instance, it created a situation in which only about 30 per cent of the senior-middle-school teachers were college graduates. After 1976, as leftist policies were repudiated, college enrolments expanded rapidly, while the growth of secondary enrolments slowed and in some areas was even reversed.

Academic standards were raised. Some schools at every level were designated as 'key' institutions; they were given the best teachers, the best students, and more funds. Some of the key secondary schools, in turn, chose to concentrate on teaching their best students, the ones likely to shed glory on the school by achieving college admission, and gave little attention to the average and below-average students. ('Key' schools and the use of streaming within schools seemed rather extreme departures from egalitarian ideals, even by post-Maoist standards, and these concepts therefore came under attack late in 1981.)

Students were once more admitted to colleges primarily on the basis of written entrance examinations. Students were allowed to proceed directly from secondary school to college, without an intervening period in productive labour. The requirement that they devote a large proportion of their time to manual labour during their years as students was also relaxed. The idea that China must import large amounts of foreign technology was once more accepted, and thousands of Chinese students were sent to study in capitalist countries. The rewards for academic excellence increased significantly; not only could one win a place in the next higher level of the educational system, but when one was through with school one could generally avoid being assigned to work in the countryside.

Competition for entrance to colleges and universities was very keen. Education seemed likely once more to be a main channel of upward mobility, and China could not, in the foreseeable future, hope to give a college education to more than a fraction of the people wanting one. In 1980, only 4.6 per cent of the graduates of senior middle schools passed the entrance examinations for institutions of higher learning.

The number of peasants in secondary and tertiary institutions may have been significantly lower under these policies than under the Maoist line. However, one should note that under these policies a small number of peasants did get a good academic education. During Mao's last years, no peasants at all had received such an education, because no such thing had been available to anyone of any class.

By 1979 the programmes for sending educated youth from the cities to the countryside were being cut back sharply, and those young people who did well in secondary school were no longer in serious danger of being 'sent down'. The government was not even able to keep in the countryside those who had been sent down in previous years. These young people became quite aggressive about asserting their newly restored status; some from Shanghai, allowed to visit their homes for a holiday in the spring of 1979, rioted and stopped rail traffic for several hours to protest the fact that they had not received permission to return to the city permanently. Of the 10 million in the countryside in late 1978, about half had returned to the cities, legally or illegally, by the autumn of 1979; most of the remainder had done so by the end of 1980. Those in the cities illegally posed the greatest social problems. They had neither a great respect for authority, nor much access to gainful employment. This combination produced the same result in China as in many other societies: a wave of crimes committed by unemployed youths.

Improvements in the status of the educated had both positive and negative implications for the economy. The extent to which technically trained people could be fitted into crucial jobs, and the extent to which the best qualified candidates could be chosen for training, clearly improved. In 1980, Hu Yaobang (soon to replace Hua Guofeng as chairman of the Chinese Communist Party) argued that recent improvements in the position of the intellectuals were not only desirable; they needed to go much further than they had.

We must value intellectuals and attach due importance to culture and education. Intellectuals play an important role. In our country there is a general lack of learning among our people, and learning is inseparable from intellectuals. We have not yet finished our job of implementing the relevant policies towards intellectuals. Intellectuals have not been used appropriately enough. They still face many practical problems, such as housing, separation from spouses, and wages. Yet, surprisingly, there are comrades who have declared that our treatment of intellectuals is overdone and that intellectuals are beginning to show conceit. The existence of this attitude shows that there are great obstacles to implementing policies on intellectuals. Now when the intellectuals have just begun to raise their heads, a few comrades are trying to beat them down. This demands that we work on these comrades.

For years our attitude towards learning and intellectuals has been in many respects neither materialist nor Marxist. Today we must change this state in which intellectuals are discriminated against.

For a brief time around 1980, it seemed that the intellectuals were gaining a privileged status. Millions of educated youths moved in from the countryside to the more desirable cities, in defiance of the restrictions that prevented the ordinary rural dweller from doing the same. Many had skills that could only be put to effective use in the cities, but many others would have been of more use in the countryside than in the cities. When they were permitted to return to the cities none the less, local officials sometimes had to create jobs for them there, jobs that often made little use of their skills and education.

It soon became apparent that the treatment of the intellectuals was not, overall, to be nearly so favourable as this initial policy led some people to expect. The flow of educated youth returning to the cities from the countryside, which had become a veritable flood by 1979 and 1980, was not allowed to continue until all who wanted to return had done so. Many found themselves still trapped in the countryside. Hundreds of people protesting this fate staged an illegal demonstration on the steps of CCP headquarters in Beijing in 1985.

In the cities, the intellectuals were often very poorly paid. One heard jokes that a man who repaired the outside of the head (a barber) could make more money than a man who repaired the inside of the head (a brain surgeon). Salaries for teachers were so low that some observers expressed astonishment at their dedication, their willingness to go on trying to educate their students when given hardly any reward.

Intellectuals were also frustrated by their lack of political influence.

The question of individual freedom

It is possible to exaggerate the extent to which personal freedom was expanded after the fall of the Gang of Four. Serious opposition to the Communist system, or actions likely to compromise national unity, were not permitted. Also, the Party maintained and even strengthened some policies that by the standards of most societies would be remarkable intrusions on the life of individuals. That secondary-school graduates were no longer shipped out to the countryside *en masse* did not mean that people were allowed to live where they wished; what it meant was that the bureaucrats who told people where they had to live were more friendly to secondary-school graduates than they formerly had been. The system that had bound the peasants to the villages was loosening, but it was not abolished. Much of the massive migration from rural to urban areas that took place in the 1980s was illegal; about one-sixth of the people in the largest cities in 1985 were there without residence permits. In the cities the government used a great array of very strong pressures to make people postpone marriage, and avoid having many children once they did marry (see below).

Some dissidents came into the open, especially in Beijing, to demand increased democracy, but they were repressed quite severely when the government felt they had gone too far. For a few months there was a 'Democracy Wall' in the middle of Beijing, near Tiananmen Square, where dissidents were allowed to display wall posters criticizing the regime. It was established in November 1978, just as the balance of power within the Communist Party was swinging decisively in favour of Deng Xiaoping. Posters began to appear demanding that the legacy of Maoism be repudiated much more completely than was occurring at that time, that a wide range of misbehaviour by cadres and officials be corrected, and that the range of personal freedom be expanded drastically. Some of these posters actually criticized Mao by name, something unheard of until that time. Once it had become apparent that the Party had decided at least temporarily not to interfere, the wall became a medium for the expression of a startling range of ideas. Some posters commented openly on the fact that the Chinese people had less freedom and less control over their govern-

PLATE 9.2 *'Democracy Wall', Beijing, 1979. Chinese reading posters critical of the Beijing government on a brick barrier around a bus depot that became the focal point of dissent. (© AP/PA Photos.)*

ment than the people of many foreign countries. The posters could reach far more than just the people who came physically to read them; foreign journalists regularly visited the wall, read important posters, and sent out of the country summaries which were then incorporated into radio news broadcasts. Chinese in many cities could listen to foreign radio broadcasts and keep track of what was appearing on the wall in Beijing. Within a few weeks the dissidents moved from writing wall posters to publishing journals and establishing formal organizations, such as the China Human Rights Alliance.

The posters on the 'Democracy Wall' represented the next stage of the development that had begun in the Tiananmen demonstrations of April 1976, when political statements defying the current Party line had been attached to many of the wreaths commemorating Zhou Enlai. Indeed one of the major demands in posters on the Democracy Wall was that the officials responsible for the suppression of the Tiananmen demonstrations be punished.

The dissident movement, in Beijing and elsewhere, was profoundly disturbing to the typical Communist bureaucrat, who had grown accustomed to an environment in which Party policy could not be questioned or criticized. Even Deng Xiaoping, who agreed with some of the criticisms voiced on the Democracy Wall, and was not terrified of the notion that views with which he disagreed could be aired in public, may have been annoyed with the more extreme of the dissidents. The most conspicuous was Wei Jingsheng, a twenty-eight-year-old electrician who had been a Red Guard in Beijing during the Cultural Revolution. Wei attacked the whole Communist political system. He argued that the Four Modernizations would be a sham unless a fifth modernization – democracy – were added. He denounced Deng for making only a pretence of introducing democracy while in fact practising dictatorship. His denunciations of past and current government behaviour were savage. He published, for example, a description of the way inmates of the political prison north of Beijing known as Q1 were starved, beaten, and sometimes subjected to more extreme forms of torture.

What an irony! These prisoners are gifted individuals who joined the Communist Party to fight for the freedom, prosperity and peace of China and of all mankind; they devoted the better part of their lives to achieving and maintaining power for the Party. Many of them were imprisoned in the past by the Party's enemies; now they are being detained by the very party they helped to create. They are at the receiving end of modern techniques of torture. Every day they face psychological and physical destruction . . .

Dictators can create any number of political excuses for eliminating their opponents. They talk glibly of 'class enemies', 'counter-revolutionaries', 'rebels', and 'traitors'. Dictatorship needs these labels, and it needs prisons like Q1. Or to put it the other way round, if political imprisonment was somehow made impossible, then one of the indispensible tools of dictatorship would have been removed. So we are dealing here not just with the humanitarian implications of imprisonment for the individual, but with the significance that such imprisonment has for the basic rights of the people as a whole. In order to avoid the disastrous consequences of dictatorship, one must first eliminate the conditions that create it and sustain it, including the dehumanizing system of political imprisonment and persecution.[2]

---

[2] The quotation comes from *Seeds of Fire: Chinese Voices of Conscience*, edited by Geremie Barme and John Minford, pp. 282, 288–9.

The bureaucrats must have been greatly relieved when Wei gave them an excuse to act against him: they inflated his willingness to talk to foreigners about the border fighting between China and Vietnam into a charge of furnishing military secrets to foreigners. He was arrested in March 1979, and before the end of the year he had been tried and sentenced to fifteen years in prison. Others were also arrested. (Wei Jingsheng served almost the whole of his sentence. Released late in 1993, in poor physical health, he promptly resumed public criticism of the government. In 1995 he was again imprisoned, but in 1997 he was released and deported to the United States.)

The Party leadership, ending the period of uncertainty that had allowed dissidents even as extreme as Wei Jingsheng to speak out for a few months, announced that the four fundamental principles under which the PRC operated were: (1) the socialist road; (2) the people's democratic dictatorship (dictatorship of the proletariat); (3) the leadership of the Communist Party; (4) Marxism–Leninism and Mao Zedong Thought. As the Central Committee put it in 1981, 'Any word or deed which denies or undermines these four principles cannot be tolerated'. The Democracy Wall in Beijing was closed down in December 1979; most of those in other cities had already been abolished. During 1980 the Party decided to remove from the Constitution a provision guaranteeing the right to put up wall posters.

The crackdown of 1979 was not remotely comparable to the Anti-Rightist campaign of 1957, when severe punishment had been applied not only to those who had seriously criticized the Communist system in the 'Hundred Flowers', but also to huge numbers of people who had not engaged in any serious criticism. Deng Xiaoping in 1979 gave severe punishments to only a minority even of those who had engaged in serious criticism during the 'Democracy Wall' period. In the years that followed, political speech remained far more free than it had been under Mao. It was sometimes possible to disagree with particular policies of the Party without attacking, or being accused of having attacked, the four fundamental principles. Perhaps even more important than this widening of the limits of permitted speech was the change in the spirit with which the limits were enforced. The citizen who wished to ignore politics and get on with his or her own affairs could do so in relative safety. Few political cadres were inclined to leap at the first sign of ideological deviation, and place the worst possible construction on it. Only through the most extraordinary bad luck did the person who had made a single careless statement, or who had said something ambiguous that might be interpreted as an attack on Party policies, get into serious trouble. It was even possible for dissidents to test the limits of the system, doing things that they knew might lie beyond the range of permissible action, gambling on the probability that if they did not venture far beyond the limits they would not be punished too severely. This was far from constituting free speech, but it represented a tremendous improvement when compared with the repression the Maoists had practiced. It created a political situation in China quite similar to the one Khrushchev had created in the Soviet Union in the mid 1950s, when he dismantled Stalinism.

Freedom of artistic creativity followed approximately the same path as freedom of political expression. There was a burst of liberalism in the late 1970s, when Deng Xiaoping and the moderates were just consolidating their power, but soon the Party renewed demands that art and literature serve the cause of socialism. There was a campaign against 'spiritual pollution', but it remained far milder than similar campaigns under Mao.

China and the world

Chinese foreign policy after the death of Mao continued to be dominated by hatred of the Soviet Union. This was extended to Vietnam, which after the end of the Vietnam War in 1975 drew increasingly close to the Soviet Union. Besides leading to the unification of Vietnam, the war had put a pro-Vietnamese government in power in Laos. At the end of 1978, after bloody border skirmishes, Vietnam invaded Cambodia, overthrew the Khmer Rouge (who had established a remarkably brutal Communist regime in Cambodia in 1975), and installed what proved, for the next few years, to be effectively a puppet government. China felt that for a Soviet ally to have this much power in Southeast Asia was intolerable. The Chinese invasion of northern Vietnam in 1979 was intended to draw Vietnamese troops off from Cambodia. When the invasion failed to achieve this goal (the People's Liberation Army performed very poorly) the Chinese withdrew instead of escalating, but they continued trying in various other ways to undermine the Vietnamese position in Laos and Cambodia.

Chinese diplomats all over the world urged other nations to distrust and oppose the Soviet Union. In a striking reversal of earlier pronouncements, China even took the attitude that strong NATO armed forces were a contribution to world peace.

China greatly expanded its contacts with the United States and Western Europe after 1976. In some areas, as with the establishment of full diplomatic relations with the United States in 1979, China was simply continuing to work on the goals Mao had set in the early 1970s. But by 1979 the

Chinese and US governments were even willing to cooperate in military matters if they could do so quietly. The United States agreed to supply very advanced equipment for an electronic observation post in Xinjiang, to eavesdrop on the communications of missile-testing ranges in the Soviet Union. The equipment was manned by Chinese, but the data that it acquired were shared with the United States. In 1980, in the aftermath of the Soviet invasion of Afghanistan, military cooperation became more public. The US secretary of defence, Harold Brown, toured Chinese defence installations, and the USA announced its willingness to sell non-lethal military equipment to the PRC. In 1981 this was broadened to include the possible sale of military weapons, but the USA continued to restrict the sale of high technology, both in regard to weapons and to civilian items such as computers which might be turned to military uses.

In 1983, the USA decided to ease the restrictions even on advanced technology, but some limits still remained, as was indicated by the arrest in February 1984 of five people charged with conspiring to smuggle over $1,000 m. worth of very advanced military equipment to China in violation of US law.

The willingness of the Western powers to sell weapons to China had much smaller results than might have been expected. The principal problem was simply money; China could not even begin to pay for all of the equipment its antiquated armed forced needed. Officers who for years had been told that they could not have a lot of modern weapons because what mattered in warfare was the human factor – fighting spirit and the support of the masses – were told instead that they could not have modern weapons because the country could not afford them. The result was a great deal of negotiation over arms purchases, but few deals actually consummated. A £100 m. agreement for Britain to equip destroyers of the Chinese navy with electronic equipment and Sea Dart missiles, for instance, fell through in 1983 because the Chinese decided they could not afford such a purchase.

Economic contacts with the West, already broadening in the early and mid 1970s, continued to develop. In Mao's last years the Chinese were buying considerable numbers of factories from foreign capitalists; by 1983 they were negotiating for the purchase of four nuclear reactors. The tourist trade continued to expand; over 200,000 foreigners visited China in 1981. China even entered into joint business ventures, in which a foreign capitalist helped to build a factory in China and remained part-owner, with a right to part of the output. Major petroleum companies such as British Petroleum (BP), Atlantic-Richfield (ARCO), Exxon, and Shell obtained contracts to explore for oil in China's territorial waters. By 1990, Western tourists visiting Tibet could stay at a Holiday Inn in Lhasa.

Educational exchanges had much more far-reaching implications. In a direct sense, China accepted the fact that the type of knowledge in which the West surpassed China was vitally important, and that China had to learn from the foreigners. This carried the implication that having learned from the Westerners could be a legitimate source of prestige and perhaps even power for a Chinese. The limited expansion of the number of foreigners permitted to study in China, and in some cases teach in Chinese colleges, seemed unlikely to have massive effects. However, a much larger number of Chinese were going abroad for study. By 1983 there were 9,000 or more Chinese studying just in the United States. Such students learned about the much higher standard of living abroad, and encountered a range of ideas and permitted behaviour incomparably greater than that found in China in recent decades. There was a clear possibility that some of them might become profoundly subversive influences when they returned home, and indeed they played crucial roles in the democracy movement of 1989.

The CCP did its best to minimize contact between Western visitors and the Chinese people, but it was aware that some such contact would occur none the less. The *People's Daily* commented that in the process of borrowing and learning from the outside world, some things would be brought into China that should not have been, but that people should not become alarmed and should not use this as grounds to cut off importation of foreign things.

There were, of course, a variety of sources of friction between China and the West. Some were momentary, such as the US decision to grant political asylum to the Chinese tennis-player Hu Na in 1983. Of the long-term problems, the most important was Taiwan, where the government of the Republic of China (the Guomindang regime) still claimed to be the government of all China. The PRC suggested that the problem of reunification might be settled by compromise, in which Taiwan would retain substantial autonomy and even its own armed forces, but the Guomindang firmly rejected such offers.

The USA, the last major power maintaining full diplomatic relations with the Republic of China, announced in December 1978 that it intended to break that tie, and establish full diplomatic relations with the PRC. The United States made this shift early in 1979, and also terminated (with one year's notice) the mutual defence treaty that the USA and the ROC had signed in 1954. But the US Congress promptly passed the 'Taiwan Relations Act', declaring that it was the policy of the United States 'to preserve and promote extensive, close, and friendly commercial, cultural, and other relations between the people of the United States and the people on Taiwan', 'to provide Taiwan with arms of a defensive character', and 'to maintain the capacity of the United States to resist any resort to force or other forms of coercion that would jeopardize the security, or the social or economic system, of the people on Taiwan'. The PRC did not mind the continuation of cultural, commercial, and unofficial diplomatic contacts between the USA and Taiwan, but it was shocked by the continuation of an unofficial security relationship, and arms sales.

In 1979 and 1980, the United States also opened up its markets, in an oddly tentative fashion, to Chinese exports. China was given what was somewhat misleadingly called 'most-favored-nation' status, meaning that the tariffs on Chinese goods entering the United States would be at the normal level, the level applied to goods from most other nations. But this was not handled as a firm, long-term commitment. Every year for the next two decades, the US Congress had to vote (often after a contentious debate) to extend China's 'most-favored-nation' status for the next year. And the United States continued to restrict the export to China of technologies having possible military uses.

By 1982, offended by US relations with Taiwan and probably also by the quirks of US trade policy, the Chinese began to distance themselves from the USA and to improve their relations with the Soviet Union. This ended, at least for the moment, prospects that the USA and China might actually become allies. Sino-Soviet trade revived to some extent, and in 1983 the two countries began exchanging a small number of students, for the first time in over twenty years. However, there was no real thaw between China and the Soviet Union; China remained sharply critical of Soviet behaviour in Afghanistan and Indochina. In the second half of 1983, after a substantial loosening of US restrictions on exports to China, the relationship between China and the USA began to improve again. Early in 1984, Chinese Premier Zhao Ziyang visited the USA as well as Canada; US President Reagan soon visited China in return.

Economic reforms

China's great problem remained its fundamental poverty. Most of the people still lived in villages not far above subsistence level, where they scraped out a living without enough machinery, fertilizer, or land. When crops failed through drought or flood, as they did in parts of two provinces in

1980, the peasants went hungry. The industrial sector of the economy was not growing rapidly; backward technology and very inefficient operating procedures held production down in most factories.

When the Four Modernizations first won acceptance as guidelines for government policy, many industrial planners assumed that they would get the large modern factories of which they had dreamed for so long. China went on a construction binge. Whole factories were purchased from abroad; others were built with local resources. Coordination was poor; sometimes two factories were built where there were only enough raw materials, or only enough electric power, for one actually to function. Besides this, the range of projects being started simply ran beyond what the Chinese economy could pay for. By 1978 the frenzy for new projects reached a level that reminded some people of the Great Leap Forward. In 1981 the government was forced to adopt stern restrictions on capital construction. China's problems could not, in any case, have been solved simply by building more factories within the framework of the existing system.

Once the moderates had consolidated their power at the Third Plenum in 1978, they initiated a remarkable variety of fundamental changes in China's economic system. The changes did not occur in a neat, orderly fashion, with policies clearly defined in directives from Beijing. Instead, provincial and local leaders were encouraged to experiment freely, and the successful experiments became models for national emulation. The unifying thread linking most of the reforms was decentralization – the shifting of power and responsibility from the central government to local governments, and from government to individuals.

In the first few years, the most dramatic changes were in agriculture. The income of each peasant family was linked directly to the production of that family, instead of being the family's share of the production of some larger group. At the same time, families were given more opportunity to decide for themselves how they might be able to increase their production.

Experiments with the 'responsibility system', in which a family or a small group of families was given responsibility for a piece of land or an enterprise owned by their production team, brigade, or commune, occurred quite widely in 1979. Soon afterwards some of the provincial officials who had played a major role in these experiments were promoted to top positions in Beijing; Zhao Ziyang from Sichuan became premier, and Wan Li from Anhui became vice-premier. The responsibility system was spread rapidly on a nationwide basis.

Families signed contracts with the collective organizations that owned land, by which the family promised to achieve a certain level of production, and would be rewarded very handsomely for exceeding the contract level. Some were even allowed simply to take any production above the contract level and sell it, for their own benefit, in local markets. In some versions of the responsibility system, there was still effective central planning. The brigade or production team decided what crops would be grown on a certain piece of land, how much fertilizer would be applied, and so forth, and the individual families were simply responsible for carrying out the plan competently. In other versions, nearly universal by 1984, individual families made more of the decisions. Even when elements of central planning remained, they could sometimes be circumvented. The government still attempted to discourage peasants from switching *en masse* from grain to more profitable crops. The contracts under which the land was allocated to peasant households sometimes specified that the peasants must deliver a specified yearly quota of grain. Some peasants put all their land in a far more profitable crop such as sugar cane, sold it on the market, and used part of the money thus earned to buy enough grain to meet their quotas for delivery to the state.

Late in 1980, the government decided to expand the scope of private marketing. The next step was to increase the amount of land assigned to the peasants as private plots to about 15 per cent of all agricultural land. The peasants were not responsible to the government for the use they made of their private plots; they could simply grow what they wished, for sale to the government or in private markets.

The peasants were still forbidden to go into commerce – to buy things that other people had produced, for resale at a profit. However, they had opportunities to adapt their productive activities to the goal of maximum personal profit which would have been unthinkable a few years earlier. In 1981, the *People's Daily* told peasants who were thinking of getting rich quickly by going into illegal commercial activities (which did exist on a significant scale) that instead they should try something like taking over management, on contract, of communally owned fish-ponds or banana groves. They were told that by doing this they could enrich themselves quite rapidly *without* violating current government policies. Three years later, even the restrictions on private commerce were loosening.

The Chinese press admitted openly that this represented an abandonment of radical egalitarianism; if incomes were keyed to results, some people would do better than others.

Let some localities in the country and a section of the peasants prosper first . . .

Facts have proved that it amounts to sheer illusion to suppose that socialism can be built by deliberately preventing people from getting rich . . .

It is equally absurd to maintain a low income level for people in relatively prosperous areas or units to prevent a possible polarization of society.

As early as 1980, it was suggested that the contracting out of land to peasant families should be carried so far that it would amount to a *de facto* dismantling of collective agriculture, in very large areas. There was opposition to this proposal, and most Party leaders emphasized that individual management of farmland operated within a framework of collective ownership, that the peasants had only the use of the land (not rights such as sale or rental, which they would have had if they had been its owners), and that cadres should not associate individual family management with actual ownership by forming the habit of assigning to people, for individual management, precisely the farms that their families had owned before collectivization. The amount of land allocated to a family was to depend on the present number of people in the family, not on how much land it had contributed when cooperatives were formed in the 1950s. By 1984, however, the government announced that almost all land was to be allocated to the peasants on fifteen-year contracts. Some peasants were in fact renting out their contract land. Collective agriculture was virtually dead.

The shift towards free enterprise methods in agriculture required that the principal showcase of Maoist methods be discredited. This was the Dazhai production brigade, located in the hills of Shanxi province in northern China. The peasants of Dazhai had, through monumental exertion, transformed unusable hillsides and gulches into fertile fields. They operated on highly egalitarian principles, without the usual amount of land devoted to private plots. The whole country had been urged to learn from Dazhai. It seemed a textbook case of Maoist ideals in action; it demonstrated that peasants working in a collectivist spirit, casting off personal greed and the desire for individual rewards, relying on their own powers rather than on money and modern technology, could accomplish anything to which they set their minds. Through correct application of Maoist ideas, Dazhai was credited with having built a prosperous agriculture in one of the least promising areas of China.

The rightists may or may not have suspected all along that this was too good to be true. In any case, after investigation they announced that it had not been true. Dazhai's supposed spirit of self-reliance had in fact been supported by substantial government subsidies, and even with the subsidies the actual level of production attained had not always been as high as the Maoists had claimed.

Capitalist enterprise also came to be accepted in industry. A Chinese who had funds could invest them in a workshop, hire people to work, and earn a profit out of the work done by the employees. In other words, he could, quite openly, engage in what was by Marxist economics a form of exploitation.

Even more startling, foreign capitalists were allowed to do the same. In 1980, four 'Special Economic Zones' were created, in which foreign investors would be permitted to build factories, using cheap Chinese labour to produce goods mostly intended for export. The Chinese Communist Party took this step very warily, but the temptations were great – not only to have foreign investors bring in modern machines and train Chinese workers in their use, but also to improve the prospects for reunification of Hong Kong and even Taiwan with China, by demonstrating that capitalist businesses could function profitably under the rule of the PRC. Shenzhen, by far the largest and most important of the four Special Economic Zones, bordered directly on Hong Kong. Of the other three, two were also in Guangdong province, not too far from Hong Kong, and the third was on the coast of Fujian, opposite Taiwan.

The word 'Special' in 'Special Economic Zones' reassured conservative Communists. The rules by which China operated were not being changed; the special zones were being exempted from the normal rules as an experiment, and could be scaled off from the rest of China if the experiment went badly.

The elimination of foreign influence from Shanghai after 1949 had left Guangdong – having extensive contacts with Hong Kong and the overseas Chinese communities – as China's main gateway to the outside world. The creation of the Special Economic Zones in Guangdong opened the gate much wider. Most of the capitalists who came through it were, naturally enough, from Hong Kong. They lived next door to Shenzhen, and many of them had local contacts and spoke the local dialect. By the late 1980s, Hong Kong businesses had more employees inside the People's Republic of China than in Hong Kong itself.

Finally, market principles were introduced into socialist industrial enterprises. In November 1981, the government began (very cautiously and hesitantly) to introduce policies under which urban workers had a certain degree of freedom to search for jobs on their own, rather than simply being assigned jobs. Soon the contract system, under which socialist enterprises contracted out certain operations to private individuals, was beginning to spread into retail distribution, service industries, and some light manufacturing industries.

Allowing people to follow their own economic self-interest worked out well in the short run, giving the economy needed flexibility. It did not, however, always produce justice. Great wealth might go to the person who happened to be in the right place to seize an opportunity, rather than to the person who worked the hardest. Consider, for example, the case of a certain tractor driver in Guangdong. Fellow villagers had helped make arrangements, and possibly paid part of the cost, for him to get training in handling a tractor. They had expected that once trained he would use his new skills to plough their fields. In the spring of 1981, however, he bought his own tractor, hired an assistant, and went into the transport business, hauling cargo on a trailer behind the tractor. He was able to earn what was by local standards a princely income. His neighbours' fields went unploughed; they could not afford to pay him, for the very time-consuming job of ploughing, the hourly rate he could earn in the transport business. At the time, it seemed fascinating that he could get away with this. Such an extreme of selfishness was in violation of CCP policy even in 1981, but local cadres could not or would not put a quick stop to it. A few years later, it would not have been against policy.

Unfortunately, one of the main reasons the CCP decided to tolerate individuals making themselves rich, sometimes without much work, was that the ones likeliest to be in the right place to seize such opportunities were the Party members, or their relatives. The Special Economic Zones, for example, offered higher wages and better living conditions than were available in most of China. After many children of powerful officials had used their families' influence to obtain jobs there, the special zones became less subject to political attacks from conservative Communists.

The weakening of central control and the fact that substantial amounts of wealth were once more in private hands permitted a revival of many aspects of traditional culture, some of which the CCP did not like at all. Male domination over women (never completely eradicated by the CCP) became more blatant, leading in extreme cases to the actual sale of women. Religion likewise revived. In Guangdong province, by the early 1980s some of the new private wealth was going to restore the old clan organizations, and even clan feuds were reviving.

When the Party decided to suppress its misgivings and permit the revival of the private sector, it at least reaped a quick reward in economic growth. Despite all the traumas of the revolution, China still possessed huge numbers of would-be capitalists, willing to jump into the private sector and make it a success. Such people did not exist in all Communist countries. When Mikhail Gorbachev introduced *perestroika* (restructuring) in the Soviet Union in the late 1980s there turned out to be far fewer people willing quickly to commit themselves to the private sector than there had been in China. This was not the only reason *perestroika* produced such disappointing results – Gorbachev's timidity must bear a portion of the blame – but it was a very important part of the problem.

If we ask why the capitalist spirit survived Communism so much better in China than in the Soviet Union, possible explanations include:

1   The Communist experience had been shorter in China than in the Soviet Union. China had been socialist for about twenty-five years when Deng Xiaoping began his reforms. The Soviet Union had been socialist for well over fifty years before *perestroika*.

2   The Maoists even at their worst had not slaughtered the practitioners of private enterprise on a scale matching what Stalin had done to the *kulaks* in the 1930s.

3   The capitalist spirit may have been stronger in China in the first place, even before the Revolution. The institution of private property had been more firmly established in nineteenth-century China than in nineteenth-century Russia.

Study questions

To what extent was freedom of speech expanded after the death of Mao Zedong?

How was it possible for the Chinese Communist Party, which had seemed firmly committed to socialism, to reintroduce significant elements of private enterprise in China by the early 1980s?

How close, and how friendly, had the relations between China and the West become by the early 1980s?

CHAPTER 10

The era of Deng Xiaoping

In June of 1981, the Central Committee of the CCP produced an official re-evaluation of the history of the Party, summing up the lessons of its thirty-two years in power. This document contained a total repudiation of the Cultural Revolution. It mentioned some constructive accomplishments that had been made during the Cultural Revolution, but at the end of the list it commented: 'Needless to say, none of these successes can be attributed in any way to the "cultural revolution", without which we would have scored far greater achievements for our cause.' One sees no mention of any useful results of the Cultural Revolution which really were connected with its fundamental goals, such as the spread of 'barefoot doctors', or the fact that individual peasants in at least some areas, however helpless they remained when faced with arbitrary decisions made in Beijing, really did have a better chance of resisting an unjust decision by an individual village cadre after the Cultural Revolution than before it. One sees, indeed, no acknowledgement that the Cultural Revolution had any goals worthy of serious consideration. Mao, seeing Communist functionaries behaving in a way he felt was unpleasantly reminiscent of the pre-revolutionary bourgeoisie, had spoken out in vague and apocalyptic language suggesting that the Party was becoming a bourgeois organization. The Central Committee position of 1981 was that since it was not true that the pre-revolutionary bourgeoisie had infiltrated and taken over the Party, Mao must simply have been suffering from some sort of delusion. The Central Committee wished to sweep under the rug the real complexity of Mao's views. It was able to do so, at least for the moment, partly because most of the people who wrote and talked about such issues were intellectuals who had suffered in the Cultural Revolution and had no desire to bring up the idea that it might have had some rational motivation, and partly because Mao had never presented his views to the public in a clear and rational form.

Repudiation of the Cultural Revolution, however, did not mean repudiation of Mao; he was still treated as a great revolutionary, whose merits far outweighed his errors. China's new leaders may genuinely have respected Mao's tremendous accomplishments during the early stages of the revolution; in any case they did not wish to see his memory become a rallying point for opposition to them, the way the dead Zhou Enlai had become a rallying point for opposition to the Leftists in 1976. They said that Mao was the man who, more than anyone else, had originally set the revolution on the correct path: 'Our Party and people would have had to grope in the dark much longer had it not been for comrade Mao Zedong . . .' He was the one who had adapted Marxism–Leninism to fit the concrete conditions of China, and the synthesis he had worked out, Mao Zedong Thought, was and should remain the guiding light of the CCP. The Central Committee dealt with the question of the Cultural Revolution, in this context, in a startlingly simple manner: it decided that Mao Zedong Thought consisted only of Mao's correct (earlier) ideas; that what Mao as an individual believed in the last decade of his life had nothing to do with 'Mao Zedong Thought', and indeed contradicted it. This seemed breathtakingly cynical, but it allowed Mao's name to be used as a symbol and a prop for a system Mao had spent ten years trying to destroy.

This was, however, only something to say on a question about which the CCP could not remain entirely silent. It was not an ideological position that could command genuine belief, in the way that Mao's ideas had commanded genuine belief for so many years. The wild swings in policy that the Party had undergone since the 1950s had undermined its moral authority; only a total amnesiac could believe that whatever the Communist Party said could be assumed to be correct. Many college students treated their compulsory courses in Marxist theory with undisguised apathy or even contempt; this would have been unthinkable a few years earlier.

Deng Xiaoping and his cohorts stressed order, stability, prosperity, and to some extent the rule of law. They were trying to restore confidence in impersonal institutions, to reverse the trend of the 1960s which had made Chinese politics so much a matter of conflicts between individuals and factions. They criticized the 'cult of personality' which often gave a single individual absolute power over his subordinates, either at the national level or in provincial and local organizations. They distinguished offices from the individuals who held them; they repudiated the unwritten rule under which Party leaders had lifetime tenure in their jobs, unless purged for some ghastly doctrinal error. They also tried to streamline administration. By the second quarter of 1982, restructuring of the central government's ministries had reduced the number of ministers and vice-ministers from 505 to 167.

Conversion to the rule of law was more difficult. Party policy for many years had taken precedence over formal law. This not only coloured attitudes and expectations; it left China with only the most rudimentary laws, and hardly any lawyers. Deng had new legal codes written, but there remained the problems of training lawyers to interpret and implement them, and persuading Party functionaries into the habit of obeying them. The networks of *guanxi* (personal relationships and obligations) among bureaucrats often remained more influential than formal rules.

The great advantage of the new policy line, which quickly won it considerable success, was that it relied much more on the carrot and less on the stick in winning compliance with its policies. Coercion was still substantial, but it played a much smaller role in government policy than it had before 1976. The Maoist line of economic development had called for self-sacrifice; it had called on the people to work hard and unselfishly to build a better China, in which all would someday benefit. Deng Xiaoping felt that the quickest way to build a better China was to improve living conditions immediately, to give people the level of morale they needed for further development. The economic readjustment of 1981 called, quite deliberately, for cutting back on capital construction to allow more production of consumer goods. This policy proved spectacularly successful, improving living conditions in the short run while at the same time creating a much higher rate of long-term economic growth.

The Communist Party's membership had expanded to over 50 million by the early 1990s, but its authority was weakened by corruption, internal divisions, and the collapse of belief in Marxist doctrine. It was far from capable of imposing order and discipline on a society in a state of dynamic change. China was plagued by social ills that the Communists had once assumed had been eradicated forever, or at least reduced to negligible proportions – smuggling, embezzlement, robbery, rape, and so forth. The Sichuan provincial government found it necessary in 1982 to issue an order forbidding anyone to carry weapons, explosives, or pornographic books into a school.

The background to the democracy movement

By 1981, a new leadership seemed firmly in place. Hu Yaobang was CCP secretary-general, Zhao Ziyang was premier, and Deng Xiaoping was most powerful of all by virtue of his prestige, though his highest formal position was chairman of the Party's Military Affairs Commission.

These three men were all deeply committed to economic reforms involving a large role for private enterprise. Many intellectuals hoped that they would also continue to expand freedom of expression (already far greater than it had been under Mao) and move China closer to democracy. Later events proved that these hopes were not totally unrealistic; both Hu Yaobang and Zhao Ziyang felt some sympathy for such ideas. When it came to a choice, however, Deng Xiaoping decided to preserve the political domination of the Communist Party, and his choice was to prove decisive.

Appeals for democracy had been muted after the abolition of the 'democracy walls' in 1979. They burst out again with much greater force in December 1986, when a few thousand people, mostly students, demonstrated for democracy in Hefei (the capital of Anhui province) starting on 5 December. Within days the same thing was happening in Wuhan. By 20 December, tens of thousands of students, joined by many people from other walks of life, were demonstrating in Shanghai. In early January of 1987, despite threats of punishment, Beijing students put on what seemed at the time an impressive protest in Tiananmen Square (it seems small in retrospect, dwarfed by comparison with the demonstrations there two years later).

The Party leadership did not retaliate against the mass of the demonstrators, but against a few ringleaders, and people of very high rank considered to have sympathized with the protests. Astrophysicist Fang Lizhi, vice-president of the University of Science and Technology in Hefei, had been a vigorous spokesman for the democracy movement and had helped create the climate for the first large demonstration on 5 December. He was demoted and banned from teaching. Less famous individuals were imprisoned.

Most important, CCP Secretary-General Hu Yaobang, who was considered to have been too sympathetic to the protesters, was forced to resign his position. Zhao Ziyang replaced him as secretary-general; Li Peng, minister of electrical power and a veteran bureaucrat less inclined toward democratic reforms than Hu or Zhao, took Zhao's former position as premier a few months later.

The forces supporting democracy had suffered a serious blow, but not a devastating one. Relatively few people had suffered severe punishment. The remainder were momentarily silent, but not terrorized into permanent submission. The trend toward greater freedom on economic matters was not even temporarily reversed. The island of Hainan become in effect a huge special economic zone, very open to foreigners and foreign investment.

Tiananmen

By 1989, China's economic reforms had achieved massive successes – far greater than those of *perestroika* in the Soviet Union. Not all had benefited equally, however. The rampant corruption, and the wealth accruing to the relatives and friends of important Party leaders, found little favour in the eyes of the less fortunate; a bout of severe inflation, the control of which involved a slowdown in industrial growth, was exacerbating the resentment of those with low incomes.

Many of the most dissatisfied were students. Inadequate funding for education, especially higher education (China's spending levels were low even by third-world standards) had left them living in very unsatisfactory circumstances, and at the same time they had more contact with foreigners and more knowledge of conditions in the outside world than most Chinese, and thus more awareness of the existence of alternatives to the Chinese system. Finally, despite the blows inflicted on intellectuals as a class in the previous decades, they still felt more willing than most Chinese to speak out openly and protest against conditions they did not like.

On 15 April 1989, Hu Yaobang died of a heart attack. Students in Beijing, remembering how he had been dismissed as CCP secretary-general two years before for showing too much sympathy for the democracy movement, seized the opportunity to stage demonstrations in his honour, demanding that the verdict against him be reversed but also demanding other reforms. University students were particularly eager for such an excuse that week; only two days before Hu's death, the government had revoked a previous declaration that university graduates would be permitted to search for jobs where they wished, instead of being assigned jobs by the state. Thousands of students demonstrated in Tiananmen Square on 17 April, and more demonstrations followed.

The 1989 demonstrations began among students at élite universities, and they sometimes seemed a little too aware of their status as an élite. The Chinese people sometimes referred to university students as 'God's favourites', and did not necessarily sympathize if the students claimed that they should be treated better than they were. In the end, however, the students overcame this handicap and achieved a remarkable degree of support from other sectors of the population of Beijing.

A list of seven demands drawn up in April called on the government to correct its evaluation of Hu Yaobang, to permit freedom of the press, to release details on the assets and incomes of high-ranking leaders and their children, to control inflation, to promise that there would be no reprisals for the demonstrations that had been occurring, to release honest accounts of the demonstrations, and to open a dialogue with the students.

When the government rejected the initial demands and attempted to suppress the demonstrations, the demands became more radical, reaching in some cases to the point of asking that Communist rule be replaced with democracy, but few of the students had a clear idea what this would mean in concrete terms. They also suffered an even more dangerous form of ignorance. China had not had the comparatively free press that had grown up in the Soviet Union by this time under Gorbachev's policy of *glasnost* (openness), so most of the students knew little about the recent history of their own country. They did not understand the events that had shaped the thinking of their country's leaders, or the ways those leaders were likely to respond when they saw a danger of 'disorder'.

In late April, the CCP produced a major policy statement, published as an editorial in the *People's Daily*, describing the protest movement as a dire threat to order and stability; if it were not suppressed, then all the gains of the preceding decade of reforms could be lost. This statement was greeted not with submission but with defiance; increasing numbers of non-students joined the protests. On 27 April, and again on 4 May, which was on everyone's minds as the seventieth anniversary of the demonstration that had done so much to shape the era in which the Chinese Communist Party had been born, over 100,000 demonstrators marched through Beijing.

The next form of protest introduced was the hunger strike. Thousands of hunger strikers, along with many times that number of sympathizers, occupied Tiananmen Square on a continuing basis instead of marching to it each day and then returning to their campuses.

China by this time had imported modern communications equipment. The students in Beijing used the new facilities, especially fax machines, to maintain contacts with sympathizers abroad and, more importantly, with students in other cities. The 1989 demonstrations were a national movement. Students on campuses across China staged demonstrations, sent delegations to Beijing to represent them in Tiananmen Square, and got regular reports of events there, which they sometimes broadcast over loudspeaker systems on their campuses.

When Mikhail Gorbachev visited Beijing in mid May, several ceremonies that had been scheduled to occur in or near Tiananmen Square had to be relocated or cancelled. He attended one meeting in the Great Hall of the People, but had to enter by a side door rather than through the main entrance facing the square.

PLATE 10.1 *CCP General Secretary Zhao Ziyang was purged days after going to Tiananmen Square and speaking to the protesters there. However, his assistant Wen Jiabao, who accompanied him, survived politically and became premier of the PRC in 2003. (© AFP/Getty Images.)*

The leaders of the CCP were naturally enraged, and the debate already going on among them, over how to deal with the protesters, must have intensified. CCP Secretary-General Zhao Ziyang favoured concessions; Premier Li Peng, and paramount leader Deng Xiaoping, argued for a hard line. Zhao soon realized that he had lost; when he visited the students in the square on 19 May, he said tearfully 'I came too late'. That evening, tens of thousands of troops were ordered into Beijing to impose martial law.

Astonishingly, the order at first proved unenforceable. Along all the routes the soldiers tried to use to reach the centre of the city, local citizens – the number has been estimated at 2 million – blocked their advance. The attempt to impose martial law had drawn the general population of the city into much stronger support of the students than had been shown before. The troops themselves did not push very hard. The failure to enforce martial law was a humiliation for the hard-liners even greater than the disruption of Gorbachev's visit. This helps to explain why Deng Xiaoping and Li Peng rejected a possible opportunity, two weeks later, to allow the demonstrations to fade out naturally. If the Tiananmen Square demonstrations had ended on a note of government humiliation, two things would have been certain: that the next democracy movement would be very large, and that it would come soon.

By the end of May, most of the Beijing student leaders were deciding it was time to end the affair. They had made their point, and could not plausibly hope to accomplish much more. They were also concerned about the very real danger of disease, with so many people packed into a limited space in hot weather without proper sanitation. Students newly arriving from distant cities argued for continuing the struggle, but by the first days of June most of the demonstrators had left the square.

Instead of waiting to see whether the number of demonstrators might shrink to a point at which a police operation of modest scale could sweep them away, the hard-liners sent in the troops once more on the night of 3 June. Up to this time there had been very little violence, on either side. Even the confrontations that had blocked the army's last attempt to enter the city, on the night of 19 May, had been essentially peaceful. On the night of 3 June, however, the soldiers were not willing to be stopped peacefully, and the people who swarmed into the streets to stop them were not willing to be peacefully shoved aside.

Many in the crowds had empty hands; the remainder were armed mainly with stones and bricks, sometimes with Molotov cocktails (bottles filled with gasoline) and other weapons. Most of the soldiers carried assault rifles or other firearms, but, especially in the early period of the fighting, were reluctant to make full use of their weapons. In the first hours, soldiers often refrained from shooting to kill even when rocks were thrown at them and their vehicles were torched. Later, as their orders were changed to allow more use of deadly force, and as fatigue, fear, and utter confusion took their toll (possibly exacerbated, according to unproven but plausible rumours, by the effects of stimulant drugs given to the troops by their commanders), they became much more willing to kill. Around dawn on 4 June, a tank driver crashed his tank into a non-violent crowd, crushing at least seven people to death, on no more provocation than some shouted insults. Parents of demonstrators were shot when they tried to walk into the square to search for their children. In the hours that followed, some soldiers seemed to be firing at random, even when under no visible threat or provocation.

The number killed is unknown; the total was probably somewhere between 700 and 3,000. Although the incident is usually called the 'Tiananmen massacre', very few people were actually killed in Tiananmen Square. Most of the dead were non-students killed in locations widely scattered across the city, starting hours before troops reached the square and continuing after the square had been cleared.

The citizens of Beijing who battled the army that night or simply interposed themselves between the troops and the square revealed a profound failure of the Chinese system. They enjoyed a material standard of living well above the average for China, and even the average had risen substantially over the preceding decade. Yet apparently they felt something so oppressive about the overall pattern of their lives that the students' challenge to the system had inspired joy and hope, and the military suppression of the democracy movement caused such outrage that huge numbers of non-students, not just a few thousand, were willing to risk their lives in a futile effort to stop the soldiers from reaching Tiananmen Square. The following day, hours after the army had occupied the square and the last protestors had left, military vehicles were still being destroyed (burned) in considerable numbers, at widely separated locations scattered across Beijing.

The hard-line leaders who turned the army loose in Beijing on the night of 3 June, in a situation that neither the leaders nor the soldiers understood, were in no position either to determine the scale of the violence or to choose its targets. There is no indication that they felt any remorse when they learned the result. The only indications even of embarrassment were the lies with which the government tried to conceal the size of the death toll.

In the government's version of events, the soldiers appeared as the heroes – the victims rather than the perpetrators of violence. Some soldiers had in fact been killed. Typically, these men had become separated from their units, and had then done something to focus the anger of a crowd upon themselves – firing on a crowd, racing an armoured personnel carrier across Tiananmen Square at high speed, and so on.

Local authorities in most other cities of China had the patience to bring their local democracy movements to an end without serious bloodshed, even when this meant tolerating protest marches and blockages of public transportation by students protesting the massacre in Beijing, for several days after 4 June. In Shanghai, the police allowed protestors to block many main roads for about four days.

Once the momentary crisis was over, the government made a more systematic effort to hunt down and arrest the leaders of the democracy movement. Thousands were indeed arrested, though a surprising number managed to escape abroad. This wave of repression lasted much longer than that following the demonstrations of 1986–87. Ringleaders of the

Tiananmen demonstrations were not even put on trial until January 1991, when the Persian Gulf crisis was distracting world attention from Chinese events.

The government attempted to arrest and imprison those accused of having been ringleaders in the democracy movement. In a few cases the accusation was false; the government was reluctant to admit the extent to which young students had been acting on their own initiative, and it searched assiduously for older people who might have been manipulating them from behind the scenes. Fang Lizhi, who really had helped trigger the 1986–87 student movement, had avoided involvement in the 1989 movement, but he was accused of having played a key role. He took refuge in the US embassy in Beijing, where he remained for more than a year before he was able to leave the country.

In accord with post-Mao principles, the government dealt with ordinary participants in the democracy movement with warnings, prolonged indoctrination sessions, and various punishments short of imprisonment. The movement had involved literally millions of people; this made for quite a few ringleaders subjected to severe punishment, which in some cases included repeated beatings of imprisoned individuals. But if one looks back at what the Anti-Rightist Movement of 1958 had done to very minor participants in the Hundred Flowers episode, or at what the Cultural Revolution had done to people who were merely suspected of thinking bad thoughts, the punishments given to the 1989 protesters look very mild by comparison. (The death penalty was applied not to leaders of the democracy movement, even the most important ones, but to some people charged with acts of serious violence – attacks on soldiers, destruction of a railroad locomotive – during the fighting that began on the evening of 3 June.)

At East China Normal University in Shanghai, some of the more obstinate democracy activists were assigned after graduation to rather undesirable jobs – as secondary school teachers. One wonders whether this was really an effective way for the government to ensure that there would be no more student democracy movements in the future.

Politics after Tiananmen

Zhao Ziyang had not been the only senior Communist leader sympathetic to the Tiananmen demonstrators. Deng Xiaoping, in putting together the coalition of hard-line leaders that deposed Zhao and carried out the Tiananmen massacre, had to rely heavily on very old men, his own contemporaries. Over the preceding years he had been pushing many octogenarians toward retirement, but in 1989 they were among his most important backers, and they continued to be very influential for a few years after Tiananmen.

The conservatives were dubious about the reform programme as a whole, not just about the students' demands for democracy. They even reversed the trend toward greater economic reform, for a while. This particularly applied in state-owned industries, where efforts to introduce more capitalist principles were abruptly reversed after 1989.

The hard-liners' grasp on power was by no means totally secure. They had been able to ram through the policy decisions they considered necessary; they were not in a position to transform the party, or even just its top leadership, in their image. Zhao Ziyang's replacement as CCP secretary-general was not a fire-breathing hard-liner, but the former head of the CCP organization in Shanghai, Jiang Zemin (1926–), a career bureaucrat not known to have strong political convictions.

The hard-liners, observing the obvious extent to which the democracy movement was inspired by foreign ideals of democracy, and the obvious sympathy of the capitalist world for the movement, inevitably concluded that the movement had been, as Premier Li Peng put it in March 1990, a result of 'infiltration and subversion by foreign hostile forces'. They did what they could to prevent further 'spiritual contamination'. They could not afford to exclude foreigners from the country – indeed the number of tourists coming to China in the months following Tiananmen was smaller than they would have liked – but the policies designed to prevent foreigners from getting into informal conversations with Chinese people were strengthened. The existence of 'English Corners' in various cities – Beijing's was in Purple Bamboo Park – where Chinese had actually been encouraged to go and practise their English in conversations with Western tourists, journalists, and so forth, had been an exception to the general attitude of the Chinese government even while they existed. They were formally closed in October 1989. Foreign journalists were forbidden to enter the campuses of Chinese universities.

One of the most dangerous forms of spiritual contamination – the return to China of students who had been deeply westernized while studying abroad – was temporarily curtailed without the need for any action by the Chinese government. Few such students wanted to return to China in the immediate aftermath of Tiananmen.

Not having expelled from the universities all the students who had participated in the democracy movement, the government tried to keep younger students, admitted after 1989, from having too much contact with them. At Beijing University, from 1989 to 1993, all first-year students were required to undergo a year of training in the army, in the hope that this would teach them discipline and immunize them against subversive ideas.

Martial law was lifted in Beijing early in 1990. The announcement, however, was only a formal gesture. The number of armed troops who could be seen in the city, ready to pounce on any new sign of dissent, remained very large.

By the early 1990s, some of the men who had helped organize the military suppression of the democracy movement, and had been elevated to very high positions in the process, were losing those positions again. Zhu Rongji, the mayor of Shanghai whose careful avoidance of force in dealing even with very disruptive protestors in 1989 had contrasted so sharply with the actions of officials in Beijing, was brought to Beijing in 1991 as vice-premier, with considerably more power, especially in the formulation of economic policy, than usually went with that position. He replaced Li Peng as premier in 1998.

Foreign relations

China in the 1980s did not really function as a great power on a global scale. In Afghanistan, which barely borders on China, the Chinese provided some support to the Mujaheddin guerrillas in their war against the Soviet Union and the Soviet-supported Afghan government, but China was not among the most important backers of the guerrillas.

The only area where China tried to exert a major influence was Indochina, where the PRC supported guerrillas fighting against the pro-Vietnamese governments of both Laos and Cambodia. In the case of Laos, the guerrillas remained modest in strength, harrassing the government rather than threatening its existence. In Cambodia the Chinese had a really effective local force to support, the Khmer Rouge who had ruled Cambodia from 1975 until the Vietnamese invasion of 1978. The Khmer Rouge forces were large enough and competent enough to create a genuine possibility that they could, with adequate outside support, someday return to power. This aid, which was estimated by US government officials as having been as much as US$100 million per year, finally ended in the early 1990s.

Mutual hostility to Vietnam, and to the pro-Vietnamese governments in Laos and Cambodia, provided the basis for a *rapprochement* between China and the non-Communist nations of Southeast Asia. This was most striking in the case of Thailand. During the 1960s, American officials had worried that if there were to be a Communist government in Laos, this government would cooperate with China in supporting guerrilla warfare against the government of Thailand. What actually did happen, in the 1980s, was that China and Thailand cooperated in supporting guerrilla warfare against the Communist government of Laos. The Thai government furnished instructors for at least one camp in China at which these guerrillas were trained. The Chinese were also able to send through Thailand their military aid for the Khmer Rouge forces in Cambodia.

In the early 1990s, relaxation of tensions with Vietnam left China with no points of serious hostility on any border, but Beijing kept a wary eye on the Muslim republics of the former Soviet Union, nervous that their having shaken off Communism might give ideas to Muslims in China, especially in Xinjiang.

Another possible trouble spot was offshore, in the South China Sea, where China and several Southeast Asian nations had conflicting claims to various tiny islands (and coral reefs that could be converted into islands with a bit of dredging, if a government was determined to establish an outpost there), the control of which might be crucial in determining the ownership of oil rights in the surrounding areas. In the early 1970s, China established effective control over the Paracel Islands, about 200 miles southeast of Hainan. In the late 1980s, as the growing economy made possible the funding of an expanding navy, China began moving into the Spratly Islands, even further to the south.

Much of the world was outraged by the suppression of the democracy movement in June 1989. The major capitalist countries agreed on a number of punitive measures, including cutting off loans from governments and from the World Bank, and a cessation of direct contacts by high-level officials. The Dalai Lama, who had been in exile since the rebellion of 1959 and was a symbol of Tibetan resistance to Chinese rule, received the 1989 Nobel Peace Prize.

The impact of the loans cut-off was very substantial while it lasted; Japan had been negotiating a loan package of about 800 billion yen (equivalent to more than US$5 billion). Enforcement of the sanctions, however, began to waver rather soon. The fact was that few of the governments involved were angry enough about the suppression of the democracy movement to give up for very long any project about which they really cared. As early as July 1989, two senior United States officials, National Security Advisor Brent Scowcroft and Deputy Secretary of State Lawrence Eagleburger, made a clandestine visit to Beijing in violation of the publicly announced ban on such high-level visits.

In June 1990, an economic summit of the seven major capitalist powers issued a declaration that accepted – though it did not really endorse – Japan's determination to go ahead with its loan package for China. The loans were to be used mainly to build or upgrade power plants, harbours, railroads, and roads. The significance of this programme for China was even greater than its US$5 billion size indicated. The reason the Japanese government was so interested in this project was that Japanese corporations wanted to make large-scale investments in Chinese industry, and needed the assurance that their new plants would have adequate power supplies and transportation facilities. Up to this time, while Japanese companies had established extensive sales networks in China, they had not put much actual investment into China.

Foreign critics pointed to a variety of human rights violations in China – not only the suppression of demands for democracy, but also such things as the ongoing repression in Tibet, and the continuing use of prison labour in China's industries, including some industries producing goods for export. Powerful elements in the United States Congress, citing these issues, Chinese arms sales abroad, and the trade imbalance between China and the USA, tried repeatedly in the 1990s to deprive China of 'most-favored-nation' trade status. Doing this would have meant massive increases in the tariffs on Chinese goods entering the USA. George Bush as president firmly resisted such ideas. When William Clinton became president in 1993 he considered using the threat of withdrawing 'most-favored-nation' status as a lever to alter Chinese behaviour, but in the end he continued President Bush's policy.

The Soviet Union did not join the chorus condemning China after Tiananmen. Gorbachev's visit to Beijing in May 1989 had been a diplomatic success despite its embarrassing circumstances, and Sino-Soviet relations continued to improve after it. Li Peng's visit to Moscow in April 1990 was the first such visit by a Chinese premier since the 1960s. By 1990 trade was expanding, there were almost two dozen Chinese-Soviet joint ventures (mostly restaurants) in the Soviet Union, and plans were being laid for a textile mill to be built as a joint venture in China. In May 1991, CCP Secretary-General Jiang Zemin and Foreign Minister Qian Qichen went to Moscow for the signing of an agreement settling some of the border disputes between China and the Soviet Union. (Agreement on the whole of the border was not reached until 2004.) By 1992, the collapse of the Soviet Union had removed most of the reasons for the former hostility between Beijing and Moscow, and Boris Yeltsin's financially strapped Russian government was eagerly selling high-technology arms to China.

During the next few years, as Russia's economy stagnated, an increasingly prosperous China extended its economic influence into Siberia.

Hong Kong and Taiwan

Hong Kong and Taiwan constituted special cases in China's diplomacy, since the populations of both were Chinese, and the governments controlling both acknowledged that all or most of the territory in question was Chinese.

The problem of Hong Kong involved a definite time limit. Most of the land area of Hong Kong (89 per cent) was legally part of China; Britain had only leased it from China, and the lease was scheduled to run out in 1997. In the early 1980s, the Chinese indicated that they intended to recover all of Hong Kong, not just the leased portion. Britain's bargaining position was weak, since China's title to the leased territories was very clear and, with these gone, what would have remained of Hong Kong would have been too small to be viable if the Chinese did not approve of it. In September 1984 the British agreed that all of Hong Kong would revert to Chinese sovereignty in 1997.

Hong Kong's prosperity was economically very important to China, and the PRC agreed to allow capitalism to persist there for 50 years after the resumption of Chinese rule, but many in Hong Kong remained fearful. The degree of toleration of private enterprise in China, in 1984, would not have come close to satisfying the freewheeling capitalists of Hong Kong.

The tension seemed to be easing a few years later. The biggest factor was the success of the Special Economic Zones in Guangdong province; increasing numbers of Hong Kong businessmen were building new factories there instead of in Hong Kong. By 1989 Hong Kong industrialists had far more employees in China proper than they had in Hong Kong.

No such agreement was reached in regard to Taiwan, but in 1986, President Chiang Ching-kuo began to loosen some of the restrictions that had formerly prevented contact of virtually any sort between people living on Taiwan and those on the mainland. Following his death in January 1988, his successor Lee Teng-hui (Li Denghui) continued the relaxation policy. After visits to the mainland were permitted, the yearly number soon grew into the hundreds of thousands. At least a few thousand mainlanders even managed to migrate to Taiwan, illegally, to find jobs in an economy with much higher wage levels than on the mainland.

Once, both Beijing and Taipei had been so firm in their refusal to send any delegation to an international meeting or sporting event attended by

PLATE 10.2 *In the Shenzhen Special Economic Zone, Guangdong Province, a modern city sprang up in the 1980s. (© Sally and Richard Greenhill/SACU.)*

the other that some events had no delegation from either side, neither having been willing to tolerate even the possibility of attendance by the other. By 1990 it was possible for a team from Taiwan to compete on the mainland when the Asian Games were held in Beijing.

Taiwanese businessmen began to invest in enterprises on the mainland, as Hong Kong businessmen were already doing. By 1992 the total of such investment was believed to be over US$3 billion. Some estimates placed it much higher than this, but reliable figures were hard to obtain. Although the Guomindang government indicated clearly that it approved the idea of Taiwanese businessmen investing on the mainland, it required that such investments be routed through Hong Kong, rather than being made directly.

The smoothness with which contacts grew was astonishing when one considered that it happened without any overt negotiation between the governments involved. Such negotiation required, at a minimum, that the People's Republic of China (Beijing) and the Republic of China (Taibei) each acknowledge that the other government existed and was a government. The PRC had been proposing for some years that there be 'one country with two systems'. The ROC finally responded with a formula defining the mainland and Taiwan as 'one country with two regions governed by equal political entities'. Despite this, when direct talks finally began in 1993 in neutral Singapore, these had to be thinly disguised by the fiction that it was two private organizations, Beijing's 'Association for Relations Across the Taiwan Strait' and Taibei's 'Straits Exchange Foundation', that were negotiating. They reached no agreement on regularizing the legal status of Taiwanese investments on the mainland, but did decide on exchanges in science and technology, particularly computers, and on technical matters like the handling of registered mail.

In the case of both Hong Kong and Taiwan, the prospect of reunification would be compromised if full democracy were to be introduced. It was the British, not the people of Hong Kong, who had agreed that Hong Kong should come under Chinese rule in 1997. It was the mainlanders controlling the Republic of China, not the people of Taiwan, who had so firmly maintained since 1949 that Taiwan was part of China. If the people of either Hong Kong or Taiwan were to obtain control of their governments, they would not necessarily take the same viewpoints.

In Hong Kong, when the Tiananmen massacre made union with China seem even less attractive than it had seemed during the preceding years, a democracy movement arose. It received a major boost late in 1992, when Chris Patten, the British governor of Hong Kong, announced his intention to allow the people of Hong Kong to elect a majority of the members of Hong Kong's Legislative Council. China protested vigorously.

On Taiwan, native Taiwanese had been rising to important positions within the Guomindang power structure since the 1970s. One of them, Lee Teng-hui, became president in 1988. This did not really mean that the Taiwanese had obtained control of the government. The mainlanders still controlled the National Assembly and some other important bodies, and President Lee could not have afforded to defy them at that time. But age would thin their ranks a little more each year.

The establishment of the Democratic Progressive Party (DPP) in 1986 finally offered the Taiwanese a legal alternative to the Guomindang, and a legal forum within which to work for Taiwanese independence. The Guomindang, however, held its own when it allowed free elections for some seats in the Legislative Yuan (this was one of three legislative bodies of the Republic of China; the other two were the National Assembly and the Control Yuan). In the 1989 elections, the Guomindang got 60 per cent of the votes, the Democratic Progressive Party 31 per cent. This gave the Guomindang the courage to place its fate much more fully in the hands of the voters; in 1991 a decision was reached to allow (over a period of slightly more than two years) elections to all seats in all three legislative bodies, ending what had previously been the lifetime tenure of mainlanders who had been chosen to represent constituencies on the mainland in 1946 and 1947. The Guomindang was rewarded with strong majorities when elections were held for all seats of the National Assembly later in 1991, and for all seats of the Legislative Yuan in 1992.

This proof that the Guomindang had forged a genuine political link with the Taiwanese population encouraged the party to hold its first free presidential election, in 1996. President Lee Teng-hui was the Guomindang candidate. The DPP nominated Peng Meng-min, who had been imprisoned in the 1960s for advocating Taiwan independence. Dissident factions of the Guomindang, who had either left the party or rejected Lee Teng-hui's leadership of it, put up two candidates. The People's Republic of China disliked both Peng (who was known to support making Taiwan an independent nation) and Lee (who was strongly suspected of holding a similar view). The PRC staged war games during the election campaign, which included the firing of ballistic missiles that landed in the seas northeast and southwest of Taiwan. If this was what it appeared to be, a heavy-handed effort to deter voters on Taiwan from supporting Lee and Peng, it failed. Lee won with 54 per cent of the vote, and Peng was second with 21 per cent. The candidates the PRC seemed to prefer got 15 per cent and 10 per cent.

Facing the future: population pressures

Controlling population growth was as vital for China, in the long run, as promoting economic growth. Even the Maoists had understood the need to limit population, despite their reluctance to admit in clear language that having too many people could be a problem. In the early 1970s they had developed one of the strictest birth-control programmes in the world. The post-Mao leaders, feeling less obligated to 'respect the people', pushed even harder. By 1979, the growth rate was reported down to 1.17 per cent per year.

Actually halting population growth was very difficult. The age structure of the population was comparatively young; the number of people reaching childbearing age each year was much larger than the number of old people who died. If every couple had been limited to two children, therefore, the population would have continued to grow quite rapidly. This explains how hard the Chinese government pushed to persuade the people to settle for one child per family.

The government continued to encourage postponement of marriage as a birth-control device, but did not rely so heavily on this tactic as the Maoists (generally hostile to selfishness and the search for individual gratification) had done. Both the government and the population assumed that virtually all young people would marry; the family system remained strong enough to make a life without marriage almost unthinkable. Some young people who really did not want marriage found that they could not defy social pressures to wed, but could arrange to marry someone whose work assignment was in a distant province, and thus ensure that the marriage would be purely a formality.

The rewards offered to couples who limited themselves to one child, once they did marry, were substantial. Preferences were made to one-child families in the distribution of ration coupons, in admission to higher education, and in job placement. The system for allocating land to peasant households either as private plots or under the responsibility system, which at first assigned land to each family in proportion to the number of people in the family and thus encouraged childbearing, was modified to reward smaller families.

When such rewards were not enough, the government turned to coercion. Every woman was required to plan her childbearing in consultation with local cadres, and although the basis of the system was supposed to be voluntary, women who became pregnant without permission were sometimes forced to have abortions. Family-planning personnel in some areas imposed compulsory sterilizations on parents having two or more children.

The Chinese had traditionally valued large families. To have at least one son was a special imperative, since sons, not daughters, carried on the family line. The one-child policy posed a severe problem if the first child was a daughter. The pre-revolutionary custom of killing female infants revived in the 1980s; some parents determined to have sons, and unwilling to defy openly government pressures against multiple children, chose to dispose of daughters. Even government pressures adequate to produce such effects as these, however, were inadequate to halt China's population growth. When the birth rate reached its lowest level, in 1984, the average woman was still having two or more children. At that point, the trend reversed itself, and the birth rate began to rise again.

The one-child family violated traditional norms. It posed the threat that the parents might have no one to care for them in their old age. There was even some question as to whether it was in the family's short-term economic interest; the government incentives offered to one-child families had to be balanced against the considerable economic value children often had in the new, more flexible economy. The Deng Xiaoping reforms were reducing the political and economic power of the Communist Party, and increasing the Chinese people's control over their lives. For the government to force people to do things they did not want to do was much more difficult than it had been under Mao Zedong. In the cities, where government power was stronger and formal welfare systems made parents less desperate to have sons to care for them in their old age, compliance with the one-child policy was widespread. Only in a few rural areas could the same be said, and the rural areas were most of China.

In the early 1990s, however, CCP leaders awoke to the danger and greatly strengthened enforcement of the one-child policy. Local officials, under threats that they themselves would be punished if they failed to reduce peasant birthrates, expanded their use of compulsory sterilizations; 12.5 million people were sterilized in 1991 alone. When hospital officials in Henan province were found to have accepted bribes to help women evade sterilization operations, two officials were sentenced to death. Parents giving birth to unauthorized children were sometimes punished with huge fines, or even the physical destruction of their homes. Such pressures reduced birthrates to levels lower even than those of the early 1980s.

By the early 1990s, parents determined that their one child (or, if they already had a daughter, their next and presumably last child) be a son were increasingly able to use selective abortion to achieve their goal. Clinics even in backward rural areas were acquiring ultrasound machines capable of distinguishing a male from a female fetus. The problem this would pose for men seeking marriage partners, when this generation of babies grew up, was obvious. The government soon began forbidding sex-selective abortions, but this prohibition proved unenforceable.

The impact on Chinese society cannot be predicted. One reason is that the true magnitude of the sexual imbalance is unknown. One possible choice for parents who wanted to have a second child after the birth of a daughter was to raise the girl, but keep her existence from appearing in government records. The number of girls growing up unregistered was believed in the early 1990s to be in the millions – not enough to bring the sexes into balance, but perhaps enough to bring them much closer to balance than the population registers showed.

Study questions

How much support was there in China for the democracy movement of 1989?

To what extent was the democracy movement a result of Western influence?

Why was the Chinese Communist Party able to hold onto power when the Soviet Communist Party collapsed?

To what extent did Deng Xiaoping expand political freedom in China?

CHAPTER 11

The boom years

Economic reform once again

The restraints conservative Communists had imposed on economic reform, after the suppression of the Tiananmen demonstrations, lasted less than three years. In January of 1992, Deng Xiaoping went on a visit to Guangdong, the province where economic reforms had been pushed the furthest and had achieved the most impressive results. While there, he launched a campaign to resume rapid economic reform and push for fast economic growth. He was going so far, indeed, that (like Mao in 1966) he had had trouble getting his views published in the national press.

Deng succeeded in overcoming the resistance of the conservatives. So many new Special Economic Zones were established that they ceased to be in any genuine sense 'special'. The rate of economic growth rose to 12 per cent for the country as a whole; the rate of growth in the rapidly expanding coastal provinces was considerably higher. This growth took place almost entirely in industry; the spectacular rise in agricultural production triggered by the first stage of Deng Xiaoping's economic reforms had slowed after 1985.

In order to evaluate the industrial growth of the 1990s, we must consider the three major sectors of Chinese industry. State industries made up a substantial portion of the total, but they showed comparatively low levels of profit, innovation, and growth. Much of their equipment was antiquated. They were often hamstrung by directives and quotas handed down by the central authorities. They were required to provide economic security, an 'iron rice bowl', for tens of millions of urban workers. What this meant in practice was that they could not fire surplus workers if their staffs were too large for the amount of work needing to be done, nor could they fire workers who slacked off when there *was* work to be done. They could sometimes offer higher wages to those who really worked, but even this proved difficult to arrange.

The rigidity of the state sector had been relaxed a bit in the mid to late 1980s. Even that limited movement was dramatically reversed after Tiananmen. Conservative Communists had been shocked by the degree of support student dissidents had won from industrial workers; they were determined to reinforce the iron rice bowl, to hang onto the loyalty of the workers in state industries. Efforts to reform the state sector by linking wages to productivity resumed in the 1990s.

What were called 'collective enterprises' were far more successful. The term conveys an image of ownership and management by the people work-ing in an enterprise, but this is misleading. Most 'collective enterprises' of the 1980s and 1990s were government-owned: established and controlled by local governments at village, township, or higher levels. But they were free of many of the encumbrances that hampered enterprises formally designated as state-owned; free to make hard work a condition for employment and reward it with good salaries, free to change products to keep up with shifts in demand, free to plough profits back into improved production facilities. In addition, few of them (except the ones that were former state enterprises, converted into 'collective enterprises' to allow them to operate more efficiently and profitably) had been in existence long enough to have a serious problem with obsolete machinery. It was no surprise that the collective sector of the economy was highly profitable in years when a third or more of the state enterprises were running at a loss, kept going by government subsidies.

Privately owned industry showed even higher rates of profit and growth than the collective sector, but the private sector had started out so tiny that even very dramatic rates of percentage growth had only brought it up to moderate size by the early 1990s. Many of the privately owned industries were not totally independent, but were tied to collective indus-tries through subcontracting arrangements. Such ties gave them valuable security in an economy that still depended so much on *guanxi* (personal ties). In the later 1990s, the private sector grew much larger, much stronger, and somewhat more independent.

In areas with strongly developing industries, local governments were wealthy, and their leaders were listened to at higher levels. Ordinary people in such areas were hardly taxed; the impressive budgets of their governments came mostly from the profits of the industries. In rural areas little touched by the reforms, where peasant agriculture made up most of the local economy, the taxes that supported local governments were a heavy burden on already impoverished peasants, and the methods used to collect those taxes were harsh. Serious efforts to lift this burden from the peasants began early in the twenty-first century (see below).

In the late 1990s, and even more in the early years of the twenty-first century, the economy was increasingly dominated by private enterprises. In the early stages of the reforms, when state-owned industries were still a very large portion of the overall economy (they employed 112 million workers in 1995), the fact that they were not very dynamic or profitable represented a major problem. But in the following decade the state sector shrank dramatically; by 2005 it had only 65 million workers. Even the collective sector, such a source of economic dynamism in the 1980s, declined in importance. It was privately owned industry that expanded hugely.

The shrinkage of the state sector caused severe social problems, especially in the old industrial cities of the northeast. Some state industries were privatized, while others were simply shut down. Millions of workers, who had thought they had an 'iron rice bowl', were left in the lurch.

The CCP resisted private ownership of land; that remained in government hands. Under a system formalized in the late 1980s, private individuals or companies could lease land for long periods, and could sell the leases to others. There was thus a market in land. But it was a market in leases, not actual ownership. This put the ordinary citizen at a disadvantage. If a large, expensive project – an office complex or luxury housing – were built on what had previously been low-value residential housing or farmland, there could be huge profits for the local governments, local officials, and/or private developers handling the project. But the people displaced often got rather little, because they had not been legally the owners of the land from which they were being evicted. Protests by people not given adequate compensation for loss of their farms or homes was becoming a significant source of social disorder by the early twenty-first century.

A new property law giving a secure legal foundation to private ownership of various sorts of property inspired considerable opposition that blocked its formal ratification in 2006. Much of the wealth in private hands had been acquired through more or less corrupt means, and many, both among the intellectuals and among Communist Party officials, felt that to give formal legal status to private wealth would be to legitimize the fruits of corruption. The law finally passed in 2007. But even this law did not give the peasants ownership of the land they farmed. They could only use it, on thirty-year leases.

China was eager for foreign investment in Chinese industry, but the government resisted opening up the economy to foreigners in some other ways. A large part of the problem was the interaction of business with politics. State-controlled banks had no choice but to make financially unsound decisions fitting the agendas of powerful officials, for example by extending large loans to shaky state-owned corporations. It seemed unlikely that they could survive if forced to compete with banks free of such handicaps. Therefore, foreign banks were for years blocked out of the Chinese banking market.

Prolonged negotiations over the extent to which the Chinese economy would be opened were required before an agreement was finally reached, in November 2001, for China to join the World Trade Organization (WTO). This agreement did not open the Chinese economy to foreign businesses as much as was normal for members of the WTO. In 2006, foreign banks finally were permitted to buy part interests in some of the largest formerly state-owned banks in China.

Exports fuelled China's economic growth. In this regard China was following the path that had been pioneered by Japan, and then followed by South Korea, Taiwan, Hong Kong, and Singapore. The bulk of the exports were industrial products, but the Chinese were quite imaginative in finding other opportunities; there were agricultural products that China exported on a significant scale. By the early twenty-first century, exports made up slightly more than one-third of China's gross domestic product.

China enjoyed a favourable balance of trade, and an odd economic relationship with the United States. China sold far more to the United States than it bought from the United States. The official US figures for the trade gap, which rose to US$201 billion in 2005 and $232.5 billion in 2006, were somewhat exaggerated. (The US government made the gap appear larger than it was by including US imports from Hong Kong in its figure for US imports from China, but omitting US exports to Hong Kong from its figure for US exports to China.) But even if one discounted for such exaggeration, it was plain that the real size of the gap was huge. The normal result of such a trade imbalance would have been a shift in the exchange rate between the two countries' currencies, increasing the value of the Chinese yuan (also called the renminbi) in US dollars. The United States, worried about the effects of the trade deficit on American manufacturing industries, pressed the Chinese to allow such a shift in the exchange rate. This would make American goods cheaper for Chinese purchasing them with yuan, and make Chinese goods more expensive for Americans buying them in dollars. It was hoped that this would lead Americans to buy fewer Chinese goods, and Chinese to buy more American goods, redressing the imbalance in trade. The Chinese government resisted American pressure, and for years kept the value of the yuan pegged at US$0.1208. In 2005, China began to allow some adjustment of the rate, but the value of the yuan had increased only to US$0.1331 by October 2007. One of the main financial tools the Chinese used to hold down the value of the yuan was to lend large amounts of money to the US government. In effect, China was importing US Treasury securities as a substitute for importing American goods and services.

The Chinese feared that if they allowed a greater shift in the exchange rate, making Chinese goods more expensive in foreign markets and thus reducing Chinese exports, this would seriously slow China's economic growth. Also, a drop in the value of the yuan would mean a financial loss for China, because it would reduce the value, in yuan, of the huge quantity of American securities the Chinese had already bought.

Aside from protesting the exchange rate, the United States also claimed that Chinese government subsidies were enabling certain Chinese goods to be sold on the American market at artificially low prices. In March 2007, the United States government imposed punitive tariffs on certain types of Chinese paper, which it said were being sold on the American market at improperly subsidized prices, and made clear that it was thinking of doing the same for other products. Many American businesses were also angry about China's lax enforcement of copyrights and intellectual property laws. Chinese manufacturers were churning out unlicensed copies of American movies, computer software, and assorted trademarked goods.

The way some sectors of the Chinese economy advanced more rapidly than others produced bizarre contrasts. China had begun earning money by putting communications satellites into orbit, for foreign customers, in 1990. But it was not until well into the twenty-first century that China started making automobiles of a high enough quality even to think of exporting significant numbers of them to Western Europe. And most agricultural production still operated on muscle power.

Money to spend

The growth of China's gross domestic product (GDP) remained very fast and indeed accelerated; the rate reached 10 per cent per year in several years early in the twenty-first century. This was so fast that many Chinese officials felt it was actually excessive, that the economy was 'overheating', and that a rate of 8 or 9 per cent would be safer. This spectacular growth

PLATE 11.1 *Shanghai: buildings of modest height, dating from the Maoist era (foreground), are being torn down to make room for much taller ones. (Photo author's own.)*

made a great deal of new wealth available. Many cities were places of dynamic, exuberant optimism. Vast numbers of people saw their incomes double in a decade or less, and had every reason to expect further large advances.

There was a huge expansion in consumer spending, especially by the rapidly growing middle class, and it was not just for small items like television sets and better clothing. China, where private ownership of automobiles had not even been legal until the mid 1990s, became the world's second largest market for motor vehicles. Roads and streets were widened, and still were often jammed with ever-heavier traffic. Chinese tourists in tens of millions visited not just distant parts of their own country, but also foreign countries. There were about 3.2 million Chinese visits to Hong Kong, and about 6 million to more distant foreign lands, in 1999. The number of visits to Hong Kong and foreign countries had more than tripled, to 31 million, by 2005.

The forests of high-rise apartment buildings that sprang up to house the newly prosperous were not just taller than those built in the 1950s and 1960s, but were in many cases far more attractive. If this added to

PLATE 11.2 *Fengdu, on the Yangzi River, shortly before the city disappeared under the lake created by the Three Gorges Dam. Across the river on higher ground was the new city being constructed to house the displaced population. (Photo author's own.)*

their construction costs, people could afford it. City governments probably applied some pressure to real estate developers on this issue – it is clear from the public parks that were being created, and the highway beautification projects, that there were officials who cared about making cities look good – but not much pressure may have been necessary. The tallest buildings were often strikingly original in appearance; in Shanghai it was said that no two of them had the same design for their tops.

Despite widespread tax evasion, government revenues expanded rapidly, and were applied to all sorts of purposes. The governmental austerity of the 1980s, when Deng Xiaoping had been reluctant to divert to any other purpose money that could go into industrial development, was over. There were huge individual projects, and huge numbers of smaller projects.

The Three Gorges Dam, on the Yangzi River in Hubei province, is the largest steel-and-concrete dam in the world. It is intended to generate electricity, to ease navigation on the river, and to control flooding. (The dam may not eliminate Yangzi River floods of the sort that killed thousands in 1998, but it should at least reduce their frequency and scale.) Construction began in 1994; the river was closed and the lake behind the dam began to fill in 2003. When the lake is full, which is scheduled to occur in 2012, it will stretch more than 600 kilometres upstream, toward the city of Chongqing. Not only villages but also towns disappeared below the waters. Because this was a very conspicuous national project, a serious effort was made to provide decent new homes – in many cases whole new towns – for those being displaced. (This did not always happen in smaller projects.)

China's first manned space mission, in which an astronaut orbited the Earth for slightly less than a day, was in 2003. A larger mission, in which two astronauts orbited for almost five days, came in 2005.

China's successful bid to host the 2008 Olympics required that the rebuilding and modernization of Beijing be carried even farther than was already occurring.

China's military forces were somewhat smaller than in Mao's day, but they had not shrunk as much as American and Russian forces, and their budget had expanded instead of shrinking. China was left with the largest armed forces in the world. The exact amount of Chinese military expenditures was difficult to define, but by the early twenty-first century, China's military budget was by some measures the second highest in the world. Its rapid rate of increase promised to make it the second highest by any measure within a few years, though still far below that of the United States. China had a modest force of intercontinental ballistic missiles, and successfully tested an anti-satellite weapon early in 2007. The quality of Chinese combat forces was unclear. The People's Liberation Army had not engaged in significant combat since the brief incursion into Vietnam in 1979, and it had not performed well in that campaign.

The government decided in 1998 to encourage a massive expansion in higher education. Hundreds of new colleges and universities opened; the number of graduates per year had expanded fivefold, to 4.1 million, by 2006. It was reported that 22 per cent of people of college age were getting some form of post-secondary education. But the economy, even growing as fast as it was, did not provide nearly that large a number of new white-collar jobs per year.

Massive inequalities

Mao Zedong had pushed a radically egalitarian vision for Chinese society. Although actual implementation of this vision had been erratic and inconsistent, it had produced something closer to economic equality than had existed in pre-revolutionary China. After Mao's death, Deng Xiaoping had

PLATE 11.3 *A two-man space capsule mounted on a Long March II rocket, shortly before its launch in October 2005. (© Zhao Jianwei/AP/PA Photos.)*

adopted a very different set of priorities. What mattered to him was that productive enterprises be built and rapidly expanded, not that the benefits from them be, in the short run, widely shared in society. As he put it, some people would get rich before the rest. He was not interested in taking wealth away from the successful, to distribute it to the less fortunate. And he did not seem to mind very much if the process that created successful enterprises was corrupt, as long as it did create successful enterprises. Jiang Zemin, after Deng's death, took a similar attitude. The result was that the gap between rich and poor went in a few years from being unusually small, by world standards, to being unusually large.

In the dynamically growing cities, mostly near the coast (though some, like Chongqing, were deep in the interior) the élite were very wealthy. They included officials who had found ways to profit from their positions, and private businessmen, the most conspicuous of whom were the owners of the industrial firms that were the engine driving the economic growth, and the real estate developers who were building and rebuilding China's cities. (There were handsome new buildings going up everywhere one looked; people joked that the construction crane had become China's national bird.) By 2007, it was estimated there were more than 300,000 Chinese whose personal wealth exceeded US$1 million. Below the élite was a large middle class, and a large class of workers who were treated reasonably well, as full members of urban society.

But below these, much of the urban workforce was made up of migrant laborers, denied many government services, paid a much lower wage than official residents of the cities, and sometimes at risk of being cheated out of even that low wage. The number of migrants, often called the 'floating' population, was about 150 million by 2006. Most of these had moved fairly short distances, but about a third were working outside their home provinces. Most of the migrants were working adults, who left their children, if any, in their home villages. But by 2004, the migrants included more than 6 million school-age children. A law passed in 2006 required city governments to allow such children to attend public schools in the cities where their parents were working. If actually implemented, this law could be expected greatly to increase the number of children brought to the cities by migrant-worker parents.

Peasants who lived close enough to wealthy cities to be able to produce high-value fruits and vegetables for urban markets could do quite well. By the early twenty-first century, some peasants in fortunate locations were even hooking themselves into the global economy, exporting apples to Indonesia, broccoli and onions to Japan, garlic to the United States, and so

PLATE 11.4 *Rice is grown in flooded fields. The seeds are initially planted very close together. When the young plants are large enough, they are uprooted by hand (above), and replanted farther apart (below). (Photos author's own.)*

forth. Fish raised in ponds near the southeast coast became a major export. Much of the interior of China, however, was made up of villages whose locations offered few opportunities either for industrial growth or for getting high-value crops to markets. Agriculture there was still based on muscle power, rather than machinery. Draft animals pulled the ploughs; farmers transplanted rice seedlings by hand; grain was harvested with small hand-held sickles. Staple crops grown by such techniques did not produce high incomes. That was why tens of millions of young men and women headed for the towns and cities, where even the low wages paid to migrant laborers were far higher than what could be earned farming the land back in their villages. The gap in educational opportunities between the advanced and backward areas, which had narrowed significantly in the last decade of Mao's life, widened again dramatically.

China's leaders spoke of the need to close the gap between the advanced and backward areas of China. Significant efforts were indeed made, and conditions indeed improved very substantially in many ways in the backward areas, but this did not really close the gap, because the wealthy areas were themselves continuing to develop at great speed. The inadequacy of government spending on health care was a particular problem in poor areas.

The new leaders Hu Jintao and Wen Jiabao, firmly in power by 2004 (see below), seemed more committed than their predecessors to reducing inequality and in particular to improving the situation of the peasants. Their slogan for this was the 'Harmonious Society'. They significantly increased the amount of government investment in the economies of backward interior provinces. They announced programmes to increase economic assistance for the poor and for the elderly, especially those who had had only a single child.

There were some hopeful trends for the status of the migrant workers. Prime Minister Wen pressed for employers actually to pay accumulated back wages they owed to migrant workers. There was significant progress – though far more was needed – toward modification of the household registry system, to allow migrants to obtain a legal status in the cities where they worked. At a more fundamental level, the one-child policy had been in effect long enough so that the number of young people reaching adulthood and looking for a job each year was declining. This improved the bargaining position of workers trying to find an employer willing to pay a decent wage.

Under Jiang Zemin, the central leadership had worked to reduce or eliminate the many taxes and fees collected from the peasants by local governments. His successors decided to abolish even the land tax, The first announcements were of a gradual process lasting until 2008, but this was soon accelerated, and the land tax was abolished by 2006. Local governments were henceforth to be supported by transfers of funds from higher levels.

The potential impact of such programmes seemed especially important in education. The Chinese population still included more than 100 million illiterates, mainly in the countryside, where schools tended to be underfunded and of low quality. Their budgets came in part from school fees, which were high enough to be a significant burden for peasants wanting to educate their children. In 2006, Premier Wen Jiabao announced that no school fees would be charged by primary and middle schools in 2007 and 2008. With rural schools becoming dependent on subsidies from higher levels of government, rather than on locally collected taxes and fees, the question was, how generous would those subsidies be? In some poor areas, the earlier stages of the programme to reduce local taxes and fees had led to serious declines in already inadequate spending on education and health care.

Tibet was a special case. It was very poor. Many of its people resented Chinese rule, and particularly resented the destruction of the religious institutions that had formerly been the centres of Tibetan culture. Many remained loyal to the exiled Dalai Lama. China's eventual response to the problem was twofold. One part was to minimize the causes of resentment by allowing a revival of temples and monasteries. Monks were recruited and trained; pilgrims could once more come openly to Lhasa to pray in temples there.

The other part was a major development programme offering better jobs, better housing, more education, a more diversified diet and other luxuries, a tree-planting programme to control erosion, and so forth. The government hoped to win the younger generation away from the traditional way of life, and away from loyalty to traditional religious leaders. But one of the problems with this was that many of the new jobs went not to Tibetans but to the swarms of Chinese who came to Tibet, especially to Lhasa, to take them. Conservative Tibetans felt that their culture was being drastically undermined.

A stable political system?

When Deng Xiaoping died in 1997, he left behind him a Communist Party that appeared to have as much unity as could reasonably be expected in a huge political organization. It did not have significant factions visibly pushing an agenda of radical reform, as it had had in the 1980s before Tiananmen. Its numerous members – just over 70 million of them by 2005 – were scattered broadly through Chinese society, including the enterprises in the private sector. Most of the CCP leaders, including Jiang Zemin, Deng's successor, were committed to carrying on Deng's programme of rapid industrial development with a dynamic private sector. This agreement on policy issues helped make this the first smooth and orderly handover of power that China had seen in more than a century. But under the surface appearance of unity there was a great deal of corruption, and also a significant minority that retained some commitment to Marxist ideals, and thought the Party's embrace of capitalism was a mistake.

Deng's reforms had left the CCP leaders with much less control of China than they had had under Mao. The fading of socialism meant that most people no longer earned their living in workplaces controlled by the Party. In general, their lives were less controlled by the Party and the institutions it controlled. At the same time, Deng had decentralized power within the Party, allowing local Party heads more freedom to make, for their areas, the decisions that were still being made by the Party. But the reduction in control should not be exaggerated. The extraordinary power of China's leaders during the Maoist era had been pathological, and everyone – not just the people but also the Party – was better off when leaders in Beijing were no longer telling peasants all over China how to farm. The Party and its leaders had much less power than they once had had, but they were still strong, and firmly in control of the country.

Trying to bring the theoretical foundation of the Party more into line with its actual behaviour, Jiang declared that the CCP represented China's advanced productive forces, China's advanced culture, and the fundamental interests of the overwhelming majority of the Chinese people. This theory was called the 'Three Represents'. The CCP formally declared in July 2001 that the capitalists themselves were eligible for Party membership. The following year, the head of the appliance manufacturing firm Haier became a member of the CCP Central Committee.

Jiang Zemin, like Deng Xiaoping, felt it was not a good idea for top positions in China to be lifetime posts. In 2003 he stepped down as general secretary of the Communist Party, and got Premier Zhu Rongji and other senior leaders to step down at the same time. The new general secretary of the CCP, and president of the PRC, was Hu Jintao. Born in 1942, the son of a teacher, he had combined political with technical skills from an early age. Hu's first job after graduating from college was as a political instructor at the prestigious Qinghua (Tsinghua) University, in Beijing, but in 1968 he went to Gansu province as a hydraulic engineer. He spent many years in Gansu, rising in the provincial construction commission and eventually becoming head of the Communist Youth League for the province. He became the head of the CCP for another backward interior province, Guizhou, in 1985. His close association with Hu Yaobang (no relation) raised doubts about his political reliability when Hu Yaobang was removed as CCP general secretary in 1987, but Hu Jintao resolved these doubts by his firm suppression of Tibetan riots in Lhasa in 1989. Deng Xiaoping promoted Hu to membership of the five-member Politburo Standing Committee in 1992.

Hu's attitudes appeared to be those of a highly intelligent but rather conventional Communist bureaucrat. He was firmly dedicated to maintaining the power of the CCP, and did not have much tolerance for dissenters. He did not seek publicity, and was not inclined to flamboyant gestures or dramatic policy initiatives. But he was more concerned than Jiang Zemin about the need to narrow the gap between the rich and poor areas of China, perhaps because of the many years he had spent in poor and backward provinces. And he was less tolerant of corruption than Jiang had been.

The new premier was Wen Jiabao, originally a geologist, who as vice-premier under Zhu Rongji had helped to manage China's economy. He had played major roles in the development of China's stock exchanges, the privatization of state-owned enterprises, and efforts to limit the tax burden on the peasants. As premier he took the lead in running the economy and the civil government bureaucracy, while Hu Jintao took the lead on political and national security issues.

Jiang Zemin, when he resigned as CCP general secretary, did not wish to give up all his power. Just as Deng Xiaoping had done in the 1980s, he held onto the chairmanship of the Party's Central Military Commission. He had an uneasy relationship with Hu Jintao until he resigned from this final position in 2004. The Party was determined to prevent public discussion of the tension between Jiang and Hu, and was furious when information about it leaked to the Western media.

The memory of Tiananmen was a lingering sore point in China. The CCP was determined not to acknowledge that the suppression of the democracy movement had been a mistake. Zhao Ziyang remained under house arrest until his death in January 2005. He was given a respectable funeral, good enough to not constitute an insult, but attendance was firmly restricted; the police made sure that no large crowds of people would be able to attend. The official assessment of his career stated that he had made major contributions to China, but that his actions in 1989 had involved 'grave errors'. In November of that year, Hu Jintao pushed through a decision (rumoured to have been disputed within the top CCP leadership) to grant a sort of posthumous rehabilitation to his old patron Hu Yaobang.

The legal system was expanded, and its role in Chinese society was strengthened. Many law schools were established to train attorneys and judges. But foreigners criticized the lack of transparency; criminal trials were often closed, and Party officials could and did intervene to ensure the desired verdict was reached in cases about which they cared. The police retained the power to place people in 'labour re-education' for years without even giving them a trial.

China made lavish use of the death penalty. Official statistics were not released, but it was believed that in the early twenty-first century there were more than 8,000, and perhaps more than 10,000, legal executions per year in China. This was more than in all the rest of the world combined. Many crimes, including non-violent ones such as embezzlement, carried the death penalty. Some of the victims were of very high rank. For example, amid a string of scandals involving counterfeit or adulterated products, the former head of China's Food and Drug Administration was executed in 2007, charged with having taken large bribes to approve pharmaceutical production licenses.

Widespread corruption, and arbitrary and oppressive behaviour by officials, inspired much discontent in China. The population, better educated and less under the thumb of the Party than it formerly had been, and in some cases probably remembering Maoist ideas about resisting abusive authority figures, did not simply assume that nothing could be done. There were protests, most of them small, some of them escalating to major riots. The number of 'mass incidents' was said to exceed 80,000 per year. The CCP was determined to prevent protesting individuals or small groups from coalescing into broad protest movements that could challenge its power, but at the same time it realized the importance of ameliorating the conditions that inspired protest. Many activities that could perform useful functions in solving social problems also had the potential to turn into protest movements. The CCP allowed elections to choose village administrative committees, and there were occasional experiments with elections at higher levels. The Party even allowed non-governmental organizations (NGOs) from democratic countries to give advice and assistance in elections, because well-run elections seemed likely to produce local governments that would be more satisfactory to the people. The CCP was nervous about lawyers and other human rights campaigners who denounced abuses by officials, but it permitted them to operate to some extent, at some risk, as long as they did not try to join together into large groups. It was nervous about foreign NGOs promoting women's rights in China, but permitted them to do so to some extent.

Local officials were more often corrupt, and more often brutally oppressive, than national ones. Leaders in Beijing were ambivalent about protests of citizens against the misdeeds (many of which were in flagrant violation of Beijing's announced policies) of local officials. They ignored most of the thousands of petitioners who came to Beijing begging for assistance, but occasionally sided with petitioners against local officials.

Foreign relations

Trade was the main driving force in China's relations with the world. It was not just that Chinese industries were dependent on foreign markets for their products. China needed ever-larger quantities of raw materials to fuel its industrial growth, and Chinese purchasing agents signed large contracts for minerals, petroleum, timber, and so forth. Chinese industries also subcontracted some of their manufacturing; a final product assembled in China often incorporated parts manufactured elsewhere.

China's relationship with the United States was complex and sometimes tense. Economically, the two had become so intertwined that a rupture in their economic ties would be disastrous for both. Politically and militarily, the PRC worried about an American 'anti-China containment policy', American support for Taiwan, the visible American desire that China democratize, and more generally the implications of America's role as the world's only superpower. But China did not wish to provoke a major confrontation. Economic growth, China's great priority, would be better served by a relaxed than a tense international environment. China opposed US efforts to obtain authorization from the United Nations Security Council for the war in Iraq in 2003, and for drastic sanctions against Iran in later years, but China kept such opposition fairly low-key.

Chinese leaders defied American sensibilities by befriending various repressive regimes, such as those in Myanmar (Burma) and Sudan. Partly this was simply a desire for commercial profit, but partly it reflected a rejection by the PRC of the very idea of one government applying criticism and pressure against another for violations of human rights. The PRC was well aware that many Americans disapproved of China's treatment of democracy activists and various religious groups. It disliked any American action anywhere that could be a precedent for American pressure regarding Chinese human rights issues.

There were occasional unexpected incidents. In 1999, the North Atlantic Treaty Organization (NATO), with the United States taking the lead, launched a bombing campaign against Serbia/Yugoslavia, in order to drive Serbian military forces out of Kosovo. China opposed this bombing. On 7 May, US 'smart bombs' hit the Chinese embassy in the Serbian/Yugoslav capital of Belgrade, killing three Chinese journalists. The USA said that it had had faulty information, and had mistaken the embassy for a Yugoslav military facility. The Chinese rejected this as an absurd falsehood. Not just the Chinese government but the Chinese people believed overwhelmingly that the Americans, with their vaunted precision bombing capability, could only have hit the embassy in a deliberate act. The police permitted crowds to run through the streets of various cities, shouting anti-American slogans and throwing stones and bottles at buildings associated with the United States. A few buildings, such as the American consulate in Chengdu and a KFC restaurant in Nanjing, were seriously damaged. But then the incident blew over; it was not permitted to compromise the long-term relationship between China and the USA.

In April 2001, an American reconnaissance aircraft was gathering electronic intelligence near the island of Hainan. A Chinese fighter plane made several close passes by the American aircraft, and finally a miscalculation by one or both pilots led to a collision. The Chinese pilot died and the American aircraft was heavily damaged. Again China blamed the United States, but again there was little lasting impact.

The withdrawal of Vietnamese troops from Cambodia in 1989 had alleviated the hostility between Vietnam and China. The relatively friendly relationship between China and Russia made possible a complete resolution of the border dispute between them in 2004. The border with India was not so easily settled, the areas in dispute being so much larger, but China and India at least became able to talk about a border settlement, and tensions were reduced to a point that in 2007 the chief of staff of the Indian army was able to visit China and discuss organizing joint training exercises for the military forces of the two countries. This left China without serious problems along any of its land borders.

Relations with Japan remained somewhat tense. China said that Japan had never properly acknowledged the evil done by the Japanese military during the Second World War, and criticized what it saw as signs that both Japan's militarism and its great-power status might be reviving. When it was proposed in 2005 that the United Nations Security Council be reorganized, giving Japan a permanent seat, a mob in Shanghai attacked Japanese restaurants and automobiles, and the Japanese consulate. But China's economic relationship with Japan, like that with the United States, was too important for such issues to be permitted seriously to interfere with it.

Hong Kong and Taiwan

Under the Sino-British agreement of 1984, the PRC was to regain control of Hong Kong in 1997, but the people of Hong Kong would continue to enjoy the freedoms they had had under the British; the Chinese system would not be imposed on Hong Kong. There would be 'one country, two systems'. By 1997, the PRC was allowing so much capitalism in China that Hong Kong businessmen no longer worried much about their economic prospects.

Political issues were trickier. In 1984, the people of Hong Kong had a great deal of freedom of speech, religion, and the press, but these freedoms depended on government forbearance; they were not well guaranteed in formal law. In addition, of course, the people could not choose their government. After signing the 1984 agreement, however, the British began allowing some members of Hong Kong's Legislative Council to be elected by the people. In the 1990s the last British governor of Hong Kong, Christopher Patten, pushed the process much farther. He enacted a Bill of Rights, and in 1995 he allowed all members of the Legislative Council to be elected, some directly and some through 'functional constituencies' – groups based on occupation. Many of the politicians elected were openly hostile to the Chinese Communist Party. The Chinese government felt that the largely democratic political system the British handed over to them in 1997 was not the system they had promised to preserve, and they promptly reversed some of Patten's reforms, but they dared not reverse them all for fear of a political explosion. The Legislative Council continued to be chosen by a mixture of direct elections and functional constituencies. The government was able to manipulate the system of functional constituencies, giving a great deal of power to conservative businessmen uninterested in rocking the boat, to prevent Hong Kong's vocal democracy movement from winning a majority on the Legislative Council.

The first chief executive of Hong Kong after the handover was Tung Chee-hwa, a very wealthy businessman who had been educated at the University of Liverpool in Britain, and had worked for years in the United States before returning to Hong Kong to join his father's shipping company. Tung had had strong financial ties to Beijing at least since the early 1980s.

The people of Hong Kong enjoyed a higher overall economic level, and far better systems for public education, health care, and so forth, than those of mainland China. Unification with China in 1997 did not eliminate these gaps, and did not give Chinese citizens a right to migrate to Hong Kong. They could visit as tourists, and did so by the millions, but legal Hong Kong residency was tightly restricted. Hong Kong capitalists continued to participate massively, and successfully, in the private-sector economy of the mainland. By 2007 it was estimated that Hong Kong businesses had about 11 million employees on the mainland – almost twice the total population of Hong Kong. But the portion of the Hong Kong economy that was actually in Hong Kong remained a part of the broader Asian capitalist economic system.

In 2003, an internal security law was proposed for Hong Kong that would have restricted political freedom, mandating heavy penalties for political offenses such as sedition and 'theft of government secrets'. It sparked massive protests. An estimated 500,000 people demonstrated against the proposed law on 1 July. On 5 September, Tung Chee-hwa announced that the law was being withdrawn. Tung announced his resignation, two years before the expiration of his term, in 2005. He said the reason was stress; he was rumoured to have been placed under pressure to resign by Beijing. His replacement, Donald Tsang, a Catholic and the son of a sergeant in the police force under the British, had risen through the colonial administration and had been knighted by the British in 1997. His position was confirmed through a tightly controlled, indirect election in 2007. He was popular enough to have probably won in a more democratic election, and suggested that a shift to actual democracy would be desirable, but Beijing was not prepared to tolerate so drastic a step.

On Taiwan, the breakoff of dissident factions from the Guomindang had not prevented the party's candidate, Lee Teng-hui, from winning a convincing victory in Taiwan's first free presidential election in 1996. The effect would be much greater in the election of 2000. The Guomindang candidate, Lien Chan, got only 21 per cent of the vote. James Soong, who had split from the Guomindang, got 37 per cent. This split allowed Chen Shui-bian of the Democratic Progressive Party to win the election and become president with 39 per cent of the vote. In 2004, Lien Chan and James Soong joined forces – Lien was the Guomindang's candidate for president and Soong for vice-president – but Chen Shui-bian managed to win re-election, defeating Lien by a very small margin.

The PRC insisted that Taiwan was part of China, and threatened to use military force if the government on Taiwan attempted to declare Taiwan an independent nation. The United States, which despite the cancellation of the mutual defence treaty in 1980 continued to regard itself as Taiwan's protector (the United States had criticized the PRC's efforts at intimidation during the 1996 election as 'reckless' and 'irresponsible' and had sent two aircraft carrier battle groups into the area), strongly urged first President Lee Teng-hui and then President Chen Shui-bian to avoid triggering a crisis. Lee as president flirted with the idea of independence, but refrained from declaring independence openly. Not until 2003, when he was no longer president, did Lee lead a huge demonstration, perhaps involving as many as 150,000 Taiwanese, asking that the government on Taiwan stop calling itself the Republic of China, and instead simply call itself 'Taiwan'. Chen Shui-bian flirted with independence even more openly than Lee had; the Guomindang criticized Chen for this. In 2004, when his government introduced a new history curriculum for the schools, in which the history of Taiwan would be taught separately from that of China, President Chen said, 'Some people fail to recognize that our national history is not Chinese history, and our national geography is not Chinese geography.' In his new year's message for 2007, he said, 'Taiwan is part of the world, absolutely not part of China.' But he avoided a formal governmental declaration of independence.

The situation was complicated by serious corruption allegations against President Chen and his family. He was charged with filing fraudulent expense vouchers, to obtain government reimbursement for imaginary expenses. He admitted that he had filed false vouchers, but claimed that this had been done to finance some sort of secret programme serving national security goals, not to obtain money for personal use. He was immune to criminal prosecution as long as he was president, but prosecutors indicated that they intended to bring charges against him as soon as his term ended, and his wife was on trial by the end of 2006. These scandals increased the likelihood that the Guomindang would regain power in the 2008 election. This must have pleased the PRC, since the Guomindang was much less inclined to support Taiwanese independence than the DPP was.

Political tensions did not block the growth of a very strong economic relationship. Taiwanese investors were involved in so many factories and businesses in China that the number of Taiwanese living and working on the mainland reached 1 million.

Issues of religion

The collapse of Communist ideology as a belief system, and the weakening of the CCP's hold over society in general, allowed a considerable revival of religious activity in China. Reliable figures do not exist, but the number of religious believers may have reached 30 per cent of the Chinese population early in the twenty-first century. There were officially sanctioned religious organizations, Christian (both Catholic and Protestant), Buddhist, Daoist, and Muslim. There were also unofficial ones, the status of which varied widely.

The Chinese Communist Party formally proclaimed freedom of religion. But it forbade its members to become religious believers, and it condemned religious proselytism, arguing that to attempt to persuade other people to convert to one's own faith was an offence against their religious freedom. It also was wary of any organization that was outside its control, and might have the potential to become a nucleus for opposition to it. This applied doubly to organizations with foreign links.

So there was an officially sanctioned Catholic Church in China, the leaders of which were all vetted by the government. It did not engage in open proselytism, and did not recognize the authority of the Vatican. There was also an 'underground' Catholic Church, which accepted the authority of the Vatican and proselytized vigorously. The PRC and the Vatican each denounced as illegitimate the appointment of Catholic bishops by any process controlled by the other. In the case of Protestantism there was no equivalent of the Vatican, and no centralized religious leadership under foreign control that the CCP was determined to block out of China, but otherwise the situation was somewhat similar. 'Underground' Protestants of various denominations made many converts.

The 'underground' churches were illegal, but their suppression was not a priority of the CCP leadership. Local officials who chose to persecute them did so, sometimes quite brutally. But in many areas, local officials ignored them. The central leadership did not care enough about the issue to punish officials who chose to ignore 'underground' churches.

A special case emerged in Falun Gong, the members of which practised physical exercises and forms of meditation that could, some claimed, give them supernatural powers. The CCP did not approve, but did not regard Falun Gong as important until 1999, when Falun Gong protested hostile articles that had recently appeared in the media by organizing a demonstration of about 10,000 people outside Zhongnanhai, the residential compound for top Communist leaders in the middle of Beijing. CCP leaders were shocked that the group had been able to organize such a demonstration, in the heart of Communist power, without the police having had any idea about what was going to happen. They also were disturbed to realize that Falun Gong had found significant numbers of followers within the CCP and the government. They denounced Falun Gong as an evil cult, and did their best to obliterate it. Persecution of Falun Gong became a genuine priority, a policy that officials in every province were required to take seriously, unlike the suppression of underground Christian churches, which local officials could ignore if they chose.

The Muslims posed problems, especially in Xinjiang. They benefited from the general relaxation of controls on religion after the death of Mao Zedong. Mosques were rebuilt, open religious study was permitted, and a significant if not huge number of Muslims – thousands per year – made the *hajj*, the annual pilgrimage to Mecca. But there was a separatist movement in Xinjiang, which the Chinese government branded a terrorist organization.

Issues of freedom

China remained, as it had been since the late 1970s, a country where the level of personal freedom was far below what it would have been in a democracy, but higher than in many dictatorships. The Communist Party was much less able to control the people's thoughts and actions, and limit the information available to them, than it had been under Mao.

Up to the early 1990s, it had been possible for conservative elements in the CCP to hope that they could minimize contact between the Chinese people and foreigners, to prevent 'spiritual contamination'. No such thing could even be imagined in the twenty-first century. By 2005, there were 140,000 foreign students studying in Chinese universities, millions of Chinese tourists travelling abroad, millions of foreign tourists swarming across China, businessmen from Western countries and from Western-influenced Hong Kong and Taiwan, foreign scholars doing research in China, and even foreign human rights activists.

Much was made, in the West, of the censorship of the internet in China. It was often said that there were 30,000 people assigned to monitor and censor the internet. What often went unnoticed was that 30,000 people, while enough to reduce the exposure of Chinese internet users to subversive material, were not adequate to do a really thorough job of censorship, in a country with more than 120 million internet users.

All newspapers, magazines, and broadcasting stations had to be owned by government organs, the CCP, or public institutions such as universities. But most of the organizations that owned the media regarded them less as tools for spreading the CCP political line than as profit-making enterprises. If investigative journalists uncovered scandalous stories of official abuses and corruption, and thus increased circulation, institutional owners of newspapers were as happy about this as purely private owners would have been. If officials wanted to prevent material of which they disapproved from being printed and broadcast, they needed to apply tools of censorship and intimidation, very much as if they had been dealing with privately owned media. The limits on acceptable public discourse were often vaguely defined, so at any given time, some publications and writers were exercising a cautious self-censorship, while others were testing or pushing against the limits of the permissible.

China's leaders did not like bad news. Stories about any disaster, even a natural one, set their teeth on edge. In 2005, the government announced that death tolls from natural disasters would no longer be considered state secrets, but the very next year a draft law was under consideration that threatened fines of up to US$12,500 for media outlets that reported 'sudden events' without first checking with government officials; these could include riots, strikes, and natural or manmade disasters. On the other hand, when the CCP leadership became disturbed over a string of scandals about dangerously contaminated or otherwise unhealthy pharmaceuticals and food, they opened the door for media publicity about such problems.

There were serious problems in connection with infectious diseases. HIV, the virus that causes the disease AIDS, was spreading in China during the 1990s, but the government denied the magnitude of the problem, and discouraged reporting on it in the Chinese press. Partly this was due to the CCP's general reluctance to publicize bad news. Partly it was due to the same squeamishness that had discouraged clear discussion of the AIDS crisis in a number of other countries. HIV was spread through drug use and through sex, especially prostitution (because prostitutes have many sex partners) and homosexuality (because an unprotected sex act between an infected and an uninfected person is more likely to cause transmission of the virus if the act is between two men than if it is between a man and a woman). The post-Mao reforms had brought an increase in sexual freedom, visible in everything from public displays of affection to prostitution and pornography, but the leaders of the CCP, who had grown up in the puritanical days of Maoism, still were not comfortable with public discussion of such issues, nor of drug abuse. Not until late in 2001 did the government publicly acknowledge that China faced a serious AIDS crisis.

An additional factor was peculiar to a local situation. In Henan province, a business grew up in blood products. Many peasants in poor villages earned badly needed money by selling blood. The technique used to gather blood was extremely careless; if one peasant selling blood had HIV, the virus quickly spread to the others selling blood at the same collection station. Corrupt local officials, who were profiting from the blood products business, suppressed reporting of the problem while huge numbers of peasants were being infected.

In November 2002, a new viral disease, later to be named severe acute respiratory syndrome (SARS), emerged in Guangdong province. It did not attract public notice until February 2003, by which time hundreds of people had become infected. The initial reaction of the Ministry of Health was to soothe public anxiety by claiming that the problem was being brought quickly under control. By April, the disease had spread to Beijing, where hundreds of people were infected and a significant number were dying. The ministry issued misleading statistics showing far less than the real number of cases, gave only limited cooperation to the World Health Organization's experts, and did not move aggressively to identify and quarantine persons who had been exposed to the virus. This policy, however, lasted only briefly. The minister of health and the mayor of Beijing were dismissed from their positions on 20 April for having covered up the problem, and vigorous measures were applied to control the epidemic. By the time the outbreak was brought to an end in July, there had been over 5,000 cases in China, with an official death toll of 348. In Hong Kong there were an additional 298 deaths.

Dissidents were sometimes arrested, beaten, or even killed, but there were dissidents, and some of them, even rather brazen ones, could operate quite openly for extended periods before provoking the government into cracking down on them.

The CCP leadership saw some value in having lawyers who would actually represent the interests of their clients, even in lawsuits against officials, because this offered a means of restraining misbehaviour by officials. Provincial and local officials were much less inclined to see some virtue in such people, and even the central leadership grew annoyed when such people went too far. Gao Zhisheng was to become an extreme example, an early twenty-first century counterpart of Wei Jingsheng. He had made a reputation in Xinjiang in the 1990s, winning a number of conspicuous cases, including one in which he represented a businessman whose company had been seized by a local government. The hostility of officials in Xinjiang finally drove him to Beijing, where he was enraged by political interference in the justice system. He actively sought out cases in which he would be pitted against the government and the CCP, representing members of Falun Gong and underground Christian churches in legal disputes with the police, and representing people whose land had been seized for construction projects. He denounced the government in extravagant terms, writing for example, 'Most officials in China are basically mafia bosses who use extreme barbaric methods to terrorize the people and keep them from using the law to protect their rights.' It may have been his public denunciation of police torture of Falun Gong members that finally persuaded the authorities, late in 2005, to strip him of his licence to practise law. He responded with further public denunciations of official abuses of power, and a hunger strike early in 2006. He was detained on vague criminal charges late in 2006.

China's prospects

China in the early twenty-first century had an economy that was growing at breathtaking speed, and showed no sign of being about to stop. It had a political system that was changing little, and showed no sign of being about to change much more. These patterns could not persist indefinitely.

Sooner or later, it seemed almost inevitable that something would happen to slow the economic growth. Demands for raw materials and water would outstrip supply, or foreign countries would become unable or unwilling further to expand the quantities of Chinese exports they purchased, or the environmental effects of rapid growth would become unsustainable, or something. But would this happen sooner, or later?

China's environmental problems were a large question mark. China had begun to take steps to mitigate the environmental effects of rapid industrial growth, but the growth was so massive that it was very difficult for mitigation efforts to cope. By 2006, it was estimated that of the twenty cities in the world with the worst air pollution, sixteen were in China. Air pollution was believed to be causing about 400,000 premature deaths per year, and China's pollution, carried across the Pacific, was beginning to effect air quality even on the west coast of the United States. When experts working for the World Bank estimated in 2007 that various forms of pollution, combined, were causing 750,000 premature deaths per year in China, the PRC asked that this estimate be removed from the final draft of their report.

Coal was the biggest problem. Most of China's electricity came from coal. China was determined to keep electricity cheap both to promote industrial growth and to allow individuals to use their new electrical appliances. (The number of air conditioners more than tripled between 2000 and 2006.) China therefore was building new coal-fired generating plants at a furious rate – it was estimated early in 2007 that, on average, there was a new plant *every four days* – but it was reluctant to spend extra money to get the equipment that would make the most efficient use of coal, and minimize pollution. A ton of coal burned in a Chinese generating plant produced on average far more hazardous emissions (sulphur compounds and particulates), and somewhat less electricity, than a ton of coal burned in modern American or Western European plants. China's massive use of coal had made the country the world's leading emitter of sulphur dioxide. Estimates of the date of China's surpassing the United States as the leading emitter of carbon dioxide, a major cause of global warming, varied from 2006 to 2008.

In the northwest, farmland was being lost to the spread of the Gobi Desert. Farther south, the destruction of forests by timber companies, and the clearing of hillsides for crops by land-hungry farmers, caused erosion and made disastrous floods more frequent. By 2005, the timber companies were being brought under control in many areas, and farmers were being restrained from planting crops on steeply sloping, unterraced fields in some areas.

The population had surpassed 1.3 billion and was still growing at somewhat more than 0.5 per cent per year. The fact that less than half the young adults were women, and thus potential mothers, must have helped hold down the growth rate. The number of female infants born remained far smaller than the number of male infants, despite government efforts to ban sex-selective abortion.

China's role in world affairs remained modest, even as its armed forces grew rapidly in strength. There was no way to tell whether, or when, or how, China might take on a more assertive role.

There was no sign that major political change was imminent, but it seemed very possible in the long run. The CCP, lacking the support of a strong belief system, might split into factions, perhaps with a regional foundation. The rapid rise in the wealth and educational level of the Chinese people seemed likely, sooner or later, to cause major changes in the relationship of the people to the Communist Party. Such changes might occur gradually and smoothly but they also might be rough, especially if there continued to be obvious reasons for the people to be discontented with the Party's rule, such as high levels of corruption, and high and rising levels of pollution

As was stated above, it seemed clear that China's rapid economic growth would slow eventually. But it would make a very large difference whether this happened sooner or later. The Party's leaders believed that continuing rapid economic growth was vital to maintaining political stability. This was almost certainly correct in the sense that if China's growth had slowed in the year 2000, or when China's gross domestic product reached twice the level of the year 2000, massive discontent would have been likely. But if rapid growth brought the gross domestic product to four times the level of the year 2000, might that represent a high enough level of wealth for the people to tolerate a slowdown in further growth? Would the gap between the rich and poor remain huge, or would efforts to promote social equality make significant progress before the end of the rapid growth?

In short, the future was extremely unpredictable.

Study questions

How did China manage to achieve so high a rate of economic growth for so long?

What was China's economic relationship with the rest of the world?

To what extent, and how thoroughly, did the CCP suppress discussion of politically sensitive issues?

Suggestions for further reading

The most important all-purpose journal dealing with China is the *China Quarterly*, which contains not only articles, but also reviews of recent books, and a 'Quarterly Chronicle and Documentation' section, which summarizes events in China's domestic and international affairs and sometimes gives full translated texts of major documents. *Modern China*, which also appears on a quarterly basis, contains only full-length articles.

The Cambridge History of China, 15 volumes covering the period from 221 BC onward (Cambridge University Press, 1978–), and *The Cambridge History of Ancient China* (Cambridge University Press, 1999) together give a detailed scholarly accounts of most aspects of Chinese history.

China's Imperial Past, by Charles Hucker (Stanford University Press, 1975), gives a good summary of Chinese history up to the beginning of the modem era. See also *The Retreat of the Elephants: An Environmental History of China*, by Mark Elvin (Yale University Press, 2004). *Sources of Chinese Tradition*, 2nd edn, edited by Wm. Theodore de Bary, *et al.* (Columbia University Press, 1999), is a selection from the writings of the early philosophers, Buddhist scriptures, and other documents. *The Death of Woman Wang*, by Jonathan Spence (Viking, 1978), gives a detailed look at life in an unimportant county of China in the seventeenth century. It is useful in establishing the background against which the later modernization of China can be seen.

Jonathan D. Spence's *The Search for Modern China*, 2nd edn (Norton, 1999) is a good overall history of China, from the seventeenth century onward. For the early stages of the Western impact, and China's reaction to that impact, see *The Opium War*, by Peter W. Fay (North Carolina Press, 1975), *The Last Stand of Chinese Conservatism*, by Mary C. Wright

(Stanford University Press, 1957), and *God's Chinese Son: The Taiping Heavenly Kingdom of Hong Xiuquan*, by Jonathan Spence (Norton, 1997).

China in Revolution, edited by Mary C. Wright (Yale University Press, 1968), is a collection of articles on the Revolution of 1911. For analysis of early twentieth-century patterns of social mobility, see 'Downward Social Mobility in Pre-revolutionary China', by Edwin E. Moise, in *Modern China*, vol. 3, no. 1.

China in Disintegration, by James Sheridan (Free Press, 1975), traces the overall history of China from 1911 to 1949. Lloyd Eastman has written two good volumes on the Guomindang regime: *The Abortive Revolution* (Harvard University Press, 1974) covers the period from 1927 to 1937, and *Seeds of Destruction* (Stanford University Press, 1984) covers the period from 1937 to 1949. *One Day in China*, edited and translated by Sherman Cochran, Andrew Hsieh, and Janis Cochran (Yale University Press, 1983), is a fascinating collection of short pieces written in 1936, discussing Chinese society and China's situation at that time. *Spymaster: Dai Li and the Chinese Secret Service*, by Frederic Wakeman, Jr. (University of California Press, 2003), is a valuable study of considerable portions of the Guomindang power structure, not just the Secret Service.

The U.S. Crusade in China, by Michael Schaller (Columbia University Press, 1979), and *Stilwell and the American Experience in China*, by Barbara Tuchman (Macmillan, 1971), give a good picture of relations between Chiang Kai-shek and the United States during the Second World War. *Two Kinds of Time*, by Graham Peck (Houghton, Mifflin, 1950), and *Thunder out of China*, by Theodore White and Annalee Jacoby (Sloane, 1946), are important contemporary accounts of the Second World War in China.

The Long March to Power, by James Harrison (Macmillan, 1973), traces the history of the Chinese Communist Party from its founding in 1921 up to its victory in 1949. *Selected Works of Mao Tse-tung*, 5 vols. (Foreign Languages Press, 1965–77), is the official canon, the writings considered to represent Chairman Mao's thinking (with the original texts altered in some places). For much more complete collections of his writings, translated from the original texts, there are two projects, not yet complete: *Mao's Road to Power: Revolutionary Writings 1912–1949*, edited by Stuart R. Schram (M.E. Sharpe, 1992–), and *The Writings of Mao Zedong, 1949–1976*, edited by John K. Leung and Michael Y.M. Kau (M.E. Sharpe, 1986–).

Two of the better studies of the civil war that finally brought the Chinese Communists to power are *Decisive Encounters: The Chinese Civil War, 1946–1950*, by Odd Orne Westad (Stanford University Press, 2003), and *Civil War in China: The Political Struggle, 1945–1949*, by Suzanne Pepper (University of California Press, 1978).

On China since 1949, see Maurice Meisner, *Mao's China and After: A History of the People's Republic*, 3rd edn (Free Press, 1999). *China's Longest Campaign: Birth Planning in the People's Republic, 1949–2005* (Cornell University Press, 2006) also covers this important topic.

For the Communist Party's policy in the villages up to 1953, see *Land Reform in China and North Vietnam*, by Edwin Moise (North Carolina Press, 1983). Overlapping this is *Peasant China in Transition: The Dynamics of Development Toward Socialism, 1949–1956*, by Vivienne Shue (University of California Press, 1980). An excellent account of the revolution in one North China village is *Throwing the Emperor from His Horse*, by Peter Seybolt (Westview, 1996). Equally good on one South China village, from the 1960s through the 1980s, is *Chen Village under Mao and Deng*, by Anita Chan, Richard Madsen, and Jonathan Unger (University of California Press, 1992).

Origins of the Cultural Revolution, by Roderick MacFarquar, 3 vols. (Oxford University Press, 1974–97), is a thorough and revealing study of the eventful years from 1956 to 1965. For the Cultural Revolution itself, see Roderick MacFarquhar and Michael Schoenhals, *Mao's Last Revolution* (Harvard University Press, 2006). There are several excellent eyewitness accounts, including *Son of the Revolution*, by Liang Heng and Judith Shapiro (Knopf, 1983), and *To the Storm: The Odyssey of a Revolutionary Chinese Woman*, by Yue Daiyun and Carolyn Wakeman (University of California Press, 1985).

On the first stages of the post-Mao transformation of China there are two good eyewitness accounts by Westerners: *Coming Alive* by Roger Garside (Deutsch, 1981), and *Alive in the Bitter Sea* by Fox Butterfield (Times Books, 1982). *One Step Ahead in China*, by Ezra Vogel, describes the remarkable transformation of Guangdong province under the economic reforms of the 1980s.

For the background to the democracy movements of the late 1980s see *Seeds of Fire: Chinese Voices of Conscience*, edited by Geremie Barme and John Minford (Hill & Wang in the US, Collins in Canada, 1988). *Bringing Down the Great Wall* (Knopf, 1990) is a collection of writings by Fang Lizhi, a key leader of the 1986–87 democracy movement. Shen Tong, author of *Almost a Revolution* (Houghton Mifflin, 1990) was one of the student leaders of the Tiananmen Square demonstrations of 1989. Also good are *Quelling the People: The Military Suppression of the Beijing Democracy Movement*, by Timothy Brook (Oxford University Press, 1992), and *The Pro-Democracy Protests in China: Reports from the Provinces*, edited by Jonathan Unger (Sharpe, 1991). For translated documents see *Beijing Spring 1989*, edited by Michael Oksenberg, Lawrence Sullivan, and Marc Lambert (Sharpe, 1990), and *Cries for Democracy: Writings and Speeches from the 1989 Chinese Democracy Movement*, edited by Han Minzhu (Princeton University Press, 1990).

Very recent events are discussed in *Oracle Bones: A Journey Between China's Past and Present*, by Peter Hessler (HarperCollins, 2006); *The Man Who Changed China: The Life and Legacy of Jiang Zemin*, by Robert Lawrence Kuhn (Crown, 2004); and *Chinese Politics in the Hu Jintao Era*, by Willy Wo-Lap Lam (M.E. Sharpe, 2006).

On the international relations of the PRC, see *Mao's China and the Cold War*, by Chen Jian (North Carolina Press, 2001); *China and the Vietnam Wars, 1950–1975*, by Qiang Zhai (North Carolina Press, 2000); *Survey of the Sino-Soviet Dispute: A Commentary and Extracts from the Recent Polemics, 1963–1967*, by John Gittings (Oxford University Press, 1968); and *Constructing the U.S. Rapprochement with China, 1961–1974*, by Evelyn Goh (Cambridge University Press, 2004). Much valuable information on China's role in the Cold War has been published, both as bound volumes and on the internet, by the Cold War International History Project, at the Woodrow Wilson International Center for Scholars in Washington, DC.

Index

Page numbers in *italics* indicate references to maps and photographs.